The New Silk Road

Road

How a Rising Arab World is
Turning Away from the West and
Rediscovering China

Revised and updated edition

Ben Simpfendorfer

palgrave
macmillan

First published in hardback 2009
First published in paperback with a new Preface 2011
Published by PALGRAVE MACMILLAN

Palgrave Macmillan in the UK is an imprint of Macmillan Publishers Limited, registered in England, company number 785998, of Houndmills, Basingstoke, Hampshire RG21 6XS.

Palgrave Macmillan in the US is a division of St Martin's Press LLC, 175 Fifth Avenue, New York, NY 10010.

Palgrave Macmillan is the global academic imprint of the above companies and has companies and representatives throughout the world.

Palgrave® and Macmillan® are registered trademarks in the United States, the United Kingdom, Europe and other countries.

ISBN 978–0–230–28485–2

This book is printed on paper suitable for recycling and made from fully managed and sustained forest sources. Logging, pulping and manufacturing processes are expected to conform to the environmental regulations of the country of origin.

A catalogue record for this book is available from the British Library.

A catalog record for this book is available from the Library of Congress.

10 9 8 7 6 5 4 3 2 1
20 19 18 17 16 15 14 13 12 11

Printed and bound in China

To Julia and Alex

CONTENTS

Preface

"China is the world." This is what Mohammed, an Egyptian trader, says to me while we sit in a Turkish cafe. The cafe is in Guangzhou, a large Chinese city neighboring Hong Kong. And it is full of Arab and Turkish traders meeting with their Chinese colleagues. Mohammed has lived in China for the past decade. He has apartments in three different cities and shuttles between each for work, buying goods for export to the Middle East.

Mohammed thinks China is the world because it has provided him with an opportunity to make money and create a better life for himself. He travels easily between China and the Middle East, faced by fewer visa restrictions than he would in Europe or the United States. China's thirst for oil has also pushed oil prices to record highs, leaving his Arab customers with plenty of cash to spend. I have heard countless stories similar to that told by Mohammed.

The East is catching up to the West. And the change is most obvious in China and the Middle East, from the gleaming skyscrapers of Shanghai to the wealthy investors in Abu Dhabi. The result is a rise of two historic economic powers, and a rebalancing of the world's center of economic gravity.

This story is increasingly familiar to readers of the *New York Times*, *Financial Times*, or any of the major international dailies. Less familiar is how China and the Middle East are reaching out to each other. It used to be that the two sold their consumer goods and crude oil mainly to the West. But they are increasingly looking closer to home, in the East. The economic crisis has only accelerated the changes taking place as a fast growing East contrasts with a slow growing West.

However, the changes are hard to observe. It is individuals, rather than governments, that are the driving force. Take the Syrian textiles trader who has established an office in Shanghai, or the Chinese entrepreneur who has constructed an exhibition building outside Damascus. They are part of a tapestry that weaves the new Silk Road together. But their stories are not easily uncovered while reading the international dailies. They are happening 1,000 feet below the surface.

Since the book's hardback edition was published, I have maintained a blog, titled the Silk Road Economy, keeping track of events in the Arab, Chinese, and English media. I have also travelled constantly between the two regions, speaking with traders, bankers, and CEOs, among others, about the changes taking place. I had fears that the economic crisis might initially disrupt the strengthening linkages of these two great powers. But, in the event, it has only reinforced them.

Chinese traders have started talking about "oumei," shorthand for Europe and the United States, as fading markets, and instead focus on "jiao dian," or hot spots, primarily in their own domestic market and the Middle East. They have good reason to be excited. Chinese exports slowed briefly during the crisis, but are now higher than they were pre-crisis, having grown to $60 billion.

There are some important, and well-observed, reasons for the increase. China entered the World Trade Organization in 2001, resulting in a drop in the import duties the Middle East imposed on Chinese-made goods. Massive outsourcing by Asian electronics factories to China also produced a sharp increase in the latter's exports of electronics goods, from DVD players to notebook computers, over the past decade. The surge in oil prices has meanwhile fuelled the Middle East's own demand for consumer goods.

Yet there are other equally important, but less well-observed, reasons. Visas remain an important explanation for the growth in trade. Europe and the United States tightened visa restrictions on Arab nationals after September 2001. They have since relaxed them only modestly and the number of Arab nationals receiving visas to the United States, for instance, remains below its pre-2001 levels. China, meanwhile, relaxed its own visa policy, recognizing that visiting Arab traders buy goods and create jobs.

And so Yiwu, the small Chinese coastal city and a virtual Arab market town, continues to flourish. I have visited the city on several occasions since the hardback edition was published, and the number of Arab restaurants and Arabic-speaking translators is still impressive. Worried that Arab traders might be hesitant to visit Yiwu, as the economic crisis and oil prices plummeted, the city's traders set up shop once a year in Dubai itself, at the China Sourcing Fair. They even created a Yiwu-city logo to advertise their participation.

It was not a surprise then when China overtook the United States in 2008 as the world's largest exporter to the Middle East, having overtaken Germany in 2006 and the United Kingdom in 2002. It was a symbolic changing of the guard. Sure China's exports to all parts of the world grew quickly during the period. But its exports to the Middle East have grown at faster rates than its exports to either Africa or Latin America, two equally important emerging markets.

And what does the Middle East think of a flood of cheap Chinese consumer goods? They are certainly welcomed by the region's growing middle-class. I recall shopping for a digital camera with a Syrian friend in Damascus. "If it wasn't for China I wouldn't be able to afford this," he said. He looked delighted at his new purchase, and spent the next week showing me the camera's many features and newly taken pictures of his family.

However, not everyone is happy. The Palestinian city of Hebron has a large textiles industry. It produces Keffiyehs, the black and white checkered scarves so popular among the Palestinians and made famous by the former Palestinian leader Yasser Arafat. But Hebron's textile industry employs just 5,000 people today, down from 15,000 a decade ago. Cheap Chinese imports have undercut local producers. Palestinian men, in their conflicts with Israeli soldiers, are now covering their faces with made-in-China keffiyehs.

While the Middle East's political problems grab media headlines, the region's economic problems are just as damaging. The Middle East has a large youth population of 177 million, or 56 percent of the total population. It is an astonishing figure, the product of high birth rates over the past two decades. Unless they are put to work, these youth will become frustrated and risk turning to crime or violence. And if China's exports to the Middle East continues to grow unchecked, resulting in factory closures, the odds of such an outcome will grow.

Nevertheless, there is an alternative trajectory. Chinese manufacturers, the type that produce the cheap clothing and microwave ovens that fill shelves in Walmarts and Carrefours around the world, are starting to look abroad in response to rising production costs and transport costs at home. They are also looking abroad for fear that rising protectionism will deny them access to Europe, their largest market. If sustained, the development is of huge importance. Whereas China once received factories from the rest of the world, it might start exporting them.

It is typical to focus on countries such as Bangladesh and Vietnam as an alternative to China. But countries such as Egypt are also compelling. Not only does it have a cheap labor force, but Egypt is also situated closer to Europe. This is a boon as oil prices rise to over $80 a barrel and transport costs surge. Moreover, Egypt enjoys preferential market access, having earlier signed a free-trade agreement with the European Union. In 2009, two Chinese air conditioner manufacturers built factories outside of Egypt for just this reason.

An increase in cross-investment would be welcome. China and the Middle East boast some of the world's largest wealth funds. Their public wealth is measured in trillions and they have not been shy to put the money to work as asset prices, especially in Europe and the United States, tumbled during the crisis. The rise of the region's wealth funds is among the most potent symbols of the transfer in wealth from West to East. And it is not surprising that Western bankers fill flights to Beijing and Abu Dhabi as they pitch for funds.

But China and the Middle East have so far invested little in each other. They are good reasons for this; the Middle East's energy assets are largely not up for sale, while it remains too difficult to buy majority stakes in China's established companies. Still, the restrictions will ease in time, especially as controls on foreigners buying domestic stocks are eased. The wealth funds are also increasingly active, such as the joint-venture agreement signed between the China Investment Corporation and the Qatar Investment Authority in late 2009. But more work needs to be done to spur cross-investment.

The Silk Road, of course, was never just about trade and capital. It was also about ideas. One of the best examples was the export of Islam eastwards and Buddhism westwards. China's rise has equally provided the Middle East with an alternative way to think of the world.

Take a study trip made by the governor of Syria's Hasakah province to China's Hunan province in early 2008. He was there to learn more about Hunan's economic reform experience. It made sense. The two provinces are largely poor and agricultural. They both export migrant labor to wealthier coastal cities. They both certainly have more in common they did with the policy planners in Washington who more often gave theoretical, rather than practical, advice. And Hunan's 12 percent average economic growth over the past 10 years must have given hope to the Hasakah's governor.

I also recall watching Song Hongbing, the author of the Chinese-language book, *Currency Wars*, appear on the Arabic-language news channel Al Jazeera in early 2009. He was invited by Bila Hudood, one of the news channel's more popular talk shows. Song's book argued that the West uses its currency policy to prevent the rise of the East. His themes might be considered conspiracy theory, but they were popular among Chinese officials, and they also resonated in the Middle East, especially among the region's former colonies.

Islam is also one of the Silk Road's more important links, but its role is often misunderstood. China's 20 million Muslim population, according to official figures, ranks it alongside Syria and Saudi Arabia. It is tempting to assume that relations between China and its Muslim population are poor because of tensions in the country's western provinces. And, as a result, China's relations with the mainly Muslim population of the Middle East will also face major challenges. But this is a superficial reading of the situation.

Certainly, China's relations with its Uyghur Muslim population are strained. Yet, the Uyghur account for 8 million of the 20 million Muslim population. The Hui Muslim minority make up 10 million.

Who are the Hui? They are the original descendents of Silk Road traders, and the later converts to Islam. They have largely assimilated with the Han Chinese majority and are indistinguishable from the average Chinese national, especially when compared to the Uyghur who share more in common with their Turkic ancestors. The Hui are more geographically diverse, living across the country rather than only in the western provinces. They speak Mandarin Chinese and hold senior positions in government. They are also, most importantly, a useful ally in China's strengthening relations with the Middle East.

Neither is China afraid to play its Muslim card. Take a speech delivered by Prime Minister Wen Jiabao at the Arab League Headquarters in late 2009. Typically, such a speech would stick tightly to a script about bilateral trade and investment relations. But this time Wen started by emphasizing China's historical relationship with the Muslim world. He spoke about the 35,000 mosques in China and the fact that public institutions are legally required to provide Halal food, suitable for the country's Muslim minority.

With the global economic crisis not yet over, what next for China's relations with the Middle East and a historical rebalancing in the world's center of economic gravity?

If there is one city that sums up the potential in the relationship, it is Dubai. The small emirate has received a great deal of bad press as a result of its credit problems. Yet, its foundations remain strong. Dubai was eliminating duties, dredging deep water ports, and building international airports decades ago, long before it embarked on the more glitzy construction projects that have since created such problems for the emirate's rulers. China is already starting to see Dubai's promise as its global reach extends.

What is that promise? Dubai has the type of geography money cannot buy. It lies in the center of three great continents: Asia, Africa, and Europe. This is important to China. For instance, while China's trade with Africa has captured media attention, over 35 percent of that trade is with North Africa, a region that shares strong cultural, historical, and religious ties with the Middle East. And it makes sense for Chinese companies with large business activities in North Africa to set up regional headquarters in Dubai, rather than a city in Africa.

No surprise then Chinese companies are already making a stand in Dubai. The city already hosts 200,000 Chinese nationals, with nearly 50,000 of them traders. Chinese banks are also increasingly active, lending to construction projects in the emirates. In time Dubai will learn to pitch itself more aggressively to China so as to encourage such activity. And Chinese companies will help to fill empty office buildings, some left by exiting Western companies, in another small sign of the changes at work in the global economy.

CHAPTER 1

The New Silk Road: The Arab World Rediscovers China

Yiwu is a small city by Chinese standards. It has fewer than a million people and lies in the shadow of its wealthy neighbors, Shanghai and Wenzhou. But Yiwu is special. It claims the world's largest wholesale market for consumer goods and is a Mecca for foreign traders. I had heard about the market from a Syrian trader, having asked him if there were many Arab traders in the city. He laughed and replied, "Not *many* Arab traders. *All* Arab traders are in Yiwu." Intrigued, I decided to find out for myself. It was winter when I arrived and the city was gripped by a chill wind. I hustled out of the small airport into the warmth of a taxi. We sped along a newly built freeway to the city's outskirts. From the outside, the exhibition hall looks like a large American mall. But, from the inside, it looks like a riotous collision of every retail shop, city market, and roadside stall in the world.

There are 18,000 individual stalls. Most are less than ten feet wide and staffed by a single stallholder. Each is stuffed with product samples and sell wholesale only. The literature claims there are 320,000 products for sale. Multiply each sample by the thousands of identical products filling warehouses elsewhere in the city and you start to arrive at the sheer volume of goods that Yiwu ships to the rest of the world. It was a mind-numbing experience to walk past a hundred stalls displaying inflatable toys, another hundred stalls displaying plastic flowers, and yet another hundred stalls displaying cutlery. Yiwu's exhibition halls are a massive temple to the twin-gods of consumerism and globalization that have captured the imagination of traders from around the world.

Even the Chinese are impressed. When the Chinese Commerce Minister Bo Xilai visited the city he was awed enough to suggest that the municipal government create an index to survey the city's trade in small consumer goods.[1] Bo recognized that Yiwu was so important to the entire country's trade in small consumer goods that the index would accurately reflect the health of that sector of the economy. The city's municipal government sensibly agreed to his suggestion; after all, Bo was a senior Communist Party leader, the son of one of the "Eight Immortals" responsible for the country's post-Mao transition. A walk through the city's exhibition halls today reveals bronze plates identifying which shops participate in the survey. The Yiwu index takes the temperature of the world's demand for small consumer goods.

Yiwu isn't widely known in the West. The city only started to make its fortune from the early 2000s, whereas Wenzhou, a three-hour drive north, was already an export dynamo in the early 1990s. But Yiwu is different. It sells mainly to individual traders, rather than to large retail conglomerates such as Wal-Mart and Carrefour so the city hasn't grabbed the Western media's attention. Yiwu is also better known in the developing world than in the developed world. As I walked through the city's exhibition halls, I met traders from Cairo, Lagos, and Budapest, among dozens of other cities. It is a true global village. Traders traveled in groups of two or three, accompanied by translators. Most were visiting the city for just a few days before returning to their home countries. All had caught the Yiwu bug.

What makes Yiwu special? It focuses on selling the type of cheap consumer goods that can be purchased for a few dollars. Vendors are also happy to sell in small volume, ideal for developing-world traders who are generally stocking their own street stalls back home and prefer to buy just a few hundred, rather than a few thousand, of any single item. And so, Yiwu has found a niche. But its timing is also fortuitous. The developing world is booming. A surge in commodity prices had injected cash into many economies even as governments have opened their domestic markets to foreign imports. It is an explosive combination and the sudden flood of traders to Yiwu represented the cutting edge of a consumer boom across large parts of the developing world. Forget selling DVDs to America and shoes to Europe. Yiwu is making its fortune selling gifts, toys, and hardware to the developing world.

At one point I found myself in a little stall selling religious icons. A Romanian trader was shopping for pictures of Christian saints while the Chinese shopkeeper stood attentively at his side. The pictures were painted in the fourteenth-century Italian style and depicted a single Christian saint robed in dark cloth and crowned by a golden halo. But these pictures were made from cheap plastic, sold for less than a dollar, and were destined for the walls of homes in Eastern Europe. A few saints had small electric bulbs inserted into their halos that flashed like Christmas tree lights. The Romanian trader was amused by this and pulled a sample from the shelf for closer inspection. I turned away to investigate the rest of the shop and found the opposite shelves filled with pictures of Islamic religious images made from the same cheap plastic. This is the genius of Yiwu. It is the world's largest consumer goods market because it is prepared to sell to anyone in the world, regardless of faith or nationality.

Thomas Friedman alluded to this in his book *The World Is Flat* when he wrote how many festival lamps for sale in Egypt are now made in China. There is a good chance the lamps were from Yiwu. An Egyptian trader had likely spotted the Chinese-festival lamps for sale in Yiwu's exhibition halls and been struck by their similarity to the Egyptian festival lamps. The trader would have asked the Chinese stallholder to modify the design to suit the Egyptian market and placed an order for several thousand. The stallholder would have produced twice that amount hoping to sell the same lamps to other Egyptian traders. If successful, other Chinese stallholders might copy the lamps for sale in their own stalls. In short time, Egyptian festival lamps will have sprouted throughout the city's exhibition halls. It's not just Egyptian festival lamps either, but a multitude of goods sold to all parts of the developing world.

The rise of Yiwu is matched by a surge in arrivals to China. In 2000, China received 445,000 visitors from Africa, the Middle East, and Latin America. By 2008, the number had risen almost five times to reach 2,395,000.[2] The biggest increases are posted in October each year when trade fairs are held in Yiwu and the southern city of Guangzhou.[3] These fairs are popular among traders who lack the sophisticated purchasing networks enjoyed by global retail giants such as Wal-Mart and Carrefour as they are an opportunity to meet wholesalers and inspect a large range of goods. The number of arrivals jumps by tens of thousands as traders flock to the two cities echoing the traders in the bazaars of the old world.

This makes the flight from Guangzhou to Yiwu an experience. It is the only flight in China I can recall on which foreigners regularly outnumber Chinese. No easy thing. I was once seated next to a group of elderly Romanian women dressed in black, their teeth capped gold. They didn't speak either Chinese or English, but we managed to communicate by drawing pictures on the airline's in-flight magazines. On a later flight, I was seated next to an Egyptian shoe manufacturer, a Christian Copt who was wearing a necklace with a heavy gold cross. He owned a factory outside of Cairo, but it was empty, and he now imports all his shoes from Yiwu. "What can I do?" he said with palms raised upwards. "I have to make a living and it's cheaper to import from China than to manufacture locally." He visits the city four times a year to meet with manufacturers and place new orders. I have met many others like him on the flight to Yiwu, all with similar stories to tell.

*   *   *

It was the Arab traders who first discovered Yiwu shortly after September 2001. These traders had found it increasingly difficult to travel to America due to visa restrictions. There were anecdotal stories of traders detained at customs when their names mistakenly matched those on a "terror watch list." The number of Arabs traveling to the United States stood at over 250,000 in 2000. By 2009, the figure had fallen to 197,000.[4] The average American household might feel safer knowing that Arab visitors are less likely to visit Atlanta or Chicago. But the world has changed. Arab traders might have stayed at home when faced with visa restrictions; today, they travel to Yiwu, China.

It was unfortunate timing for the West. The Arab traders had money to spend for the first time in almost a decade. Oil prices have hit record highs and the Arab economies were booming. Average economic growth was an impressive 5.3 percent, between 2004 and 2009 versus 2.5 percent in the developed world.[5] Dubai's construction industry was the most visible sign of the region's new wealth as it built a palm-shaped island, the world's largest mall and the world's tallest skyscraper. But most importantly, the Arab countries, in a bid to revive their stalled economies, had opened their doors to foreign imports during the 1990s. The World Trade Organization admitted seven Arab countries, including Saudi Arabia and the UAE, between 1990 and 2005. After a decade of stagnation, not only did the Arab world have money to spend, but it was also easier than ever for Arab traders to import foreign goods. And so, Arab traders headed abroad in their thousands. However, struggling to obtain visas to enter Western economies, they looked for alternatives.

China was a timely alternative. The country entered the World Trade Organization in December 2001. Its exports of consumer goods were rocketing at 30 percent annual growth. North Asian manufacturers were also outsourcing huge amounts of production to mainland China. But the real masterstroke was Beijing's unofficial decision to relax visa restrictions around the same time as the events of September 2001. There was no explicit change in policy, but Beijing was increasingly eager to attract foreign investors and foreign dollars. The Chinese embassy in Egypt claims to issue visas to Egyptian nationals overnight,[6] whereas it takes the average Egyptian 18 days to apply and receive an American visa.[7] Indeed, most Arab traders I spoke claimed to have received their visas in less than 24 hours. China is open for business.

The results of this are most evident in Yiwu where Arab traders are a common sight on the city's streets. While on a visit to the city I caught a taxi to the Red Guest House. It is an institution among the Arab community and the first stop for new arrivals. The Red Guest House is a rambling complex built around a central courtyard with sickly looking trees. It serves as a hotel, office, restaurant, and mosque for the Arabs in Yiwu. Walking through the complex I came across a Palestinian man sitting in the courtyard, drinking tea and reading a magazine. We talked for a while until I probed more about the Arab community. "You don't want to ask me," said Rashid. "Ask my cousin." He grabbed my arm and steered me through the lobby entrance. We walked ten minutes down North Chou Zhou Street, chatting the whole way.

Rashid finally ushered me into an Arabic restaurant. "My cousin works here. You should talk to him. He has lived in Yiwu for years." The restaurant was an odd fusion of cultures. Arabic ornaments decorated what was otherwise an ordinary Chinese restaurant. A large plastic palm tree positioned in the corner was a small attempt at authenticity. I was introduced to Rashid's cousin and we chatted for the next hour. He had lived in Yiwu for ten years and was married to a local Chinese girl. "We opened one of the first Arabic restaurants in the city," he said. "But it's all changed since then." He pulled on his cigarette, "So many Arabs have turned up in the past few years. It's unbelievable. The number of Arabic restaurants in this street has tripled in the past year. But there are still more Arab traders than restaurants, so it's good for business. I'm not complaining."

The city had just three Arabic restaurants in 2004. But the number jumped to nearly 20 by 2008. No other city in China, including Beijing and Shanghai, could match the figure. The restaurants are all clustered a few blocks from each other in the vicinity of the Red Guest House and cater to every part of the Arab world – the Al Aqsa was filled with Palestinian diners while the Al Damashq was occupied mostly by Syrian customers. In this small Chinese coastal city a trader can eat anything from Lebanese tabouli to Egyptian koshari.

It was the Yemeni traders who first started to arrive in numbers in 2004. Yemen is a mountainous country hugging the southern end of the Gulf peninsula. It is still an intensely tribal country. It is also a poor country and many Yemenis migrate to neighboring Saudi Arabia for work. As oil prices jumped in 2004, Saudi Arabia was among the first to benefit. The government started to spend again after nearly a decade of austerity, while ordinary households increased their purchases of consumer goods, mainly imported. A few of the more entrepreneurial Yemeni workers realized there was money to be made from this revival in consumption. And so they quit their jobs as construction workers and, tossing hard hats aside, traveled to China, eventually settling in Yiwu. They found cheap consumer goods in the city's exhibition halls for export back to Saudi Arabia.

I shouldn't have been surprised to find Yemenis in Yiwu. They are natural traders. The best are from the Hadramouti tribe, which has its origins in the eastern provinces of Yemen. The region is favored by the trade winds and as a result Hadrami traders have spread across the world. Intriguingly, Osama Bin Laden's family was originally Hadrami, and Bin Laden has built a loose network of followers[8] not unlike his compatriots who have developed trade routes reaching from Saudi Arabia to China. It was ironically the actions of Osama Bin Laden that contributed to the tightening of visa restrictions on Arab traders, including those from Hadramout, and drove them into the arms of China. It is a reminder of how seemingly isolated events in recent years are in fact often related.

The Palestinians followed shortly after. They were fleeing an outbreak of violence at home as well as hoping to make their fortune in China. Mohammed Nasser's story is typical. A 20-year-old Palestinian from the West Bank, he had arrived three years earlier on the advice of cousins already living in Yiwu. His cousins had settled in the city and opened a number of Arabic restaurants. I met Mohammed in his office on North Chou Zhou Street. We sat for an hour talking and drinking sweet heavy coffee. Mohammed sold leather belts to Saudi Arabia. "This is the Arab world's biggest consumer market," he explained. He spoke Chinese slowly and with a heavy accent. But it didn't matter, as Mohammed wasn't planning to live in China for good. "I'll return to Palestine once I've earned enough money to buy a house and marry." He found it tough both living away from his family and living outside an Islamic community.

The Egyptian and the Syrian traders were the last to arrive in Yiwu. The rise in oil prices had a less dramatic effect on these two relatively poorer countries. I bumped into a Syrian trader from Damascus in the city's exhibition halls, examining screwdrivers in the hardware section. I recognized his Syrian accent when he turned to speak with his friend. Walking over I struck up a conversation. He was in the city for just three days, buying goods to sell back in Damascus. I said I hadn't expected to see so many Arabs in the city. "This is just another Arab city," he said gesturing at the traders in the surrounding exhibition stalls. He was exaggerating for effect, but his point was valid. Yiwu is flourishing as trade between the Arab world and China increases. It has benefited from rising oil prices and economic reform across the Arab world.

These Arab traders are following the footsteps of their ancestors. The original Arab traders had arrived centuries earlier along the Silk Road, the route connecting China in the east with the Mediterranean in the west. It was along this route that dates, spices, and Islam traveled east, while oranges, roses, and silks traveled west. Trade caravans raced from one walled city to the next, or alternatively slept out in the open, running the risk of marauding bandits and dehydration. Along the way, they skirted the fearsome Taklamakan Desert and rested in the fortified cities of the Persian Plateau. Trade between the Arab world and China flourished between 200 and 1500 CE, but faded thereafter as political turbulence in Central Asia made the Silk Road too dangerous for the caravans, while the newly emergent European powers opened up sea routes to commerce.[9]

The earlier Arab traders might be gone, but they are not forgotten. Many Arab traders settled permanently in China and assimilated with the majority Han Chinese. Their descendants look Chinese, speak Chinese, but still observe Islam. They are known as the Hui Chinese. The Hui are a visible reminder that relations between the Arab world and China have a long history. They are the only Chinese minority to be recognized by their religion, not their territory. There are other Chinese Muslims, but the Hui account for half of the total 20 million. They are also the most geographically diverse, their ancestors having spread across the country.[10] So, while the number of Arab traders traveling the Silk Road slowed to a trickle after 1600, it was the Hui who kept the memories of the early Arab traders alive.

It wasn't just the Hui who welcomed the Arab traders. The Yiwu authorities realized that the arrival of Arab traders was good for the city's economy and decided in 2004 to build a mosque. This was a remarkable decision. The Yiwu authorities are mainly majority Han Chinese. At most, a few are practicing Christians. It is most unlikely that any are practicing Muslims. Nonetheless, they recognized that a mosque would help attract more Arab traders to the city. Their pragmatism was already evident in the decision to build a handful of five-star hotels. The authorities had recognized that more affluent traders wouldn't travel to Yiwu if they had to stay in dirty and noisy lodgings. This "If you build it, they will come" mentality has so far worked.

The Yiwu authorities didn't stop at the mosque. They also later requested an Islamic cleric, or Imam and the Beijing authorities dispatched Ma Chunzhen. Ma had studied with a friend of mine in Xinjiang before completing his studies in Beijing. He studied at one of the many Islamic colleges scattered across China. Working as an Imam was a good job. The government paid an annual income of $13,000 more than six times the average national income. When Ma arrived in Yiwu the mosque was still not finished. The congregation numbered less than a hundred people and used an upper floor of the Red Guest House. But after Ma's arrival the congregation swelled quickly to six hundred people who were soon "jostling for room." The congregation had grown to over a thousand people when the mosque opened in September 2005.

Even then, the Yiwu authorities continued to search for new ways to welcome the Arab traders. Jin Kechang, the bureau's head, happily told reporters from the China Youth Daily that he was still searching for ways to make life easier for Muslim Arab traders. There were plans to build an Islamic school as the bureau had discovered that while a number of Muslim Arab traders' children were studying at local schools, the school meals generally contained pork so their parents were obliged to send their children to the mosque for lunch. The bureau planned to first build a kindergarten attached to the mosque, followed later by primary and secondary schools. The bureau believed that with their construction more Muslim Arab traders would bring their wives and children to live in the city. The Yiwu authorities were taking decisions that would result in a large Arab community settling there.

Yiwu isn't an exception. There are newly constructed mosques in many other Chinese cities. There are also far older mosques spread across the country, such as in the southern coastal city of Quanzhou,[11] an old trading port, which was once a popular destination for Arab traders arriving by sea. The mosque is a reflection of how China and the West have diverged since 2001. It is tough to imagine Western governments building a mosque today to encourage Arab traders to visit a city. A mosque is more likely to be viewed as a security threat by the local community. In recent years, there have been protests against the construction of new mosques in many Western cities such as Boston, Cologne, and London.[12] Opposition is especially fierce in Southern Europe.

It certainly helps that the Chinese authorities have a more intrusive security apparatus. The Arab traders I spoke with freely admitted that they faced restrictions on their activity. Hong Kong newspapers reported stories of Arab traders facing more intrusive security surveillance after 2001. But the behavior of the Chinese authorities isn't all that different from the behavior of the Imperial rulers centuries earlier. The Tang Dynasty rulers, for instance, compelled not just the Arab traders but also all foreigners to live in specific sections of a city.[13] So long as the rules were obeyed trade was freely permitted. It was a compromise that didn't prevent trade along the Silk Road from flourishing. The same is true of events today.

Yiwu may struggle to remain competitive as production costs rise and the Chinese currency strengthens. Arab traders may buy fewer novelty gifts and hammers from China in the coming years. But they will buy more plasma TVs and automobiles. Moreover, the stories related are about more than just cheap consumer goods. Yiwu's bustling exhibition halls are testimony to the fact that China, relative to the Western countries, took a different approach to the Arab world after 2001. The city's municipal council was prepared to build a mosque to attract Arab traders. Other Chinese cities have employed Arabic-speaking officials to attract Arab investors. It is an approach built on shared economic interests and historical ties. So far it has paid off handsomely.

*   *   *

The events taking place in Yiwu bubble below the surface of the global economy. Each individual story so far described is easily overlooked. Instead, America and Europe are focused on the more easily observed phenomena, such as Wal-Mart's billion dollar purchases from Chinese factories, Europe's struggle against a flood of Chinese-made clothes and shoes, or China's thirst for oil and the rise in international oil prices. These are all newsworthy items. Nonetheless, the stories in Yiwu are symbolic of a gradual rebalancing in the global economy. The arrival of Arab traders in

Yiwu echoes the arrival of their ancestors hundreds of years ago and is helping to resurrect one of the world's great trading routes. The rebalancing is made all the more stark as it occurs simultaneously with a worsening in relations between the Arab world and the West.

Comparisons with the Silk Road are apt. The road was never a single route. It was instead made of thousands of smaller routes stretching across China, Central Asia, and the Middle East. Traders only rarely traveled the full distance between China and the Mediterranean. It was too expensive a journey, too long a time to stay away from home. More often traders traveled just part of the way before selling their goods. But it was through this long chain of buyers and sellers that Chinese silk eventually found its way to Europe. The Silk Road is a memorial to the power of thousands of individual traders. The same is true today. However, Yiwu lies at just one end of the Silk Road. So I decided to search for more evidence of change at the other end, in the Arab world. It seemed appropriate to start in the Syrian capital of Damascus for the city was once an important terminal point for the early Silk Road traders.

*   *   *

Damascus is a long way from Yiwu. It is also considerably older. The city dates back to at least 8000 BCE. But the Syrian capital wears its age well amid an eclectic muddle of architectural styles dating from Roman, Islamic, and European eras. The old city is a warren of narrow streets which makes it relatively cool as the midday sun struggles to penetrate between tightly packed buildings. The street called "Straight" slices straight through the old city, from its eastern to its western gates. It was here that Paul the Apostle was directed to ask for Saul of Tarsus after his arrival in the city. Saladin was buried nearby after his long years fighting the Crusaders. The main shopping street, Souq Al Hamidiyyeh, was built by the Ottoman Empire in the 1800s. Small doors punctuate the alleyways and give access to large open-roofed khans (markets) decorated in the alternating strips of black and white stone that are a feature of the old city. It was in the khans that traders journeying along the Silk Road would camp temporarily while they bought and sold goods.

I had met Syrian traders in Yiwu, so it wasn't a surprise to find evidence of the Chinese city in Damascus. It was a taxi driver who tipped me off, an old man driving a beat-up car. The front seat was broken so I sat in the back. After chatting for a while I switched the conversation to China. I explained I had met many Syrian traders in China and asked his opinion on the sudden flood of Chinese imports to the city. "You should visit Souq Al Hamidiyyeh," he said. He told me about a small alleyway leading off the main street that sold gifts and toys. "Everything is imported from China," he declared triumphantly. I bet him everything was imported from Yiwu. I was right. I later visited the alleyway. It was a riotous mess of brightly colored gifts and toys spilling out onto the streets in cardboard boxes and strung across the alleyway itself. I could have been walking through Yiwu's exhibition halls, specifically stalls B1 670 to B1 1040, which sold the same gifts and toys.

The stalls in this alleyway date back centuries. A single family might have traded in the same stall for generations, the stall passed down from father to son. That was the case for Fadi Al Shamsi. Fadi's stall was built out of large slabs of worn stone. A rickety wooden awning kept out the midday heat. The stall wouldn't have looked any different selling fruits and spices a century earlier. But it sold gifts and toys instead. Fadi's father had started trading with China in the late seventies, about the same time that China opened its doors to the outside world. Fadi's father had later visited Yiwu and immediately saw the opportunities. He reported back to his son and advised that he make the trip himself. Fadi did and is now a regular traveler to Yiwu, making five trips a year. I looked around his stall and asked him how much of what he sold was from Yiwu. "Everything is from Yiwu, except me." He laughed. "And I'm not sure about that anymore."

As I worked my way along the stalls it seemed that all the vendors were visiting Yiwu. What I saw made me laugh. It was Valentine's Day at the time. Valentine's Day isn't a big event in Syria, but the Yiwu factories must have been cranking out Valentine's Day gifts when the traders last visited because the alleyway was full of furry Chinese-made "Love Me" pillows, an odd sight in the old city of Damascus. But I wondered if they were really any different from the Chinese-made silks that would have been for sale in the same stalls centuries earlier. Fadi's ancestors may have owned the stall even then. It is this historical continuity in trade links that makes the changes taking place in cities such as Damascus and Yiwu so important.

Abdul Midani was yet another thread in the new Silk Road. I met him in his office in Damascus one summer. He was a yarn trader, as was his father before him. His office was five centuries old and deep inside the old city's walls. Wooden struts supported walls made out of a mix of straw, plaster, and stone. The building itself leant precariously over a narrow dusty street. It wasn't the first place you'd expect to find a profitable Syrian trader. But the Syrians have a keen sense of history and Midani was happy operating from the same office. He wasn't alone, as many of the city's most profitable traders also maintained offices in the old city. The offices also help to disguise the traders' true wealth from an intrusive government.

Midani used to import yarn from the United States. The yarn was used in Syrian mills or shipped to a third country without ever having arrived in Syria itself. But after 2001 he started to import from China. He was just one of the many Arabs traders who had benefited from the rise of China. "I became afraid of traveling to the United States," he says. "I didn't want to wait hours at customs while they checked my background. Who knows? My name might accidentally match that on a list of suspected terrorists," he said. "But when I arrive in China they welcome me like an old friend. They pay for my hotel. They pay for my meals. Nothing is too much." Midani might have exaggerated his story for my benefit, but if so, not by much. The decision by the Yiwu authorities to build a mosque, hire an Imam, and establish Islamic schools for the traders' families echoed his experience.

Midani wasn't like the other Arab traders who visited Yiwu. He had ambitions. He had recently established a representative office in the Xuhui district in Shanghai. I visited it a few months later. The Shanghai office is located in a steel and glass multi-storey building. It contrasts starkly with his office in Damascus. Midani employs four Chinese staff and speaks with them via Internet everyday from his office in the old city of Damascus. His staff has no qualms about working for a Syrian, although they might have questions about the state of the firm's headquarters in Damascus. In an ironic twist, Midani is now exporting Chinese yarn to America. He used the contacts he had earlier established in America to find buyers. Occasionally he risks a visit to America itself, but he generally prefers to shuttle between Damascus and Shanghai.

The Arab traders reshaping trade flows are one reason China is fast catching up to the West. China's exports to the Arab world were worth just $6 billion in 2000, behind the United Kingdom ($9 billion), Germany ($12 billion), and far behind the United States ($18 billion). But by 2009 its exports had accelerated to $60 billion, overtaking the United Kingdom and Germany, and overtaking the United States ($43 billion).[14] But statistics don't tell the whole story. A large share of America's exports to the Arab world is accounted for by aircraft, for instance, orders placed by Emirates, the UAE's national carrier. Emirates is enjoying surging demand for seats on its flights between Dubai and Beijing, Shanghai, and Hong Kong, meaning it is the growing number of Arab traders traveling to China who, ironically, help explain America's rising sales of aircraft to the UAE's national carrier.

In fact, Emirates offers a useful way to measure the impact of trade between the Arab world and China. The airline added 840 staff and flew an extra 4.7 million passengers in the 2009/10 financial year.[15] It had 58 Airbus 380s, the new double-decker aircraft, on order. Moreover, its total order book of 208 aircraft, worth $69 billion, was the largest in aviation history.[16] Dubai itself meanwhile has plans to build the world's largest passenger and cargo hub. Al Maktoum airport will be able to handle 120 million passengers a year. London Heathrow handles just 68 million.[17] The airport is not just a statement of intent. Dubai sits at the crossroads of Asia, the Middle East, and Africa. It is already benefiting from flourishing trade flows between the three regions and is now planning for a huge expansion.

* * *

Trade along the Silk Road was never one way. Even as Arab traders travel to China, there are Chinese traders who travel to the Arab countries. As I travel through the Arab countries I am always amazed to encounter Chinese in the most unusual places. It is popularly believed that the greatest Chinese export is the cheap consumer goods – the $1 pair of socks or the $100 DVD player. But the greatest Chinese export is people. In the mid-1800s, the opening of "treaty ports" by foreign merchants permitted Chinese to migrate abroad.[18] The result was a flood of Chinese labor to work in the goldfields from California to Australia. It was a decision that resulted in the creation of Chinatowns, which are still found in most of the world's large cities. A similar phenomenon is evident today. The Chinese authorities have again recently relaxed restrictions on Chinese migrating abroad, after travel was heavily restricted from the 1950s to the 1980s. The result is an outward flood of Chinese traders. Indeed, the number of Chinese leaving the country annually has risen by 30 million since 2000.[19]

Take for instance, the Chinese traders I met in Syria. The Adra Free Zone is a 30-minute drive from the Syrian capital. It is a dirty place full of heavy industrial equipment and large second-hand lorries imported from the European Union. The lorries belch diesel fumes into the air and leave the ground slick with oil. Although the Adra Free Zone isn't a pleasant place, it is flourishing as a staging point for shipments into Iraq. When I visited, the guard at the gate waved his arm expansively toward the lorries and jokingly said, "We've got to thank America for all this." Hardened men from Iran, Iraq, and Syria, wrapped in ex-military jackets, had the run of the place. These were the truck drivers who risked their lives to make the run to Baghdad. A representative of one of the trucking companies claimed that 10 percent of the trucks that left the Adra Free Zone never reached their destination at the peak of the conflict. But the money is good and there is no shortage of new drivers. The Adra Free Zone is profiting from the relative stability in Syria even as its immediate neighbors convulse.

I had arranged to meet Zhou Dongyun, the General Manager of a company called China City. Initially I struggled to find the building. None of the truck drivers I spoke with had heard of China City. Only after walking around the Adra Free Zone did I spot the company name written in bold red letters on a squat two-storey building. The recently constructed building was designed as an exhibition hall, with space for several dozen stallholders. I had first read about China City on a website run by the Chinese Embassy in Damascus. The website included a forum for Chinese traders to enquire about trading opportunities in the country. A trader had asked, "I am an independent trader. How can I sell goods to Syria without an established network?" An embassy official had posted the phone number of China City in reply and suggested the trader get in contact. I called the same number and arranged to meet Zhou while on a visit to Syria.

It was Chinese New Year and Zhou had kindly interrupted her celebrations to meet me. She was waiting at the entrance to the building dressed in her best clothes and heavily made up. We first walked around the exhibition halls. It was an odd collection of furniture, electronics, and industrial equipment. Zhou explained that Iraqi officials were her best customers. "They travel from Baghdad on buying trips since security has worsened." Zhou later showed me the staff canteen. It still wasn't finished and there was a layer of sawdust across the floor. I asked what sort of food the canteen would sell. "Shanghai food," she said. When I explained how I preferred northern-style cooking, she turned up her nose. Zhou and her business partners were all born in Zhejiang province, a few hours drive from Yiwu. It made sense. The majority of Chinese traders hailed from just a handful of provinces along the eastern seaboard, in particular Guangdong, Fujian, and Zhejiang provinces.

Zhou had a compelling sales pitch. "We will allow only two companies selling the same product to exhibit here. No more than that, otherwise exhibitors start competing with each other and bidding prices down." It is an irony that many Chinese traders travel abroad in order to escape the relentless competition at home, yet they often end up competing with other Chinese traders who have the same idea. Syria is still fresh territory and the number of Chinese traders is small compared to other parts of the developing world. But eventually more Chinese traders will arrive and profit margins will fall. Zhou and her partners hoped to forestall that outcome by restricting entry to their exhibition halls. They also offered their exhibitors advice on dealing with Syria's tortuous import and investment regulations, hoping that other Chinese traders would find it too tricky to set up their own operations and so choose to stay away. It was a good strategy.

I can understand why Zhou and her partners want to protect their profit margins. I had earlier purchased a box of electronic Qurans from a Chinese manufacturer. The devices contained the full text of Islam's holy book and audio recitations. The wholesale price was thirty dollars, which I thought was expensive. My Chinese friends I'd spoken with thought the same. I had brought the electronic Qurans with me to Damascus as a way to test the market. It turned out that the devices were still a novelty and I found just a single Korean model for sale in the city. When I asked my Syrian friends what they might pay for the devices, their estimates ranged between $60 and $80 retail. I hadn't expected such a high figure. After all, the average annual income in Syria is just $3000. It is a handsome profit margin and it's no surprise that Chinese traders are traveling to developing economies, such as Syria, to sell their goods. Zhou and her partners will eventually face fierce competition as more Chinese goods flood the market, but for the time being, profit margins are wide.

Zhou and China City are no exceptions. There are copy-cat versions of China City dotted across the Arab world. But like the Arabs in Yiwu, these places are largely unobserved in America and Europe. They all share similar features. First is the tendency for Chinese traders to club together in order to lower operating costs and attract customers to a single location. Second is the tendency for Chinese traders to live and eat together rather than mix with the local community. This was why China City had built its own canteen. It was why Zhou herself lived not far from the Adra Free Zone. But China City and its imitators are a lesson in the importance of Chinese traders to the rise of trade relations between the Arab world and China. There are thousands of Arab traders traveling to Yiwu, but there are just as many Chinese traders traveling to the Arab world. And by locating themselves in a single building these traders are establishing beachheads in what are difficult markets to penetrate.

Dubai claims the largest of these buildings. It is called Dragon Mart and was built on the parched outskirts of the city. It claims around 150,000 square meters of exhibition space, making it the largest building to sell exclusively Chinese-made goods outside of China. The Dragon Mart is built in the shape of a large snaking dragon. A yawning mouth welcomes visitors who wind their way through a long body before finishing up in the tail. I visited one summer and was impressed. The stallholders are a mix of Chinese manufacturers and independent Chinese traders who lack the distribution networks to make it on their own. They sell both retail and wholesale; so during the weekend the place is packed with families. It's a true crossroads of cultures. Watching Zhejiang traders haggle with Emirati women dressed in traditional costume is like stepping back into history.

It was a Dubai property development company, Nakheel, who built Dragon Mart. It also built Palm Islands, or the world's largest artificial islands built in the shape of a palm tree. Nakheel's parent company, Dubai World, owns one of the world's largest port companies and was in a unique position to watch the sudden surge of trade flows with China. It constructed Dragon Mart in 2004, or not long after the number of Arab traders traveling to Yiwu jumped. The company hopes it can capture part of this trade by encouraging Arab traders to make the shorter visit to Dubai rather than Yiwu. Nakheel had initially contracted management of Dragon Mart to the China Middle East Investment Corporation, a body associated with the Chinese government. But, unhappy with the service, Nakheel has since taken over responsibility for management of the complex. Today, Dragon Mart is a monument to the rise in trade relations between the Arab world and China.

Not all Arab countries possess a China City or Dragon Mart. Indeed foreigners are not allowed to sell retail in some Arab countries. Saudi Arabia is a good example; Egypt is another. But this hasn't stopped everyone. I have heard stories of Chinese traders knocking on residential doors in Cairo selling clothes and electronics, or even traveling through rural Egyptian communities. But you won't find thousands of Chinese traders selling goods in local markets in Cairo and Riyadh. Most traders are operating through official channels, such as the China Cities in Dubai or Syria, or meeting Arab buyers through the Internet and making periodic visits to the Arab countries in order to display their products at trade fairs. The Internet is especially popular among Chinese traders. In fact, the largest trading website has ironically taken its name from the Arab world.

Alibaba is just one of the tales in the book *A Thousand and One Nights*. But it wasn't included in the original Arabic version. Antoine Galland added it to his eighteenth-century translation. Galland was an Arabist who had lived in Syria for two decades and claimed to have heard the tale from a storyteller in the northern city of Aleppo. His claim is disputable, but regardless, the tale of Alibaba is now famous across the world, including in China. It was for this reason that Jack Ma decided to name his fledgling company Alibaba. Ma had global ambitions and wanted to find a name that both Chinese and non-Chinese speakers could associate with. While eating at a restaurant in the United States he thought of the name Alibaba. Ma called the waiter over and asked him if he knew the story. The waiter didn't just know the story, he also knew the secret password. "Open Sesame," he replied. Ma asked the same question in a number of countries and always received the same positive answer.

Alibaba.com is now one of the world's largest business-to-business websites. It has spawned many imitators, not just in China, but also abroad. Alibaba has separate Chinese and English language sites, but it is the Chinese language site that helps to explain why Chinese exporters have so successfully penetrated foreign markets. The website brings together buyers and sellers from China. But more importantly it allows users to swap experiences and post questions on chat forums. Want to export to the Arab world? Join a forum and start posting. A Zhejiang tools manufacturer might ask other users how he should receive payment when exporting to Egypt. A Chongqing auto parts manufacturer might post a comment noting that Saudi Arabia had reduced its tariffs on auto imports. A Guangdong company might advertise its services shipping goods to the Syrian port of Latakiya.

A virtual community of Chinese traders is a powerful tool. Take for instance a question asking, "Recently my company received an order from an Egyptian customer. The customer demanded a contract, receipt and consular notification. I've yet to do a consular notification. Please, can someone advise me how to go and do this thing? My company generally ships after 40 days. When is the best time to go?" The request received several replies. A blogger called Longfengqi said, "It's possible to ask the customer directly. If you're worried about losing face, don't ask him directly, but slowly ask specific questions, then he will tell you all." There are thousands of requests and replies similar to this on Alibaba. It's a powerful resource for small and medium-sized traders.

Alibaba.com never receives the attention it deserves for driving China's export growth. Economists, including myself, tend to focus on the big numbers, as these have attracted media headlines and politicians' ire in Washington. But Alibaba allows buyers to bid among manufacturers regardless of where they are in the country and this fierce competition helps to drive prices lower. This was made clear to me by the sales manager of Green Technologies, based in Shenzhen, a major Chinese city neighboring Hong Kong. I asked the sales manager what he thought of Alibaba. "We don't use it so much anymore," he said. "It's too competitive. There are too many manufacturers who use it. It's better to sell direct into Saudi Arabia where there is less competition."

The individual stories related in this chapter are important. Trade flows are already responding to the efforts of thousands of individual traders. It is because of their efforts that China may shortly rank as the Arab world's most important trading partner. The implication is lost jobs and lost output in the West. At first glance, the same is happening elsewhere in the world, as China has captured market share in both the developed and developing world. But the stories are part of something far grander. They are the individual threads of a new Silk Road. By themselves they are easy to ignore. But when woven together they are symbolic of powerful economic forces at work in the global economy.

The following chapters focus on bigger themes, such as oil, wealth, and the media. But it is individuals that are fuelling the rise of the Silk Road. In a world dominated by large Western corporations it is easy to overlook the stories of these individuals. Yet as I travel through the Arab world I find a growing number of Arabs who have a story to tell about China. At times it is a personal anecdote. More often it is a story about a friend or relative who is trading with China. These are equally important signals about the changes taking place in the global economy. They tell a story that isn't always apparent from the economic data or corporate reports. They are easily overlooked amid the recent clamor of economic and financial crises.

Ironically, America and Europe recognize the power of individuals, but mainly through the rise of the Internet. The growth of blogs, Facebook, and eBay is testimony to the power of individuals. These activities are widely documented by the Western media. It is easy to observe and participate in these activities from the security of our own home. Not so the changes taking place in the Arab world and China. These are changes that need to be observed first hand, whether in the exhibition halls of Yiwu or in the old markets of Damascus. But collaboration between an Arab and Chinese trader is potentially no different from the collaboration between two friends who met on Facebook. Indeed, their collaboration is already felt in the rising volumes of goods and money flowing between the Arab world and China.

The challenge for the West is to decide whether it needs Arab traders. Security concerns will likely win out in the immediate future and Arab traders will continue to find it difficult to visit America and Europe. Fortunately, the Western economies are increasingly selling the type of high-value goods and services that can be bought and sold by phone, so the value of goods traded will continue to grow. However, this approach risks building a wall between the average Arab and the average Westerner. These are challenges the West needs to think about, for the new Silk Road traders are already voting with their wallets and turning their backs on the West in favor of China. In doing so, they are relaying the foundations for a new road between two once great trading partners.

CHAPTER 2

Chinese Petrodollars and the Competition for Oil

In March 1937, an American geologist, Max Steinke, made a fateful trip across Saudi Arabia. He was part of an exploratory team working for the Standard Oil Company of California. Steinke and his colleagues had established a base camp in the eastern coastal city of Dhahran. Their American wives later arrived on the boat from Bombay. It was a harsh assignment. The team lived in two-bedroom portables. There wasn't a tree in sight. Summer temperatures reached upward of 130 degrees. Two Chinese cooks, Chow Lee and Frank Dang, served up a steady diet of fried noodles and bread. But for the geologists, at least, there was the reward of exploring the vast and still untamed Arabian Peninsula. And so in March that year the exploratory team set off in a convoy of two sedans and three pickups. An American journalist, Wallace Stegner, later recorded the events.[1]

Traveling to Riyadh the exploratory team stopped at Hofuf to pay their respects to the Amir, Ibn Jiluwi. The Amir had a habit of playing tricks on unsuspecting guests by murmuring "coffee" under his breath and having his bodyguard repeat the order "in a sudden savage shout that startled the uninitiated out of their cushions." Later, they traveled onwards to Riyadh and paid their respects to Crown Prince Saud in Badia Palace. They were woken up in the morning by the shriek of wooden pulleys as hundreds of donkeys pulled buckets of water from the well to pour into the channels that watered the gardens. The Crown Prince later showed them his palace, including a room full of old-fashioned clocks, each telling a separate time. The Crown Prince said he wanted his clocks to tell the time of each country in the globe.

Throughout the trip Steinke took notes of Saudi Arabia's geological structure. He didn't know it at the time, but his notes helped in the discovery of the world's largest oil field, Ghawar, more than a decade later in 1948. Ghawar lies between Dhahran and Riyadh. It is a monster. It stretches nearly 280 kilometers. It accounts for 5 percent of the world's total oil reserves and pumps nearly 5 million barrels of oil a day, or enough to supply America with one quarter of its daily oil consumption.[2] Standard Oil of California grew rich because of Ghawar. But its luck didn't last forever; in 1980 the Saudi Arabian government took full control of the concession, renaming the company Saudi Aramco. Today Saudi Aramco is the world's largest oil company, its market capitalization almost double that of ExxonMobil.[3] It is just 70 years since Steinke made his first trip across Saudi Arabia, yet the discovery of oil has changed the future of the Arab world permanently.

The Arab world accounts for 28 percent of the world's total oil reserves.[4] Most of this is exported. So when oil prices surged from less than $30 a barrel to near $150 a barrel between 2004 and 2008 it represented a remarkable windfall. A barrel of oil is still, after all, just a barrel of oil. Yet suddenly there were more buyers than sellers. All the Arab world had to do was keep pumping the same amount of oil. Its combined trade surplus surged from $100 billion to $180 billion, an increase that almost matched the rise in China's trade surplus.[5] The gain was worth an extra $3,000 annually to every resident of an Arab Gulf oil producing state.[6] The health of the Arab economies is intimately linked to the price of a barrel of oil. The risk, therefore, is that oil prices will return to $30 and stay there. If so, this would put an end to the party, as funds available for consumption and investment start to drain away.

But is this likely? The Arab oil producers have a single reason for why oil prices aren't likely to return to $30 a barrel for a long period. It is a goliath that has reshaped the Arab world.

China has an unquenchable thirst for oil. Oil imports surged as its economy shifted up into top gear after 2001. I watched this from Hong Kong while working as a China economist for JPMorgan. It was as if the whole world had suddenly discovered China. There was a sudden flood of clients clamoring to learn why the country's oil imports had surged. First, the export factories were using oil as a basic input in manufacturing of goods, such as personal computers or winter jackets. The factories also used oil to fuel their electric generators and run their delivery trucks. Second, an explosion in private car ownership was pushing up demand for gasoline. Third, the Chinese government started filling its newly constructed strategic oil reserves from 2006. These were just three of the more important explanations.

It's not that China lacks oil reserves. It produces 3.7 million barrels per day, making it the world's fifth largest oil producer, ranked just below Iran (4.3 million barrels) and on a par with Mexico (3.7 million barrels).[7] The problem is that oil production is stuck at this figure because of a lack of new discoveries. Estimates suggest that existing proven reserves will peak early in the next decade before declining through to 2030 if not supplemented by imports.[8] No doubt new discoveries will be made, for example in the Bohai region neighboring Beijing. But such discoveries are unlikely to change the fact that the domestic production is still falling a long way behind domestic consumption. And after turning into a net oil importer in 1993, China's oil imports have surged, doubling around every five years.

The figures tell the story. China's share of global oil consumption was a tiny 3 percent in the 1980s. But by 2009 its share had rocketed to 10 percent.[9] On the way, China overtook Japan to rank as the world's second largest consumer of oil. The United States is still the world's largest consumer, accounting for a huge 22 percent of global oil consumption, and it isn't about to give up that ranking anytime soon. However, for the global oil markets it's not the absolute share that is important, but rather the change in the share. And whereas China accounted for 10 percent of global consumption, it accounted for nearly 50 percent of *the increase* in global consumption between 2000 and 2009.[10] It was this extra demand that put the squeeze on global oil markets and sent prices spiraling higher after 2004, to the gain of the Arab world.

Of course, China wasn't the only explanation for the rise in prices. The global economy was enjoying its most robust period of growth in decades, having shrugged off the bursting of the high-tech bubble in 2001. Like China, many developing economies were also growing robustly, further spurring the demand for oil. There were also supply-side constraints – most oil producers had relatively limited spare capacity owing to a lack of investment during the 1990s. In addition many oil consumers had limited inventories, owing to a growing preference to manage inventory levels more efficiently. Geopolitical tensions were also playing a role owing to the continuing war in Iraq and the risk of unrest in Nigeria and Venezuela. These additional factors also helped to push oil prices to historic highs.[11]

The rise in oil prices had an immediate impact on the Arab economies. Arab traders flooded the streets of Yiwu flush with petrodollars. Their numbers started to rise in 2004, or around the same time as oil prices, and continued to rise in the subsequent years as they sourced toys, gifts, and household items for hungry consumers. The Arab oil-producing economies meanwhile boomed. Dubai's skyline grew steadily taller as the city built a financial sector to intermediate the region's windfall. Bahrain and Qatar attempted to follow in its footsteps. Saudi Arabia embarked on grand infrastructure projects planning for a post-oil future. The link between oil prices and the Arab economies is strong, and the rise in prices, in part due to China, had a transformational effect.

But will oil prices remain high? Global recession has put a serious dent in oil demand. Oil prices have fallen from their peaks. Yet the International Energy Agency expects oil prices to average around $90 per barrel through to 2015, after which prices rise above $180 per barrel by 2030.[12] The International Energy Agency was established after the oil price shocks in the 1970s. Its initial mandate was to coordinate management of emergency oil supplies in the event of another oil price shock. However, its mandate has since widened and the agency now has a team of over 100 analysts collating and interpreting data from its member countries. Investors pay attention to what the agency has to say. *The Financial Times*, the *Washington Post* and the *New York Times* likewise regularly cover its annual reports.

The agency warned of a supply-side crunch after 2010. It worried about the sheer scale of investment needed saying, "if actual capacity additions fall short of this amount, spare production capacity would be squeezed and oil prices would undoubtedly rise – possibly to new record highs."[13] The large Arab oil producers already have a strong grip on the world's oil markets, but odds are their grip will strengthen even further in the coming decade. It is the Arab world where most of the world's remaining

oil reserves are located and therefore where most of the investment in oil production is expected to take place. The agency
estimates that the Arab world, together with Iran, will account
for a rising share of the world's oil production, from 26 percent
in 2008 to 28 percent in 2030, as a result.[14]

If so, Arab oil producers will continue to speak of China in
reverent tones. The International Energy Agency estimates that
China will account for over 42 percent of the increase in the
world's oil demand through to 2030. This scenario assumes an
average economic growth rate of 6 percent. There are risks the
growth rate will periodically slow sharply, for instance, if inflation rises too fast and the central bank has to hike interest rates
too rapidly. Indeed, growth was slowing sharply in late 2008 to
its lowest level in nearly a decade. Yet, in spite of such short-
term volatility, the country's medium-term growth prospects look
robust as a result of rising urbanization and steady economic and
financial reforms. Its demand for oil is expected to continue rising as a result.

* * *

Saudi Arabia is the giant of the oil industry. Its capital, Riyadh,
is a classic Arabian city, lying inland, surrounded entirely by desert. There are few buildings more than four storey tall. A relentless sun has beaten the city flat and leached the color from its
walls. It is a harsh environment, in which to build a capital, far
from the nearest seaport. The contrast with its neighbor, Dubai,
is stark. Dubai has more than a dozen buildings higher than 40
storeys; Riyadh has just 2. I visited the city as the temperature
cooled from the summer furnace to a more tolerable 35 degrees.
It was my first visit to Saudi Arabia, having so far lived mainly
in the Arab countries bordering the Mediterranean Sea, and I
thought its bleak deserts a sharp contrast to the orange groves of
Palestine, the lush valleys of Lebanon, and the marble palaces of
Syria.

Saudi Arabia accounts for 13 percent of the world's oil production.[15] It is also the only major oil producer able to increase
its production significantly.[16] This gives it a firm grip on the
world's oil supply. It can't set the price of a barrel of oil, but it

could certainly nudge the price in either direction by regulating its own production. Not surprisingly, the oil market listens when the Saudi Arabian Oil Minister, Ali Al Naimi, speaks. A reporter friend who worked for Bloomberg Television attended the OPEC meetings in Beirut, Riyadh, and Tehran and recalled, "Al Naimi was the only official we wanted to speak with. The press was waiting out the front of the building like paparazzi and, when he appeared, we chased him like he was a pop star."

Saudi Arabia is China's major oil partner. China's Saudi imports, at 0.5 million barrels per day, account for more than half its total imports from the Arab world.[17] After Saudi Arabia is Oman at near 0.3 million barrels per day. Oman produces mainly low-sulfur "sweet" crude oil and so was a logical target in the early years, given the restraints on China's high-sulfur sour crude oil refining facilities. Yet China's imports from Oman are almost stagnant even as its imports from Saudi Arabia are rising sharply. China's imports from Yemen are ranked third, but negligible at less than 0.1 million barrels per day. President Ali Abdullah Saleh visited China in March 2004, and signed an energy agreement with the Chinese leadership. The agreement included the right for Chinese firms to explore for oil in Yemen. But China's imports from the country have nonetheless fallen since the President's visit.

Iraq is still an unknown quantity. The country is struggling to raise output to its prewar levels. But it is the world's third largest holder of oil reserves.[18] There is also speculation that its oil reserves are perhaps even larger, given that only limited oil exploration has taken place since the late 1980s.[19] China had signed a number of agreements with Saddam Hussein's regime in the 1990s, including an agreement about the Al Ahdab field in southern Iraq. But the new Iraqi government effectively put these agreements on hold while rewriting its oil laws. The Iraqi president, Jalal Talabani, visited China in June 2007, accompanied by Iraq's Oil Minister who publicly declared the Al Ahdab field contract was still valid.[20] And it seemed that the China National Petroleum Corporation (CNPC) was likely to be among the first international oil companies to sign an agreement with Iraq.[21]

Saudi Arabia ranks number one. It also has good reason to want a stronger relationship with China. Saudi Arabia is worried by its near 70-year dependence on America. It was American oil firms, such as the Standard Oil Company of California, which financed the early expansion of Saudi oil production after oil was discovered in the 1930s. Many electricity sockets in the country's oil producing regions require American-style plugs, in mundane testimony to the earlier importance of relations. But the September 11 attacks and an anti-Saudi Arabian backlash have strained relations between the two. The Iraq and Lebanon wars further aggravated tensions, as America was accused of imperialist ambitions and acting unfairly in Israel's favor. It isn't surprising that Saudi Arabia views China as a way to hedge its reliance on America.

Relations between the two countries have a relatively short history. An orthodox Islamic state and socialist Asian state are not natural partners. But relations started to shift gears after Chinese President Jiang Zemin visited Riyadh in 1999. The visit resulted in the signing of an oil cooperation agreement between the two countries. It stipulated that Saudi Arabia would make oil exploration and development opportunities available to Chinese investors. In return China agreed to open its refinery sector to Saudi Arabia.[22] The agreement helped to open the doors to oil imports from Saudi Arabia, but the increase was still small – most of Saudi Arabia's new reserves consisted of sour crude oil, unsuitable for China's refining facilities.

However, real progress was made in 2006. King Abdullah visited Beijing in January that year with a retinue of several hundred Saudi Arabian businessmen. Jiang's successor, President Hu Jintao, reciprocated in April 2006. It was part of a world tour; his first stop was Washington, his second stop was Riyadh. It was a grand declaration of intent. Moreover, Washington had termed President Hu's stay an "official visit" rather than a "state visit," meaning there was no formal dinner at the White House.[23] Beijing viewed the decision as a snub. But when President Hu arrived in Saudi Arabia, he was met with full pageantry. He was also only the second foreign leader permitted to address Saudi Arabia's legislative council, in sharp contrast to events in Washington. It appeared as if relations between China and Saudi Arabia were strengthening rapidly.

A relationship with China also has few strings attached. President Hu Jintao did not talk politics while in the Kingdom. His only words of caution were that "war and military force is never a permanent solution to a problem," advising his listeners to "persist with a just and fair handling of conflicts and bridging of differences through political means."[24] Likewise, he made no mention of democracy or human rights. I watched the speech on television. It hit the right tone for the Saudi legislators. Saudi Arabia faces many challenges, not least rising unemployment, growing domestic militancy, and a neighbor engulfed in civil war. This is what makes China and its policy of noninterference in domestic affairs so appealing.

There is also growing financial and technical cooperation in the petrochemicals sector. In 2007, Saudi Aramco signed an agreement with Sinopec, a major Chinese oil company, to expand capacity of the Quanzhou refinery in Fujian province from 80,000 barrels per day to 240,000 barrels per day, a figure equivalent to the daily oil production of Brunei.[25] The joint venture includes a 25 percent stake for ExxonMobil, a 25 percent stake for Saudi Aramco, and a 50 percent stake for Sinopec. The refinery will be designed to handle sour crude oil and is situated next to one of the country's newly built strategic oil reserves. Such refineries are expected to help spur Chinese imports of Saudi Arabian sour crude oil significantly, at the expense of African sweet crude oil. In return Saudi Arabia also granted Sinopec a concession to explore and produce natural gas in Saudi Arabia in 2004.

Commercial relations are also growing. The Saudi Arabian General Investment Authority (SAGIA) has, for instance, set up a branch office in Hong Kong. The authority is the new face of Saudi Arabia. The Kingdom has recently taken ambitious steps toward encouraging foreign investors. Indeed, the World Bank ranked it "number one" in the Middle East in 2008 for ease of doing business, albeit still large bureaucratic and regulatory hurdles remain.[26] The authority's Hong Kong office is typical of this new welcoming stance. Likewise, a few Saudi Arabian investors have established factories in China, such as the Zamil Group, one of Saudi Arabia's largest investment companies. The company owns factories producing construction materials mainly in Saudi

Arabia. However, it has also constructed a steel factory in China to supply the local market.

Is there reason to worry about a growing relationship between the two countries? America's oil imports from Saudi Arabia peaked in 2003, before declining slowly as a share of the total.[27] The falling share may simply reflect greater demand for sour crude oil from a rapidly growing Asia. But for some, it signals a shift in the strategic balance. Take an op-ed piece written by Richard Russell, an academic at the National Defense University, in the *Wall Street Journal* during President Hu Jintao's visit to Saudi Arabia in early 2006. Russell argued that China and Saudi Arabia "are laying the foundation for a strategic relationship that challenges American interests," and that "the danger is these developments will pass largely unnoticed in Washington."[28]

I wasn't convinced. I found few Chinese traders walking the streets in Riyadh. It wasn't like this in Dubai. The Saudi Arabian government had encouraged foreign investors, but it still required that foreign traders have an invitation from a local company in order to visit the country. It also banned foreigners from selling retail in the country. This was a huge obstacle to Chinese traders wanting to sell their goods. It prevented the construction of a "China City" in Riyadh. Saudi Arabian officials said there was interest among local businessmen to build a "China City," but still no planning approval.[29] For the moment, it was mainly Saudi Arabian trading firms that were importing goods from China, as well as the Yemeni traders who had established a base in Yiwu.

Of course, China has made an effort. The provincial Chinese governments have dispatched dozens of missions to Saudi Arabia. Omar Bahlaiwa from the Saudi Arabian Chamber of Commerce recalls this with a shake of his head, "It was all too much too organize. In the end we had to request the Chinese limit their annual missions to just four. We didn't mind how many businessmen attended each mission. But more than four missions a year and we would have ended up working for the Chinese government." I laughed sympathetically when I heard this story. It is a popular mistake to view China as a single entity. It is instead a collection of over thirty provinces, many similar in size to a large European country, all competing furiously with each other for export markets.

So I tried the Chinese Economic Affairs Bureau attached to the Chinese Embassy. The bureau lies in a small suburban street near King Fahd road. There wasn't any flag flying over the building so I spent an hour trying to locate it. Many streets look the same in Riyadh and few people pay attention to road names. But eventually, with assistance over the phone from the Egyptian security guard, I found the bureau, a small bronze nameplate attached to the outside wall. I was scheduled to meet an official working for the bureau. We chatted for a while in Chinese. His English was also good, but he spoke no Arabic. This official was reluctant to go on record. But during our conversation he offered nothing to convince me that relations between China and Saudi Arabia were especially deep, at least not compared to relations between China and the rest of the Arab world.

The story was the same in Beijing. I spoke with Jeffrey Towson, an American investor based in Riyadh and a regular visitor to Beijing. "When I first arrived in Beijing I was receiving calls from Chinese officials all eager to build relations with Saudi Arabia," he recalls. I hadn't expected this. Towson had lived in Riyadh for nearly a decade. But why call an American? Why not a Saudi Arabian? It turned out Towson was one of the few people in Beijing with experience of the Arab kingdom aside from embassy officials. I myself had met few Saudi Arabian nationals in China. I put the question to Arab traders I met in Yiwu. "Have you seen any Saudi Arabian traders in the city?" They all shook their head in reply. "None," they said.

It isn't hard to find reasons why Saudi Arabia might feel cautious toward China. Though wanting to reduce its dependency on America, it isn't about to cut the relationship entirely. After all, America is still the world's largest oil consumer. It also provides significant military support to Saudi Arabia. As Prince Turki Al Faisal, the Saudi Arabian Ambassador to the United States, said in an interview, "China is not necessarily a better friend than the United States, but it is a less complicated friend."[30] Omar Bahlaiwa made a similar remark, "We are in a Catholic marriage with America. But we are also Muslims – we can have more than one wife." Riyadh is indeed building bridges with Beijing. But this says as much about the state of its relations with Washington as its docs the state of its relations with Beijing.

For its part, China also worries about its addiction to oil. It worries in particular about its addiction to a single oil producer. Saudi Arabia is especially challenging. Yes, it has plenty of oil, but it is also an orthodox Islamic state with volatile neighbors and, historically at least, strong relations with the United States. So even as China works to strengthen its relations with Saudi Arabia, it works just as energetically to strengthen its relations with alternative oil suppliers, such as Angola and Kazakhstan. President Hu Jintao's visit to Riyadh was important, but he has also made two visits to Angola since 2001. For the moment, there is little hard evidence of a new strategic axis between Beijing and Riyadh, for all the state visits and handshakes, which might challenge the West's oil security.

*   *   *

In 2003, a Chinese language novel was published online titled *The Battle in Protecting Key Oil Routes*. The novel depicts a naval battle between China and the United States. It's a gripping read.

> International oil prices had broken one hundred dollars a barrel and remained high. Seventy percent of China's oil consumption relied on imports, the majority of which passed through the Strait of Malacca. After careful preparation, the imperial powers who feared China's peaceful rise brazenly declared they intended to carry out naval exercises, codenamed 'Control the Vital Passage,' at a strategic exit from the Strait of Malacca, just 100 miles from Singapore.

The story continues in this tone for several pages before the tension increased dramatically as, "Suddenly an American Tomahawk missile was launched, aimed at the destroyer Qingdao ....."[31]

Bang. The novel was hugely popular and spawned several competing online versions. It is wrong to assume the story is a statement of official policy, for its fictitious battle is the work of an active imagination and reads no differently than a Tom Clancy novel. But *The Battle in Protecting Key Oil Routes* neatly captures an increasingly public debate about the country's growing addiction to oil. The first concern is oil prices. The second is oil security. It is these two fears that keep state planners in Beijing awake at night and explain why China is eager to diversify its oil supplies. Events in recent years have worsened, rather than eased, the state planners' worst fears.

In 2008, oil prices nearly reached $150 a barrel. The rise rattled state planners in Beijing. The state media openly accused the foreign oil companies of acting like "international petroleum crocodiles" by colluding to drive prices higher.[32] Many Chinese officials believe that foreign governments have deliberately driven oil prices up in order to curb China's economic development.[33] Li Hongjie, writing for the *Arab World Journal*, claims that "America constantly pressures China's room for development in the Middle East in order to prevent China's rise."[34] Suddenly, officials were left scrambling for a way to protect themselves from the risk that oil prices continue to rise and derail the country's economic development.

Meanwhile, tensions between America and Iran the same year highlighted the vulnerability of oil imports to what are called "chokepoints." The first major chokepoint is the Strait of Hormuz, the only entry into the Persian Gulf. At its narrowest it is only 21 miles wide, separating Iran to the north and the Oman to the south. The United States Department of Energy estimates that 24 percent of China's oil imports travel through the Strait of Hormuz.[35] Beijing rightly worries about the risks of armed conflict in the Persian Gulf, especially considering the buildup of American military forces there since the start of the Iraq War in 2003. In the past, Iran has also carried out military exercises in the strait in a none too subtle reminder of its capacity to shut the strait to traffic.

The second major chokepoint is the Strait of Malacca. At its narrowest, the strait is just 34 miles wide, separating Singapore to the north and Indonesia to the south. The United States Department of Energy estimates that 80 percent of China's oil transits through the Strait of Malacca.[36] The strait ranks among the world's busiest and most dangerous shipping lanes. In his description of maritime China, John Wills writes that the early Dutch traders, who had experience in most of the world's major maritime areas, considered the strait exceptionally hazardous even in the 1600s.[37] Modern naval forces and surveillance are increasingly effective against piracy and it is now rare for large ships to be attacked. But a major naval power, such as the United States, would have the ability to block shipments through the strait.

So China has scoured Africa for oil and for good reason. First, oil shipments from Africa avoid the Strait of Hormuz. Second, it is possible for Chinese state-owned oil companies to profit from a rise in oil prices, and potentially shield the country from the "international petroleum crocodiles," by buying equity stakes in African oil assets. The Western media started to report aggressive efforts by Chinese oil companies to acquire African oil fields. The Chinese government underwrote these efforts by extending an estimated $19 billion worth of aid and concessionary financing to the African governments.[38] President Hu Jintao visited Africa three times in three years, and his efforts appeared to pay off. In February 2006, Angola temporarily overtook Saudi Arabia as China's largest oil supplier.[39] It appeared as if Africa was indeed pulling ahead of the large Arab oil producers.

But the reality was more complex. China's oil refining facilities are constructed to refine mainly sweet crude oil with low-sulfur content, rather than sour crude oil with high-sulfur content. This favored the African oil fields over the Arabian fields. African fields produce mainly sweet crude oil.[40] Arabian oil fields produce a mixture of both sweet and sour crude oil, but the newer fields produce mainly sour crude oil. So when Chinese oil demand suddenly surged, Chinese oil companies naturally turned to Africa where sweet crude oil supplies are more available. But this balance will change in time. China is already building new refining facilities capable of processing sour crude oil, and Saudi Arabia is helping to finance these efforts, in particular through its participation in the Quanzhou refinery.

Of course, China will still buy equity stakes in African oil assets. This helps shield Chinese oil companies from a further rise in oil prices. The activities of the China National Petroleum Company (CNPC) in Sudan are typical. CNPC owns equity stakes in oil fields across the country. There are an estimated ten thousand Chinese workers in the country, most employed in building refineries or pipelines to the Red Sea, although a report in May 2007 suggested that decommissioned People's Liberation

Army soldiers were also employed to protect oil fields in the south.[41] The Chinese government has also provided loans to build infrastructure, including hydropower plants and transmission lines. As a result, Sudan was China's sixth largest oil supplier in 2008, accounting for nearly 6 percent of total imports.[42]

Yet China has chosen Sudan partly by default, rather than design. The United States Department of Energy estimates that China had secured equity oil worth 400,000 barrels per day in 2006. The three largest United States oil companies – ExxonMobil, Chevron, and ConocoPhillips – had secured equity oil worth 3,900,000 barrels per day, or nearly ten times the amount by the same year.[43] China's bid for equity stakes in African oil assets appears exceptional only when viewed in isolation. Yet it has targeted Africa largely because these are the few oil assets not already owned by the Western oil majors. It is also following a path already taken by the Western companies. As the International Energy Agency wrote in a report, "China's manner of entry into the global energy markets carries no surprise. Its strategies bear strong similarities to others' and are equally aggressive."[44]

The problem for China is that troubled states are not the most reliable business partners. They are vulnerable to regime change, and there is no reason for a newly installed government to honor existing agreements, especially if they must repay their military backers. Iraq was a case in point. A series of Chinese, French, and Russian firms had all signed agreements with Saddam Hussein's regime during the 1990s. But the new Iraqi government refused to honor these agreements after it was installed by the United States. It was widely assumed that the United States and its allies would sweep the field once new contracts were signed, although the new Iraq government appeared willing to at least consider offers from other countries, especially as the country's security situation remains tense.

Troubled states are also vulnerable to armed militants even if there is no regime change. In April 2007, the separatist Ogaden National Liberation Front (ONLF) attacked a Chinese oil facility in Ethiopia, killing nine Chinese oil workers and sixty-five Ethiopian oil workers and security personnel.[45] The ONLF claimed that the oil facility was attacked because ethnic Somalis had been cleared to make way for the facility's construction.[46] Earlier, in January 2007, militants attacked China's oil facilities in Nigeria, kidnapping nine Chinese oil workers. In this instance the militants had also kidnapped other foreign oil workers in a bid to extort a ransom.[47] There is no doubt that Chinese oil companies have a higher tolerance for risk, but this still doesn't reduce the vulnerability of oil supplies from troubled states.

So China is also looking toward Central Asia. It's a good idea in theory. Importing oil overland eliminates the Strait of Hormuz and the Strait of Malacca entirely. China's neighbor, Kazakhstan, claims 3 percent of the world's oil reserves.[48] Its largest oil fields are not far from the nearest Chinese border post. Nomads have inhabited the country for most of its history. Even the early Silk Road traders preferred to skirt along its southern border to avoid its barren deserts before continuing on toward the Persian Plateau. Not surprisingly, China has focused on Kazakhstan in its search for an alternative oil supplier because of the country's proximity. A pipeline running from the Kazakh oil fields to Chinese oil refineries would be of huge strategic value to the state planners in Beijing.

There is also a compelling historical argument for the relationship. The early imperial Chinese capitals were located inland, thousands of miles from the coast. Their rulers were more inclined to look west across the land, rather than east across the sea, as it was from the west that merchant caravans and invading armies were more likely to appear. Trade relations with Central Asia reached their peak by the Yuan Dynasty (1279 CE–1368 CE).[49] The Yuan Dynasty was a creation of the Mongols led by Kublai Khan. The Mongols also pacified Central Asia and as the threat of bandits faded the number of merchant caravans traveling along the Silk Road proliferated. Trade relations flourished for several centuries as stability was returned to the region.

However, history is not always forgiving. Relations between China and Central Asia took a turn for the worse after the fall of the Yuan Dynasty. The Qing Dynasty (1644 CE–1911 CE), fought a series of battles with the Muslim Chinese in the northwestern provinces during the seventeenth century. Morris Rossabi, a historian, writes that a large force was dispatched led by the Governor General of Shanxi province. "He accomplished his mission in the most brutal way and by 1650 had crushed the Muslims, with great loss of life on both sides. Tens of thousands died, and the bitterness engendered by these campaigns did not dissipate."[50] The battles fought by the Qing Dynasty strained relations between China and the Muslim populations of Central Asia. And today many of the large Central Asian oil producers remain suspicious of China.

Kazakhstan has also taken a nationalist stance toward its oil assets. The CNPC financed the construction of an oil pipeline between the two countries in 2005 with a potential capacity of 0.4 million barrels per day. But its efforts to purchase the formerly Canadian-owned PetroKazakhstan, which operates the Kumkol fields in the Turgai Basin, were not easy. Indeed, CNPC eventually had to give up a third of its purchase to the Kazakh authorities. In 2008, Kazakhstan's Prime Minister meanwhile threatened to seize oil fields from private investors in order to "restore the balance of interests in favor of the state."[51] This growing national assertiveness raises risks for all foreign companies, not just Chinese companies, operating in the country.

Neither is China alone. Russia also has ambitions in Central Asia. An incident in the winter of 2006 underscored the difficulties ahead for China. The oil pipeline from Kazakhstan to China operates safely only seven months a year. During the winter months the oil must be mixed with other less viscous oils, supplied by Russia, to prevent it from freezing. But the Russian state-owned pipeline firm Transneft delayed its deliveries in winter 2006, arguing that its own pipeline had a capacity of just 140,000, or only enough to feed refineries in Kazakhstan. Independent analysts claimed the figure was far higher.[52] China's CNPC was forced to transport less viscous oil by rail from another part of Kazakhstan at great cost, but this was the only way to keep the pipeline unfrozen.

No doubt Central Asia will remain a strategic oil supplier for China, but it will struggle to play a more major role. Even if the region was to sell China every barrel of oil it pumped out of the ground, the total would amount to less than half China's daily requirements.[53] This is comforting to defense officials in Beijing. It means China is better shielded from the type of oil blockade that impaired Japan during World War II. But China's factories would still grind to a halt in the event oil shipments were disrupted for an extended period of time. Moreover, China must navigate nationalist sentiment in Central Asia and a complicated historical relationship. Russia will also remain a major strategic competitor in the region, periodically squeezing oil supplies to China as a means of obtaining political leverage.

It is difficult for China to buy oil security. Early successes are stalling in the face of this litany of challenges. But there isn't anything unusual about this story. The major oil importers, including the United States, have all taken a path similar to China's. Most have eventually retreated to buy their oil again from the international market. Maybe the logic will change if oil remains at near $100 a barrel. However, it is likely that China will eventually opt to buy more of its oil from the international market rather than purchasing expensive oil equity assets. It is also likely that China will also have to return to the Arab oil producers, admitting it was unable to diversify as fully as it would like.

Indeed, only the Arab oil producers have the capacity to absorb a significant increase in Chinese demand. The estimates make for compelling reading. The International Energy Agency estimates China's oil demand will rise by nearly 4.0 million barrels per day to 11.3 million barrels per day between 2006 and 2015, even as domestic oil production peaks.[54] The figure is vastly greater than the current daily output among China's largest alternative suppliers; Angola produced 1.4 million daily barrels per day, followed by Kazakhstan (1.4 million) and Sudan (0.4 million).[55] The Arab world is still in a class of its own; Saudi Arabia produces 10.9 million barrels per day, followed by the UAE (3.0 million), Kuwait (2.7 million), and Iraq (2.0 million).[56] Iraq will also increase its production in time. Its pre-2003 daily output was 2.6 million, but the true figure may be significantly higher, as only limited exploration has taken place in the past decade.

So it is inevitable that China will attempt to bind itself closer to Saudi Arabia and the other large Arab oil producers. It may not be a comfortable relationship, but necessity will ensure that China is prepared to overlook the risks of allying itself with orthodox Islamic states. What is not clear is how China will attempt to achieve this. So far its preference is to use economic force. This strategy has worked well in Africa. In 2006, Beijing announced it would double its aid to Africa and also establish a $5 billion investment fund, largely intended to finance infrastructure projects, such as railways and stadiums. But there is a catch. It is Chinese companies, employing Chinese laborers, who are the main beneficiaries of the construction contracts. In this way China has also profited from its relationship with Africa.

This model isn't likely to work in the Arab world. For a start, most Arab governments are better funded. For instance in 2005 Saudi Arabia started construction on the King Abdullah Economic City. Its total construction cost is estimated at $27 billion, or more than five times the total amount that China has allocated to its African investment fund.[57] The other Arab oil producers have embarked on similarly ambitious construction projects. Who needs China? There is greater scope for China to offer aid to the less developed Arab oil producers, in particular Egypt and Syria, but these two countries are able to provide only a fraction of China's total oil demand.

Meanwhile, Arab governments are reluctant to permit foreigners to take equity stakes in their oil assets. Many have spent more effort keeping Western oil companies out rather than in, and China will find the competition more aggressive relative to Angola or Sudan. Moreover, the Arab Gulf governments are seeking technology, not financing, especially as many are grappling with the problem of trying to extract oil from mature fields. And it is not yet clear whether the Chinese oil companies, although well funded, will be able to compete directly with their Western competitors in terms of providing technology. If not, then the Chinese oil companies may be limited to countries such as Syria that require not just technology, but also financing.

Even if China clears these hurdles, it still has to face America. China is projecting its economic force in the Arab world, but America is still the region's most powerful military and political force. Its influence is even more pronounced among the major Arab oil producers, in particular, Kuwait, Oman, Saudi Arabia, and the UAE. If China wants seriously to challenge America in the Arab world, it will have to start likewise projecting its military and political force. This wasn't a problem in Africa. There China caught America largely unawares. The American military didn't create a unified African command (AFRICOM) until

2007, or over two decades after it created a unified command for the Middle East, East Africa, and Central Asia (CENTCOM).

Sure, troop levels in Iraq may now be falling, but the American military retains the ability to surge its forces rapidly. In March 2006, the military published contracting documents revealing it has prepositioned everything from food to missiles at "forward operating sites" in Bahrain, Kuwait, Qatar, and Oman. In addition it contracted for the maintenance of equipment on air bases in Saudi Arabia, even as more routine operations shifted to air-bases in Bahrain, Kuwait, Qatar, Oman, and the UAE.[58] It also relies heavily on "reach back," or the ability to conduct operations from bases in America itself, such as the control of unmanned reconnaissance planes.[59] Meanwhile, the permanent presence of a naval battle group in the Persian Gulf, navigating the same sea lanes used by the world's largest oil tankers, is a visible deterrent to strategic competitors.

China has few options. It has no military force in the region and its naval force is limited. Indeed, the United States Defense Department has concluded that "China's concept for sea denial appears limited to sea control in the waters surrounding Taiwan and its immediate periphery."[60] The lack of an aircraft carrier is a major challenge. So far, the Chinese navy has relied on subma-rines as a more effective use of national resources. If China were to build an aircraft carrier this would represent an important change in strategy. But, the debate in Beijing on how to proceed is inconclusive for the time being. Moreover, building an aircraft carrier is no easy thing. The hull is straightforward. But the com-mand system is not. So it is unlikely China will try to exert mili-tary force in the Arab world for years, perhaps decades, to come.

Of course, there are alternative strategies. In May 2002, Pakistan started construction on a deepwater port in Gwadar, a remote fishing village in the western provinces. China invested $200 million in the first phase of the port's construction in return for "sovereign guarantees to the port facilities."[61] The timing was important. It was just a few months after the American invasion of Afghanistan and the buildup of American naval forces around the Persian Gulf. The Gwadar port is just 400 kilometers from the Strait of Hormuz and enables China to monitor traffic through that channel. In 2005, *Newsweek* quoted an internal Pentagon report as claiming China had already set up electronic listening posts at Gwadar.[62]

The port is a part of what India and other countries suspicious of China refer to as a "string of pearls." The pearls are ports located along China's key oil supply routes. For instance, China has ambitions to build another "pearl" in Burma.[63] Yet these ports are not ideally situated. Tribal groups seeking autonomy from the Pakistani government constantly threaten the Gwadar port and three Chinese engineers were killed in a car bombing in May 2004. The Burma port is also hostage to the durability of the Burmese regime itself. It is economic force, not military force, which has built this "string of pearls," and each of the pearls is hostage to militant attack or regime change. And until China is able to project its military force, especially through the development of an aircraft carrier, it will struggle to secure its oil supplies through the Strait of Hormuz and Strait of Malacca.

What about political force? China has indeed started to play a more active role in shuttle diplomacy. In September 2002, shortly before the American invasion of Iraq, the government appointed a special representative to the Middle East, Wang Shijie, a veteran diplomat. Wang had first traveled to the Arab world in the early 1960s to study Arabic as part of a small group of students. Most of the students rose to senior positions in the subsequent decades working as diplomats and journalists. In 2006 Wang was replaced by Sun Bigan, another veteran diplomat. Sun had previously worked in Iran, Iraq, and Saudi Arabia. He had only recently retired as head of a working group dispatched in 2002 to reestablish the Chinese embassy in Iraq. But he agreed to accept the position of special representative stating, "if they [the government] call you to complete your mission, you can't retire."[64] Sun was plunged almost immediately into an emergency, as fighting broke out between Hizbollah and Israel in July 2006. He shuttled between Beirut, Damascus, Amman, Jerusalem, and Cairo during the hostilities, but his public statements were limited to requests for the cessation of hostilities.

In addition to its increased diplomatic activity, China may more actively wield its power as a permanent member of the United Nations Security Council. In 2003, it sided with France and Russia in threatening to veto any resolution permitting an

American-led invasion of Iraq. Yet, China has used its veto just three times in the past decade.[65] It has likewise only sparingly initiated its own resolutions. Although the Chinese government has more warmly embraced the United Nations in recent years, even sending a team of over 300 peacekeepers to Lebanon after the end of the 2006 war, it has largely maintained a minimalist approach.[66] This accords with its preference for economic, rather than political, issues.

*   *   *

No doubt, Chinese diplomats are working hard to improve relations with Arab governments. But there isn't anything so exceptional about their activities as to suggest an imminent political rebalancing in the region. Instead, China will continue to rely on its economic force in the Arab world. However, it is not the large state-owned companies who are the major source of this economic force. It is instead the thousands of individual Chinese traders already operating in the Arab countries. It was events during the war between Hizbollah and Israel in August 2006 that brought into relief how the public and private sectors have come together to fuel China's economic force in the Arab world.

Shortly after the war's conclusion, the Chinese embassy in Damascus issued a statement noting that international funds pledged for the reconstruction of Lebanon totaled $1.2 billion.[67] It also stated that Chinese support for the embattled Lebanese government during the war should now translate into trade opportunities. It then advised Chinese firms to seek advice from the Chinese Embassy in Beirut about the trade opportunities with Lebanon, while also advising firms to use the embassy's extensive Lebanese contacts to identify trade opportunities, in particular the supply of building materials and household goods. This simple statement was indicative of the fact that economic force, not military force or political force, is the basis for how China behaves in the Arab world.

This event slipped below the radar of the Western media; the statement was written in Chinese and advertised to a domestic audience only. Individual Chinese traders traveling to Lebanon likewise attract little attention. The Chinese have an expression for this: "speak little do more" (*shao shuo duo zuo*). The former leader Deng Xiaoping referred to the policy in the early 1980s and it has since characterized China's foreign policy. This will likely change in time, especially as China grows more assertive in exerting its economic influence, but until China can project a military and political force equivalent to its economic force it is likely to prefer to "speak little do more," and its economic influence may not be fully registered by the Western media.

China will likely find more reason to agree with America about the Arab world. All parties desire stability in the Middle East, if only because this helps cap increases in international oil prices. Attitudes toward Iran are also not so dissimilar. I have heard Chinese academics worry that the "Iranians are trying to build another empire." I once asked an academic at the Chinese Academy of Social Sciences whether the government was worried about Chinese religious students studying in Cairo and Damascus. "No," he said. "But they do worry about the Chinese religious students in Tehran." China is now prepared to deal more directly with troubled states, thus complicating America's relations with the Middle East, but that doesn't mean China seeks instability in the region. The prospect of a war between Iran and Saudi Arabia, for instance, would be horrifying to Beijing.

The risk for China is that American "adventurism" in the Arab world pushes oil prices higher. The Iraq war is a case in point. The war is now popularly viewed as a mistake, as there were no weapons of mass destruction, while the links between the regime of Saddam Hussein and Al Qaeda were tenuous at best. Yet the war has added a premium to oil prices. And China must pay this higher cost to sate the thirst of its rapidly growing economy. It is a cost it is increasingly unwilling to pay. If there is a risk, it is that China will start opposing such American "adventurism" more vigorously for fear of higher oil prices. It cannot exert its military force directly in the Middle East, but Beijing has alternative means of leverage over Washington, such as through the threat of force against Taiwan or negotiations with North Korea.

It may require that America cede some influence to China among the Arab oil producers. This may be an abrupt change for a country that has enjoyed a relatively free hand in the region for the past two decades. Yet it's a change worth considering as

China's thirsty cars and factories consume growing volumes of oil. A good start is to recognize that relations between China and Saudi Arabia are still in their infancy, so there is room for Washington to pull back modestly if only to reassure the state planners in Beijing. It is equally important to recognize that co-opting China as a force for regional stability may have surprising benefits if the Chinese government is able to exert its influence in the Arab world to prevent regional conflict and curb a dramatic rise in oil prices as a result.

Most intriguing is whether the politics in the Middle East, and specifically the Arab world, will force China to drop its policy of "nonintervention." The region has a way of forcing foreign parties to choose sides. It is hard to sit on the fence for long. If so, then it is imperative for Western governments, in particular the American government, to emphasize the mutual interest all parties have in keeping international oil prices low. It is unlikely China is yet willing to join such a group as the "Quartet," a body created to help mediate the peace process and composed of the United States, the European Union, Russia, and the United Nations. But China could be encouraged to act more often as a relatively independent intermediary between all parties.

CHAPTER 3

The Arab Wealth Funds and the Rise of an "Islamic Corridor"

In July 2005, the currency trading desks burst into action across the world. The euro had suddenly strengthened against the dollar. It wasn't clear why. But the traders scrambled to dump their long dollar positions regardless. This wasn't the time to stand in the way of the market. The traders had to pay widening spreads as the market gapped higher. The foreign currency market is the largest of the world's financial markets, trading over $3 trillion a day.[1] A one-point miss on a €100 million trade would cost a trader $10,000. A ten-point miss would cost $1000. A large enough move might wipe out weeks of profit. Tempers flared and keyboards were smacked hard in frustration. Losing money was bad enough, but losing money without knowing why was gutting.

Then the news wires flashed a headline across the trading screens. The United Arab Emirates Central Bank had announced it would switch 5 percent of its foreign exchange reserves from dollars to euros.[2] The United Arab Emirates (UAE) isn't a large place. Its total population is less than two million. A decade earlier most currency traders couldn't have pointed to the country on a map. But the United Arab Emirates now strides across the foreign currency market like a giant. Its central bank had managed to move the world's largest financial market with a single statement, scrambling foreign currency trading desks from London to Tokyo. The UAE Central Bank wasn't alone. The entire Arab world was exerting a growing influence on the foreign currency markets. For the first time, trading desks were responding to statements out of Dubai, Kuwait, Riyadh, and even Damascus.

The Arab world was always rich. But it has recently leapt into the ranks of the super rich and its status as a player in the world's financial markets had grown. What happened? Three events had converged to change dramatically the fortunes of the Arab world. First, a surge in oil prices. Second, the rise of China. And third, a decision by Western households to embark on a historic, and largely debt-fuelled, consumption binge.

Soaring oil prices were the first pivotal event. Oil prices tripled in price from less than $30 a barrel to near $150 a barrel between 2004 and 2008. The Arab oil producers had a choice either to spend or save the windfall and they chose to save it. The International Monetary Fund estimated that Arab oil producers were spending just 15 percent of the rise in oil revenues versus around 70 percent in the 1970s.[3] The 1970s was a mistake. The Arab governments spent lavishly, but were unable to pay for their extravagant outlays when oil prices collapsed in the 1980s. Saudi Arabia, in particular, had accumulated enough debt to put it on a par with Turkey in 2001.[4] It was a far fall from grace for the world's largest oil producer. "Never again!" was the country's rallying cry as oil prices surged after 2004.

Since then the Arab world has accumulated a staggering amount of wealth. In 2008, pre-crisis, it was estimated to own $1,400 billion in foreign assets.[5] A few simple comparisons will put this figure in perspective. That same year, Warren Buffett, the world's richest man, was worth an estimated $62 billion, or just a small fraction of the total. The Californian Public Employees Retirement System, America's largest public pension fund, was worth an estimated $230 billion, again not even close. The best benchmarks are the world's largest asset managers, such as State Street, which managed around $1,700 billion each.[6] By this measure, the Arab world is now definitely punching in the heavyweight division, albeit the financial crisis continues to hurt all investors.

Oil prices were soaring partly because of China. From the trading desks in Hong Kong it was possible to watch a filthy haze drift over Victoria Harbor. The haze had grown worse after 2004, or about the same time that Chinese factories across the border started to work overtime pumping out consumer goods for the rest of world. Everything from Nike Airs to iPods used oil in the manufacturing process. Oil fed the electricity generators. Oil fueled the delivery trucks. The entire country was hungry for oil. China accounted for one-third of the total increase in world oil consumption, between 2004 and 2007, racing past

Japan as the world's second largest consumer. Arab oil producers had good reason to thank China, as the country was partly responsible for their sudden accumulation of wealth.[7]

The third pivotal event was the growing indebtedness in the English-speaking world. This was especially true in America. The average American household started to spend more than it earned and between 1990 and 2007 household debt rose from 84 percent to 133 percent of annual personal disposable income.[8] The increase in debt was staggering. The U.S. trade deficit required around $500 billion to finance the shortfall in 2009. This has implications for the dollar. The dollar is like a canary in a coal mine. It acts as a balancing agent between the financing needs of the United States and the willingness of foreigners to supply that financing – if foreigners stop supplying financing, the dollar weakens. Luckily, the Arab oil producers, among others, have been willing to bankroll America. But the currency trading desks fret that if foreigners stop financing the shortfall there will be a dead canary.

There were fears that foreign investors were doing just this as a result of the economic crisis. The U.S. Federal Reserve slashed interest rates and the dollar slumped. Falling house prices and bank failures weakened confidence in America's economy. Many investors still liked the security of United States government debt. But others sold their American assets in response to weaker economic growth, financial market turmoil, and worries about a falling dollar. Moreover, there were lingering fears that Arab investors would sell their American assets if relations between America and the Arab world worsened, for instance, if American politicians targeted Arab investors in the aftermath of another terrorist attack, or if political relations worsened as the result of a war between America and an Arab state.

The upshot was that the Arab world, China, and America appeared increasingly indivisible. They were the financial world's holy trinity. First, the Arab world sold its oil to Chinese factories. Second, Chinese factories used the oil to produce consumer goods, which in turn were shipped to America. Third, American shoppers purchased these goods from their local Wal-Mart, using their credit cards to fund the purchase. Fourth, the Arab world invested its oil revenues in America, thereby supporting the dollar and reducing the average cost of financing for the American shopper. The result? The Arab world is one of America's largest creditors, at a time the American military is entrenched in Iraq and battling terrorist networks. It is like fighting with your bank manager. It doesn't make a great deal of sense, but breaking the cycle is not easy.

America's financial crisis might yet act as a partial circuit breaker. American households, burdened by their large debts and forced to save more of their monthly income, will struggle to purchase as many consumer goods from China. However, it's a change that will play out over years, rather than months. Moreover, American consumers aren't likely to stop shopping altogether, so Arab investors will continue to play an important, if reduced, role in financing an American trade deficit. Alternatively, investors may find the American government increasingly in need of funds, as was the American consumer during the past decade. After all, bailing out the country's financial sector isn't going to be cheap. The result? The financial world's holy trinity isn't finished yet, and the Arab world will remain an important creditor to the American economy for the foreseeable future.

*   *   *

It isn't easy investing over $1,400 billion. Responsibility lies with the Arab wealth funds. The first such fund was established by Kuwait in 1953, but most were established after oil prices surged in the 1970s. The Arab oil producers, left swimming in dollars, created these funds as a way to invest their surpluses and allocated each a share of the oil revenues earned by the mainly state-owned oil companies. The funds were initially small in size but after 2004 they grew rapidly into the heavy-hitters they are today. The largest funds are in the Arab Gulf states, in particular Kuwait, Qatar, and the UAE. They appear no different to the average fund manager – they have logos, websites, and corporate brochures – and are headquartered in newly built skyscrapers that you might find in Hong Kong or New York.

But the Arab wealth funds are unusual. The Arab Gulf states are largely an artificial creation of the British and Ottoman Empires. They are lines drawn in the sand. A single family rules each state or emirate, many of which claim ancestry from the same tribe. There is only limited democracy, and it is still common for citizens to petition the Sheikh, as was the practice for centuries. This has implications for the Arab wealth funds. First, they are often largely indistinguishable from the wealth of the ruling family itself. Second, the funds operate in relative secrecy and estimates of their worth are exactly that, estimates. Third, as a consequence, the personal politics of the ruling families are important to the funds' investment decisions.

The Abu Dhabi Investment Authority (ADIA) is the largest of these funds. It is estimated to be worth $800 billion (smaller than Fidelity, but larger than Calpers).[9] Abu Dhabi is the largest of the seven emirates which make up the United Arab Emirates. The emirate originally scraped a living from pearl fishing, but the discovery of oil in the 1950s changed the equation permanently. Abu Dhabi is now the world's seventh largest oil producer.[10] The Al Nahyan family has ruled Abu Dhabi since the 1700s and invests the oil wealth on behalf of Abu Dhabi's small population.[11] Luckily the emirate's native population numbers less than half a million, so after providing free education and health care, subsidized utilities, and a one-off payment toward wedding costs, the ruling family is still able to save what is left over.[12]

Its neighbor Dubai operates a collection of funds, or quasi-funds, including the Dubai Investment Company, Istithmar, and Dubai World. But its oil reserves are far smaller than Abu Dhabi's, so the emirate has branched out into commercial ventures, including Emaar, Dubai Aerospace Engineering, and DP World. The Al Maktoum family has ruled the emirate since the 1800s after it split from Abu Dhabi. Dubai skirmished with its larger neighbor in the subsequent years until borders were finally settled. But times have changed. Relations between the two are strong. It now takes less than 90 minutes to drive between the two emirates along a multilane freeway. Abu Dhabi hosts the country's central bank, while Dubai is its unofficial financial capital. Together, they are the Washington and New York of the UAE.

Saudi Arabia rightly claims its status as the world's largest oil producer. Yet it is estimated to own just $300 billion in foreign assets, less than Abu Dhabi.[13] Why the shortfall? Saudi Arabia is the largest of the Arab Gulf countries. Its native population totals 20 million, or around 20 times the size of the UAE's.[14]

Consequently it spends more and saves less. Moreover, its enormous defense budget is estimated to account for more than one-third of the government's total outlays and is a considerable drain on the treasury.[15] Saudi Arabia announced the establishment of a small wealth fund in May 2008 worth $5 billion, but it pales in comparison next to the riches of the Abu Dhabi Investment Authority. The Saudi Arabian Monetary Authority and the Finance Ministry, through its pension funds, are for the time being responsible for recycling the country's petrodollars.

The Kuwait Investment Authority isn't the largest of the Arab Wealth Funds but it is the oldest and has blazed a path for the rest of the region. It bought a stake in a newly privatized BP in the 1980s, attracting the wrath of British Prime Minister Margaret Thatcher, and purchased a stake in Mercedes-Benz not long after. The Kuwait Investment Authority also helps explain Kuwait's rapid recovery after the Iraq War. In 1991 the Kuwait Investment Office, based in London, served as the country's central bank during the war. It also released funds for reconstruction.[16] Indeed, Kuwait rebuilt itself partly thanks to dividends from BP and Mercedes Benz. Today, the Kuwait Investment Authority is estimated to be worth around $260 billion, less than Abu Dhabi and Saudi Arabia.[17]

There are also smaller funds. Qatar, for instance, operates the Qatar Investment Authority, estimated at $50 billion. Oman has likewise established a small fund worth $8 billion. Even Libya has joined in the act, announcing in 2006 it was setting up a fund estimated at around $40 billion.[18] These are just a few examples. But they are indicative of the sudden creation of new funds after 2004, as surging oil prices left the Arab world flush with cash for the first time since the late 1970s. Not all the oil rich parts of the Arab world have set up funds. But they may yet try. For instance, Egypt and Syria owned $34 billion and $20 billion respectively worth of foreign assets.[19] But the assets are still managed by central banks, rather than a fund.

*   *   *

The Arab Wealth Funds have already invested billions in America. But their world changed after September 11. The funds suddenly faced hostile suspicion. Osama Bin Laden was, after all, born into a wealthy Arab family. Suddenly many Arab investors were receiving a cold welcome from customs officials. Relations between America and the Arab world remained strained as Washington launched its war on terror and later invaded Iraq. The trading desks worried that the Arab Wealth Funds might respond by investing elsewhere, or worse yet, sell their existing assets. All this was bad news for the dollar. Forecasts were trimmed as anecdotes suggested the Arab wealth funds, among others, were diversifying away from the dollar, buying instead euros and sterling.[20] Indeed, the two currencies reached historical highs in 2008.

American lawmakers weren't helping. Legislators from Florida and New York were particularly fierce in their attacks on Arabs. Grant Smith, Director of Research at the Institute for Research: Middle Eastern Policy based in Washington, identified nine pieces of legislation proposed between 2003 and 2004 targeting the Arab countries. Two bills in particular stood out. The first (H.R. 488) aimed to "limit the issuance of student and diversity visas to aliens who are nationals of Saudi Arabia." The second (H.R. 3137) aimed "to prohibit assistance or reparations to ... Saudi Arabia" regardless of the program.[21] The bills eventually stalled and failed to make passage into legislation, but they left a bad taste. As a result many Saudi Arabian investors, in particular, felt less comfortable with the security of their investments in America.

But what really shook the Arab world was the attack on DP World in 2005. DP World is one of the world's largest port operators, owning or developing facilities in nearly 30 countries. In October 2005, the company announced its intention to take over the Peninsular and Oriental Steam Navigation Company (P&O). The deal would have left the firm in control of six American ports. But it was two years after the September 11 attacks and national security was a sensitive issue. A Wall Street Journal/ NBC News poll showed that 73 percent of the American public opposed the bid.[22] American lawmakers, including Senators Hillary Clinton and Charles Schumer, prepared legislation in an attempt to block the bid. DP World eventually yielded and later agreed to sell the American ports to an American firm.

A reporter for Dubai's *Khaleej Times*, Mark Townsend, was invited by Voice of America to participate in a live radio interview from Los Angeles. The furor was still at its peak and DP World had yet to yield to lawmakers. "I'm used to the rough and tumble of live debates, but the vehemence of the opposition surprised me," he recalls. "I was effectively cross-examined. Did I know that Dubai could be used to smuggle radioactive materials or terrorist weapons. I was asked to clarify earlier UAE support for Hamas. It seemed to me the debate was running away from itself and rapidly becoming polarized. I began to feel that I wasn't being questioned as an impartial journalist, but as a defender of the bid. I later invited Senator Schumer to address his concerns to the UAE public. He never replied."

The Arab world was stunned. The incident raised doubts about the security of its other investments in America. After all, DP World wasn't a prime candidate for national security concerns. Not only was the company's Chief Operating Officer an American from New Jersey who had worked at the Brooklyn and Newark docks, but Dubai was also host to dozens of American warships. If DP World was a target, then who was next? *Al Hayat*, a popular Arabic-language newspaper, worried in its economic section and editorials about the change in stance toward the Arab world. Majed Al Sheikh, in an editorial for the newspaper, wrote, "The Dubai Ports company case has exposed the ugly face and the lies of so-called free trade, and other lies invented in the context of globalization."[23] The scandal appeared to have shocked the Arab world into action.

The reality was in fact more complex. At the time P&O was engaged in legal battle with Eller & Co, a U.S. ports operator.[24] An Eller subsidiary, Continental, operated stevedore operations at the Port of Miami in a partnership deal with P&O. Continental alleged that P&O wanted to increase control over Continental's share of the operations. It was Eller lobbyists who first approached lawmakers in Washington. Their 52-page lawsuit was largely devoted to the dispute with P&O. But it also quoted liberally from the 9/11 Commission report, noting that "several of the hijackers" traveled through Dubai on their way to America and saying Continental didn't want "to become involuntarily a business partner with the government of Dubai."[25] The Eller lobbyists did their job. Lawmakers jumped up in opposition. And the DP World bid failed.

China was also seen as a spoiler. The Chinese oil company CNOOC had attempted to buy the American oil company Unocal six months before the DP World bid for P&O. The bid met with similarly fierce public resistance – the Chinese government was a majority stakeholder in CNOOC and it was feared that a successful bid would put American oil assets in the hands of the Chinese government. Chinese oil companies had already aggressively bid for African oil assets and there was wild speculation the Chinese government was attempting to lock up the world's oil reserves. The United States House of Representatives voted 398 to 15 for a nonbinding resolution against the purchase, stating that the takeover "would threaten to impair the national security of the United States."[26] CNOOC dropped its bid. Six months later Continental's lawyers successfully fanned the flames of this protectionism to challenge the offer by DP World for P&O Ports.

DP World was unlucky. Admittedly, it suffered from anti-Arab sentiment resulting from September 11. But Continental's lawyers aggravated the situation, whereas the CNOOC bid for Unocal had already pushed Washington's protectionist panic button. In October 2006, just six months after DP World dropped its bid for P&O, Dubai International Capital made a $1.2 billion bid for an American manufacturer of military components for the Department of Defense. Surely this was just a clear case of national security. Yet the purchase raised little opposition from either American lawmakers or the public. By this time, the furor had faded. There were also no lawyers attempting to spoil the bid. And, lawmakers were increasingly focused on the Iraq war, as President Bush was arguing for a surge in military forces. Dubai International Capital later successfully acquired the manufacturer.

Fears that the Arab world will stop investing in America for political reasons are exaggerated. In the years following the DP World incident, a unit of DP World purchased 1,300 acres in Orangeburg County, South Carolina, to build warehouses serving ports in Charleston and Savannah. The warehouses would employ up to 8,000 people in a part of the country suffering from unemployment rates near 9 percent.[27] Saudi Basic Industries Corporation purchased GE's plastics business for $12 billion. The Abu Dhabi Investment Council spent nearly $1 billion to buy New York's iconic Chrysler Building. Not least, Dubai Aerospace Enterprise (DAE) spent $1.9 billion purchasing Standard Aero Group, an American commercial and military engine company, and Landmark Aviation, an American aviation services company, to create one of the world's largest aircraft maintenance service providers.

It helps that the Arab wealth funds have since also spent millions hiring lawyers and investment bankers in order to prepare American lawmakers in advance. Before bidding for a 20 percent stake in NASDAQ, the Dubai Group, an Arab wealth fund based in the UAE, hired a team of Washington lobbyists led by George Salem, the former head of the National Association of Arab Americans. According to a *Business Week* report at the time, the lobbyists called some 120 lawmakers to soften up any opposition to the bid.[28] United Arab Emirates also paid the lobbying firm Harbour Group $5 million to establish the United States–Emirates Alliance, which has since helped to influence public opinion. These efforts have helped to ease the passage of deals by Arab wealth funds through the Committee on Foreign Investment in the United States.[29] They are also a strong indication of the intent by the funds to continue investing in America.

It also helps that America is in desperate need of more funds after its economy was struck by the sub-prime mortgage crisis. American banks were recording large losses as home-owners defaulted and credit markets seized up. The Arab wealth funds, alongside funds from China and Singapore, stepped up to inject fresh liquidity into the largest American banks. The Kuwait Investment Authority purchased a $3 billion stake in Citigroup and a $2 billion stake in Merrill Lynch.[30] The Abu Dhabi Investment Authority purchased a $7.5 billion stake in Citigroup.[31] Charles Schumer, who was a major critic of the DP World bid, was now receptive to the funds and indeed had spoken at "some length" to Citigroup ahead of the deal.[32] It was a sign of how much had changed in just two years.

So for the time being, America remains open for business. The Arab wealth funds will certainly have their troubles. There is always the risk of another terrorist attack. The funds are also vulnerable to attack from hostile lawyers on national security grounds. But experience suggests the funds simply have to wait until such angst dies or, at the very least to prepare lawmakers in advance with the help of lobbyists. Most importantly, America is still the world's largest economy, with nearly 700 of the world's 2,000 largest public companies.[33] And the Arab wealth funds would find it difficult to invest their $1,400 billion if they turned away from America entirely. So for now, they remain buyers rather than sellers of American assets.

* * *

However, there is no denying September 11. The event has strained relations between America and the Arab world. I traveled to Dubai to examine these fears more closely. In the past decade Sheikh Maktoum, the ruler of Dubai, has spent billions building a financial industry. The city is now a major financial hub for the Arab world, playing much the same role Beirut did during the 1970s. Ironically, while enjoying almost limitless room to expand outward, the city has instead decided to expand upward. Its strip of skyscrapers now rivals those in Hong Kong and New York, and includes Burj Khalifa, the tallest building in the world after it was opened in 2010. Hundreds of thousands of workers from the Indian subcontinent and, increasingly, from China are employed in the city's constantly growing construction and service sectors.

When I arrived tension was high. Fighting between Israel and Hizbollah was still at its peak. The local Dubai newspapers were fiercely critical of America and its perceived support for Israel. Front pages carried images of children killed by the bombing of South Lebanon. Editorials demanded Washington use its influence over Israel to prevent more civilian deaths. The strength of Sunni Arab support for Hizbollah had left governments in Egypt and Saudi Arabia backpedaling. The events in Lebanon underscored just how much relations with America had soured. The financial markets were worried that Arab investors would sell their dollar assets as a way to leverage American foreign policy. In the event their worries were unfounded.

But as I met with officials and financial analysts in the city there was general concern about the security of Arab investments in America. "Sure, relations have improved today. But who knows if there will be another attack?" says one official. "It took nineteen men to commit September 11. How do you stop nineteen men?" This pessimism weighs heavily on Arab investors. The speed at which the U.S. government introduced the Patriot Act in 2002 was a common reason for worry. The speed at which relations with America deteriorated during the Lebanon war was also a timely reminder of how fragile the relationship remained. I traveled to Dubai regularly after the Lebanon war and, although relations between the Arab world and America subsequently improved, the sense of uneasiness lingered.

There are other worries. I have met Arab investors who argued an American withdrawal from Iraq would result in a sharp fall in the dollar. I was taken aback the first time I heard this claim. I thought it just another of the many conspiracy theories, or *mu'amara*, that are a feature of life in the Arab world and are rarely supported by evidence. But Arab investors argued that withdrawal from Iraq would signal the failure of American foreign policy and the decline of American economic hegemony. Fair enough. American military spending has certainly exacerbated the savings shortfall, requiring foreign investors, especially Arab investors, to step in and support the dollar. The sub-prime crisis and string of bank failures, including Lehman Brothers and Merrill Lynch, appeared to confirm the worst fears.

I heard a similar view while visiting the Syrian Central Bank. The bank lies grandly at the intersection of six major roads and I had to thread my way carefully through the traffic to reach the front gate. A guard waved me through and after entering the building I walked up the stairs to the fourth floor. My contact was seated in an office with an old Persian carpet on the floor and textbooks on the shelves. He was an experienced economist who had studied and worked in America. We drank tea and spoke about the Syrian economy for an hour before finally switching to the dollar. It was then that he repeated the same mantra I had heard six months earlier in Dubai: "if America withdraws from

Iraq it spells trouble for the dollar, as it means the failure of American foreign policy." I can only imagine the financial crisis has left him more convinced of his view.

It strikes me that the Syrians have an appreciation for history. They have participated, for the most part unwillingly, in the rise and fall of many empires. The Roman, Mongol, Ottoman, and European empires all left their mark on the county. The Arab world often refers to America as another empire, or colonizer. I wondered if the Syrian official was making a similar point. After all, the Roman, Mongol, Ottoman, and European empires all collapsed in the years following their retreat from the Arab world. It is an unusual point of view. But the financial markets, when determining the value of the dollar, are often too focused on purely short-term dynamics of supply and demand. There is value in stepping back and examining events from a historical perspective.

The Syrian Central Bank official isn't alone in his opinion. In any airport bookstore there are dozens of books debating the same topic. Most are written by American authors, among them the prominent being *The New American Empire; America's Failing Empire; Are We Rome? The Fall of an Empire and the Fate of America; Blowback: The Costs and Consequences of American Empire*. These books all have a similar hypothesis. First, the American government has used the events of September 2001 to justify a new period of military expansionism. Second, the American economy is increasingly indebted, and meltdown isn't far away. The financial crisis and, more recently, a new president may soften talk of empire in the coming years. But the Arab world was worried about America's imperial ambitions long before 2001.

So perhaps the currency desks do have reason to worry. Arab investors are still investing in America despite the outcry over DP World. And yet they are worried about another September 11. They are anxious about the security of their investments in the event of a backlash against the Arab world. They are also worried about the gradual decline of America, if not as an empire, then at least as the world's dominant economic power. The currency desks aren't likely to fret over any grand historical theories. They worry about events a few days, or even a few hours, in the

future. But the implications for the dollar are nonetheless important. The million dollar question, or more accurately, the trillion
dollar question, is where will the Arab wealth funds invest if not
in America?

The United Kingdom is a good candidate. First, it shares a long
relationship with the Arab world. It helped Arab governments
overthrow Ottoman rule in the early 1900s, later ruling Egypt,
Iraq, Jordan, and Palestine itself. Second, the United Kingdom
has one of the world's most liberal investment regimes. It welcomes, if not encourages, foreign investors. Arab investors first
started purchasing London property during the 1970s oil boom.
It was the Egyptian investor, Mohamed Al Fayed, who purchased the iconic Harrods in 1985. More impressively, the United
Kingdom has kept its doors open to foreign investors, in particular Arab investors, even after September 11 and the London
bombings in 2005.

So it makes sense that the Arab wealth funds have more
recently chosen the United Kingdom as a place to invest their
oil revenues. The Qatar Investment Authority purchased a 25%
stake in Sainsbury's, an acquisition that raised little opposition.
The Dubai Investment Corporation made a tentative bid for the
Liverpool Football Club, although they eventually failed to agree
on terms. Meanwhile, Arab investors poured money into London
property. A Jones Lang LaSalle survey suggested that Arab investors accounted for almost 10 percent of luxury properties sold in
the city.[34] The inflows of capital helped to drive the British pound
to record highs. In December 2007, it took two U.S. dollars to
buy a single British pound.

More importantly, though, the Arab wealth funds are looking
at the developing world with great interest. For perhaps the first
time in centuries, America and Europe are competing with the
developing world for foreign investment capital.

Jeffrey Towson, the American investor based in Riyadh, has
worked extensively with Prince Al Walid. The Prince was ranked
by Forbes in 2008 as the world's nineteenth richest man and is
the Middle East's most famous businessman.[35] Towson says,
"Prince Al Walid is the real pioneer of global investment. He
moves between purchasing a stake in Citigroup, buying hotels in
Europe, developing skyscrapers in the Middle East, to building

private equity funds in Africa. In a globalized world, he is the first truly global investor." It was an interesting point. I thought it contrasted with the experience of Warren Buffett, another famous businessman. Buffett has a deserved reputation as the "Sage of Omaha," having delivered regular, and large, returns for his shareholders in Berkshire Hathaway for many years.

Yet, Berkshire Hathaway has invested heavily in the type of companies that built America in the early 1900s. Many have grand histories, such as Acme Brick, which has manufactured brick and masonry-products since 1891, or See's Candy, which was established by Charles See in Los Angeles in 1921 and produces high-quality candy. I can't question Berkshire Hathaway's investment strategy. It has taken a bet on the twentieth century's most powerful economy, and, not surprisingly, made out handsomely. Why bother with the rest of the world? Berkshire Hathaway will likely continue to perform exceptionally well. But look through a list of its investment holdings and there are just a few foreign assets. Indeed, Berkshire Hathaway bought its first foreign asset only in 2006.[36] Is the company missing out on opportunities?

The Arab wealth funds say yes. They have made a range of investments since 2007 that contrast starkly with those of Berkshire Hathaway. It is the UAE's wealth funds that have led the way. Dubai International Capital purchased 3 percent of ICICI Bank, India's largest bank. Abu Dhabi Investment Authority acquired 8 percent of EFG-Hermes, one of the Middle East's leading investment banks. Istithmar purchased a stake in Daallo Airlines, in the East African state of Djibouti. Mubadala Development Company bought an aluminum mining operation, in the West African state of Guinea. Arab companies meanwhile embarked on a buying spree that included Islamic banks in Malaysia, residential property in Pakistan, and telecom companies in Kenya.

I find this pattern of investment intriguing. Djibouti, Guinea, India, Kenya, Malaysia, and Pakistan were all once trade partners for the Arab world. They also have large Muslim populations. The Arab wealth funds, and Arab companies, are exploring familiar markets. They are following in the footsteps of their ancestors, investing along the same historical trade routes.

Try this with an atlas. Trace a journey with your finger. Start in North Africa, travel east through the Middle East, then onward to India, continue to Indonesia, before finally turning north to China. It's the same route along which Arab traders traveled centuries earlier in their wooden ships. It's also the same route along which Islam was spread centuries earlier. I don't believe the Arab wealth funds have a grand strategy in mind. They may have even made the wrong bet. Isithmar may make more money from its investment in Barneys in New York than Daallo Airlines in Djibouti. But the Arab wealth funds believe that countries situated along this historic trade route are worth investing in.

I call this route an "Islamic Corridor." It stretches from Africa through the Middle East and into Asia. It includes the majority of the world's Islamic population. The Islamic Corridor isn't a grand religious alliance. It simply follows the same trade routes that early Muslim traders traveled. And just as America is comfortable territory for Berkshire Hathaway, the Islamic Corridor is comfortable territory for Arab investors. It's part of their history. For instance, whereas most Western students learn about Marco Polo, most Arab students learn about Ibn Battuta, a contemporary of Marco Polo. In the fourteenth century, he traveled from Morocco, across the Middle East and finally to China. Along the way he visited most of the countries on the Islamic Corridor. The countries he visited are the same ones that Arab investors are now targeting.

Iyad Duwaji is CEO of Dubai-based Shuaa Capital, one of the Middle East's leading investment banks. The Syrian-born Duwaji is rated among the region's most influential investment bankers by Middle East Business Intelligence. He says, "It only makes sense for GCC companies after exhausting their domestic opportunities to look for expansion opportunities and investments into their immediate neighbors. The Dubai footprint extends today to countries located in North and East Africa, Turkey and Central Asia, the subcontinent, and even South East Asia. We understand this region. We have a shared history, tradition, and enjoy geographical proximity." Today, Shuaa Capital is expanding rapidly thanks to the breadth of Dubai's footprint.

America is competing not just with the UK, but also with much of the developing world, for Arab investment funds. The periodic hostility toward Arab investors after 2001 has only accelerated this trend, as Arab investors have taken a second look at the opportunities closer to home in more familiar markets. Likewise, the financial crisis has led the same investors to reassess their investments in American companies and securities. No wonder the trading desks are watching the Arab wealth funds closely to see how they are responding. The secrecy of these funds makes it difficult to track changes in their investment behavior, but changes are observable nonetheless. Two changes in particular warrant attention from the financial markets. The most striking is the decision by Arab investors to invest in the Arab world itself.

The Arab world has recycled most of its oil revenues in the developed markets for decades, even as parts of the Arab world struggled to raise investment capital. But the more recent surge in oil prices coupled with a decade of economic reform are making it more attractive to invest in the Arab world itself. It is a landmark change that symbolizes the region's growing confidence in its own potential. Events after September 11 also have forced the Arab world to look for opportunities closer to home. If so, the Arab Gulf economies may help to sustain economic growth in the less developed Arab economies, such as Egypt, Jordan, and Syria, in the event that oil prices do fall back to earlier lows.

United Nations data suggests intra-Arab investment only started to flourish after 2001. Nearly 90 percent of this investment is concentrated in just a few countries, namely Lebanon, Syria, Saudi Arabia, and the United Arab Emirates.[37] This concentration is important. It suggests Arab investors are investing mainly in real estate, such as an apartment in Beirut's wealthy districts or a seaside property near Syria's coastal city of Latakiya. This is a good start. But what is needed is more investment in such things as textile factories and power stations in order for the Arab economies to generate job growth, tax growth, and export dollars much like the South East Asian economies have.

There are more recent signs of change. Simon Kitchen, an economist at the Egyptian investment bank, EFG-Hermes, and a ten-year veteran of Egypt says, "Arab companies are reaching maturity. They used to invest mainly in property. But now they are investing in services and manufacturing. Dubai's Etisalat is a good example. It enjoyed a monopoly in Dubai for a long time. But it is now looking to expand abroad." These companies, quasi-Arab wealth funds, have often acquired successful Western firms and are now looking to bring new technologies to the Arab world, rather than simply investing in a fancy beachside property. The change is perhaps most evident in Egypt. In the financial year 2006/07, Arab Gulf investors accounted for 26 percent of total foreign direct investment in the country.[38]

The decision by Arab investors to invest in the Arab world is indeed striking. However, there was a second change that was arguably more important for the world's financial markets. This was speculation that Arab investors are starting to invest in China, the country where Ibn Battuta finished his journeys. The idea that the Arab world is recycling its oil revenues in China rather than America hints at a gradual economic rebalancing. The Arab world has enough oil. China has enough cheap labor. Surely, the two can go it alone, especially as the American economy was slumping under its burden of sub-prime mortgages and bank failures. This oversimplifies the change, but it nonetheless points to a transformational shift in the global balance.

I heard a similar point made by an academic from the Chinese Academy of Social Sciences. We met in a teahouse in the southern suburbs of Beijing. My contact had arranged a private room fitted with couches, a dining table, and a small bathroom. It was warm inside with the winter sun filling the room with a pleasant glow. We chatted for a while about the Middle East. Then, unasked, the academic said, "Saudi Arabia wants to invest its trade surplus in China. They are looking for ways to diversify away from America." I was surprised to hear his claim. I thought it was just the financial markets that were talking about diversification. To hear an academic in Beijing speak on the same theme suggested more investigation was warranted. So during the next year I spent a great deal of time meeting with Arab investors, trying to determine just how much money they were investing in China.

It wasn't an easy task. This academic had referred specifically to an investment by the large Saudi Arabian oil company, Saudi Aramco, in a southern Chinese refinery. But the investment was worth just $1 billion and was largely funded by local currency loans. The investment also had a functional purpose, as it was intended to alleviate bottlenecks in the refining of sour crude oil from Saudi Arabia and, in so doing, spur Chinese imports of Saudi Arabian heavy crude oil. A planned investment in a northern Chinese refinery was meanwhile still not realized by early 2008 after several years of negotiations.[39] It wasn't clear to me that Saudi Arabia was in fact diversifying away from America and toward China. Its decision to invest in one of its largest trade partners was simply good business.

Emaar, the Dubai property development company, had opened an office in Beijing in July 2006, intending to invest in residential apartment blocks. But again, there wasn't anything surprising about this decision, as Emaar had also recently opened offices in Cairo, Damascus, Lahore, and Singapore. Damac Properties, another Dubai property development company, planned to build a nearly $3 billion mix-use project in the port-city of Tianjin, a two-hour drive from Beijing. The Dubai property trade fair, Cityscape, also held its first event in China in June 2007, but not before holding similar events across Asia.[40] The Dubai property developers had certainly found China, but they were relatively late to the game. Moreover, they had already made sizeable investments elsewhere in the developing world.

Arab investors have made their largest investments through stocks. The Chinese stock market has surged in recent years, its stock market capitalization tripling from $580 billion in 2001 to $2,200 billion in late 2008. For a long time it was closed to foreign investors, but in late 2002, the Chinese authorities created the Qualified Foreign Institutional Investors (QFII) program which allowed foreigners to invest in local stocks, albeit with restrictions. The Arab wealth funds are active investors and it is only natural for the large funds, such as Abu Dhabi Investment Authority, to actively trade in Chinese stocks. The foreign investment banks in Hong Kong regularly dispatch equity sales teams to Dubai and the rest of the Arab world to win new business. The eight-hour flight is fully justified by the trading commissions.

But fears that the Arab wealth funds are abandoning America and Europe in favor of China are overdone. Arab investors are definitely thinking about China. After all, China is one of the world's largest and fastest growing economies. It makes sense for the Arab wealth funds to gradually recycle more of their oil revenues into Chinese assets. But the change in their portfolios is no different from the change in investment portfolios among funds operating in the developed world, not least America. Indeed, foreign equity funds invested around $106 billion into developing economies between 2000 and 2007.[41] Middle-class American and European families were also taking an interest in Chinese stocks, not just the Arab wealth funds.

Importantly, China has weaker Islamic ties with the Arab world relative to other parts of Asia. The Chinese Hui claim ancestors from the Arab world. But the ancestral linkages with the predominantly Muslim Asian countries are far stronger. Take Yemen's Hadramouti tribe for instance. There are an estimated 4 million Indonesians who share Hadrami ancestry, including former Indonesian Foreign Minister Ali Alatas.[42] The Malaysia central bank governor Zeti Akhtar Aziz is also reputedly half Hadrami.[43] It appears that China will have to attract Arab investment on the basis of its growth potential and regulatory environment, albeit the Hui Chinese do play a useful role acting as translators and ensuring that there are operating mosques throughout China.

*   *   *

The Arab wealth funds are not alone. China has also recently established its own sovereign wealth fund. The coincidences are striking. Like the Arab world, China has accumulated foreign assets rapidly after 2004, as a result of rapid export growth. And again similar to the Arab world, China was estimated to own upward of $1,800 billion in foreign assets with the largest share invested in American assets. There are no obvious linkages between these wealth funds, no grand alliance. But they are part of the same story as the world's financial markets and governments take notice of their activities. Inevitably, they will face the same challenges as they attempt to bid for foreign assets, such as during the recent financial crisis. Yet the Arab Wealth Funds appear better positioned, at least for now.

The challenge for China is that its $2,450 billion worth of assets is split between just two agencies. The State Administration for Foreign Exchange (aptly named SAFE) manages the large share of foreign assets, while the China Investment Corporation (CIC) was set up in 2007 to manage a smaller share of foreign assets more actively like, for example, the Abu Dhabi Investment Authority. But the fact there are just two agencies makes life harder. It means SAFE and CIC are responsible for investing nearly $30 billion a month, the proceeds from their rapid export growth. By contrast, Abu Dhabi, the wealthiest of the Arab oil producers, is responsible for investing less than $10 billion a month.[44] The number of investment managers working at SAFE grew from 70 to 200 between 2001 and 2007, but the task was still enormous.[45]

The easiest solution was for SAFE to buy U.S. federal government debt. It is a large and liquid market. Holdings jumped from less than $20 billion in the early 1990s to $870 billion early 2010.[46] Its purchases were also relatively transparent to the financial markets, so when the United States Treasury produced its monthly survey on foreign holding of U.S. long-term securities, it was immediately apparent how rapidly China was in fact purchasing U.S. federal government debt. Estimates suggested China owned 10 percent of the total federal government debt stock whereas the Arab world owned just 3 percent.[47] It also overtook Japan as Washington's largest foreign creditor, and its purchases exposed it to criticism from American lawmakers.

Senator Hillary Clinton wrote a letter to Treasury Secretary Henry Paulson and Federal Reserve Chairman Ben Bernanke in February 2007 in which she claimed that the "economic policies of the last six years have contributed to an erosion of U.S. economic sovereignty and have made us more dependent on the economic decisions of other nations."[48] Earlier that year Senators Byron Dorgan and Ben Cardin had proposed legislation that would require the government to respond when foreign ownership of U.S. debt reached 25 percent of GDP. China periodically slowed its treasury purchases as the financial crisis worsened in 2008, but it will inevitably be back for more as it struggles to invest around $30 billion a month.

Likewise, in the currency markets China is a bigger presence than the Arab wealth funds. In 2008, I was working next to the currency traders at an international bank in Hong Kong. It was evident that there were a few investors who had the power, if only briefly, to shake the foreign exchange market. At the top of the list was China. Further down were Korea and Russia. And finally, the Arabs. The Arab oil producers are certainly fabulously wealthy, but their oil revenues are shared across a number of countries and an even larger number of funds, while the proceeds are invested in a variety of assets. As a result the Arab world leaves a less obvious footprint in the world's financial markets. This enables the funds to operate below the radar of investors and politicians, enjoying greater freedom of action, along with the ability to shield themselves from criticism.

China also has the challenge of dealing with a larger financial community. There are hundreds of analysts observing China on behalf of investment banks in Beijing, Shanghai, and Hong Kong. Like paparazzi, they chase after SAFE and CIC and report every move to the investment community. Yet there are still only a handful of investment bank analysts watching the Arab world. It helps that the Arab economies and financial markets are far smaller in size, relative to China, so there is less need for so many analysts. The investment banks had also largely ignored the Arab world throughout the 1990s, so the few experienced Middle East analysts worked mainly for sovereign ratings agencies or research institutions. The situation has started to change as rising oil prices inject new cash into the Arab economies. But the number of Middle East analysts is still relatively few.

* * *

The rise of the Arab and China Wealth Funds are yet another indication of the forces at work beneath the surface of the global economy. Moreover, the Arab wealth funds are about more than just their influence on the world's financial markets. The funds are responding to the same historical tide that is driving Arab traders to Yiwu. At first glance, the two are nothing alike. Abu Dhabi Investment Authority's 40-storey office in Abu Dhabi is a world away from the Red Guest House in Yiwu. Likewise, the Savile Row suits worn by Arab investors in London are very different to the white *galabiyas* worn by Yemeni traders in Guangzhou. Yet they are all part of a rebalancing of global power reflected in the rise of the Silk Road and the even larger Islamic Corridor.

Sure, the Arab wealth funds are still buying American assets. After all, America is not just the world's largest economy it also claims the world's largest financial markets. However, it still isn't clear how the financial crisis and the failure of a number of well-known American banks will affect Arab confidence in the American economy going forward. It may be that the crisis will spur investors to look elsewhere, either in Europe, China, or the Islamic Corridor. Alternatively, it may be that Arab investors will consider American assets cheap after the recent sell-off. Most likely, the implications will take years to emerge. They will also depend as much on the performance of the rest of world's economy versus America's. However, on balance the financial crisis will leave Arab investors more cautious about American assets over the medium term.

Moreover, the Arab wealth funds still expect to face periodic challenges to their investment. They are cautious about the risks to their investments in the event of another terrorist attack on American soil. It is only natural they are looking for alternatives, especially in the Arab world, where rising oil prices and economic reforms have created new investment opportunities. The upshot is that America and Europe are losing their grip on some of the world's largest investors, not just for economic and financial reasons, but also for reasons related to culture and religion. So far, this isn't a major challenge for America, and the West. The financial crisis is for the time being a bigger risk. But another major attack would act as an accelerant on the pace of change.

Like the rest of the world, the Arab wealth funds are also looking at the opportunities in the developing markets. They are looking particularly hard at the Islamic markets. Arab investors will make decisions based purely on risk and return. Yet there is also an appeal to investing in countries where mosques are a common sight and restaurants serve Halal food, or food prepared according to Islamic prescription. Yiwu's mosque and Arabic restaurants have certainly attracted thousands of Arab traders. Nonetheless, it would be wrong to overplay the importance of the Islamic markets. They are an alternative, but not a substitute, for the Western markets.

The experience of the UAE is instructive. It claims some of the richest Arab wealth funds. Yet, the UAE has also benefited from centuries of regional strife. It was Sunni Persian immigrants who, in the 1800s, fled persecution and brought with them their trade links to India.[49] More recently, Dubai has received Iranian immigrants during the Iranian revolution in 1979, Lebanese immigrants during the Lebanese civil war of the 1980s, and, two successive waves of Iraqi immigrants. The city is a mix of race, religion, and tribe. Its population appreciates the subtleties of the political situation. Its sees grey where the rest of world sees black and white. It isn't likely that Dubai will disinvest from America unless forced to, or unless the city's investments no longer make financial sense.

Ultimately, the sovereign wealth funds are among the most significant innovations to take place in the Arab world in the past century. They are laying the foundation for a non-oil future. For smaller economies, such as the UAE, foreign assets are now of sufficient size for the indigenous population to live in perpetuity on the profits of their investments in such companies as Citibank, Barneys New York, and MGM. For Saudi Arabia there is still a large shortfall, especially given the size of its defense expenditure. But the region's financial health has nonetheless improved. The Arab wealth funds are also spurring growth in their domestic non-oil sectors. For instance, Borse Dubai's acquisition of a 20 percent stake in the American stock exchange NASDAQ has bolstered the Dubai stock exchange's ambition to be the region's financial hub.[50]

The West's experience of the Arab world was largely limited to oil and politics for almost a century. It is these two issues that have dominated life in the Arab countries since the early 1900s. However, events of the past decade have added a third element to the mix. The Arab investor is a new force in the global economy. Indeed, the Arab investor may have a more durable impact on the

Arab economies than has oil. The Arab world's oil will run out eventually. But Arab investors will continue to earn a return on their billion dollar investments in the Western, and increasingly Eastern, economies for decades. It is still early days. However, the Arab investor has emerged as important foundation stone for the rise of the Arab world and the creation of a new Silk Road.

CHAPTER 4

Syria Learns from China while the Chinese "Go Global"

The Silk Road was once the heart of global commerce, a land bridge stretching thousands of miles, connecting China with the Middle East. A caravan might begin in Changan, the Chinese imperial city better known today as Xian, famous for its collection of terracotta warriors. It was here that jade, silk, and musk were collected from around the country before they started their journey west. The caravans traveled to the last fortified Chinese barrier at Dunhuang before attempting to skirt the Tarim Basin and its deadly Taklamakan Desert. There were many routes, but all were difficult and the caravans faced problems with food, water, sandstorms, and marauders. After passing through the fortified cities of Samarkand and Bukhara, the caravans traveled across the Persian Plateau before finally connecting up with the Great Desert Route, which linked the cities of ancient Mesopotamia to the Mediterranean Sea. The Syrian city of Damascus lay at the end of the route, a few days ride from the trading ports of Beirut, Sidon, and Tripoli.[1]

Damascus is one of the world's most ancient cities. Its old quarter remains largely unchanged and is a maze of narrow streets surrounded by a defensible wall. Its markets still capture the smells and noises of the caravan trade centuries ago. Wooden barrels filled with spices and sweets spill out into the streets. The air is rich with the scent of olive soap and musky perfume. Large doors lead from the narrow streets into big open-air khans. It was here that the caravans traveling along the Silk Road pitched camp and sold their goods. The grandest khans had fountains to cool the air. They were major distribution hubs centuries ago, receiving goods imported along the Silk Road for sale in the region or for shipment further onward to Europe.

However, trade along the Silk Road dried up in the 1600s when the collapse of the Timurid Empire in Central Asia resulted in chaos along the caravan routes. There was also political unrest in China itself. Non-Chinese groups in the Northwest harassed the border areas, striking as deep south as Beijing. The ruling Ming Dynasty no longer had the will or resources to protect the caravan trade and was more worried about the potential for rebellion within China itself.[2] The Ming rulers forced many Arab traders, who had settled permanently in China, to assimilate with the larger population through a policy of "sinification" (*han hua zheng ce*).[3] The links between China and the Arab world gradually faded. The rise of seaborne trade dealt the final blow to the caravan trade by offering a cheaper and safer way to transport goods between the East and West. Was that the end of the Silk Road?

Maybe not. In June 2006 a convoy of Chinese cars returned to the once great caravan city of Damascus. The convoy numbered twenty vehicles, all brand new. It was a striking sight and the convoy attracted large crowds as it entered Damascus. A Chinese journalist covering the event for the *International Business Daily* wrote of "women leaning out from their balconies to wave at the passing cars, while smiling children ran alongside in the street."[4] The convoy was part of a tour arranged by the major Chinese auto manufacturers. Over the next two weeks it traveled to Syria's largest cities, including the ancient caravan city of Aleppo. The aim, of course, was to sell more cars. The Chinese auto manufacturers had only recently entered the local Syrian market and were issuing a challenge to their more established competitors from Japan, Korea, and the United States. The auto manufacturers were also retracing a journey their ancestors had made centuries earlier.

The Silk Road was back, but the Chinese traders were driving cars rather than camels. They had also arrived in force. The tour included auto manufacturers, industry representatives, journalists, and diplomats. The Chinese auto manufacturers were all fierce competitors at home, but they had joined together for this tour, realizing that in order to sell more cars they first had to convince the rest of the world that Chinese cars were worth owning. The Chinese Machinery Industry Federation, a body with ties to the Chinese Ministry of Commerce, had provided logistical support. It had already held two similar events in Cambodia and Vietnam.[5] But this year it had chosen Syria, and had drawn together the country's nine major car manufacturers, including Dongfeng, Hafei, and Foton to participate in the tour, an impressive feat of cooperation, logistics, and publicity.

It is still early days. A lot has happened in four hundred years and Chinese cars are not as desirable as Chinese silks once were. First, the cars are not built to cope with Syria's hot temperatures and poor road conditions. Second, there were complaints that the seats weren't large enough to fit the "larger proportioned" Syrian male. I found it a tight squeeze myself. If the auto manufacturers were going to succeed they had their work cut out. "It's all about price at the moment. That's all we compete on," said one Chinese auto manufacturer at the time. "That's a great way to enter a market, but we need to do more if we want to keep selling cars. We need a strategy of 'high quality and low costs'."[6] After-sales service was another problem. It was difficult for local mechanics to fix problems or obtain parts when the cars broke down. Foton, one of the first entrants into the market, has responded by establishing a warehouse in the city from which parts can be distributed to any part of the country in 24 hours.

I visited Damascus a year later and decided to go shopping. The car dealerships are on the outskirts of town alongside the road north to Aleppo. They are all newly built. My taxi driver complained throughout the trip about the sudden rise in car ownership. "Look around. The infrastructure was all built in the 1970s. It can't handle this sort of increase. I'm losing money sitting in traffic jams." As I walked through the mud to get to one of the showrooms I could only agree. The infrastructure wasn't ready for this type of growth in car ownership. But to be fair, the old city is a bottleneck for the rest of the city. Its roads are narrow and there are strict prohibitions on demolishing the old houses. Not so in Beijing, where the government is more cavalier about demolishing parts of the old city to make way for eight-lane freeways. It is a different appreciation of history and a different approach to development.

The tour must have worked. The large Chinese car manufacturers – Chery, Geely and Hefei – were all represented in the dealerships. I stopped to examine a Geely. It looked sleek from the outside. But the car had been left out in the recent rain, and water had seeped inside to spoil the interior. When I asked the dealer his opinion of the car he was quick to point out that Volkswagen had built the car's engine. I visited a number of showrooms that day and all the dealers pointed out that the cars' engines were not made in China. The Chinese car manufacturers were winning on "low price," but still had to start winning on "high quality." Nonetheless, their arrival in Syria is testimony to the reestablishment of historic trade routes and a gradual rebalancing in the global economy.

*   *   *

The rise of China is not an isolated event. It is part of a powerful historical tide sweeping across Asia and the Middle East. Former economic powers are resurfacing after centuries of slumber. It is a remarkable change of fortunes. In the 1600s, China is estimated to have accounted for 29 percent of the global economy. By the 1980s, its share had fallen to near 3 percent.[7] There is no consensus over why the economy declined; historians still debate the issue fiercely. Blame it on the Ming Dynasty's hostility to foreign trade or its failure to license private armed trading, or blame it on sudden population growth in the interior provinces or shortages of raw materials.[8] Irrespective of the reasons, the decline of China was an event that did not pass unnoticed in the Arab world.

Indeed, the parallels between events in the Arab world and China are compelling. It was the decline of China that contributed to the collapse of trade along the Silk Road in 1600s. The Ming Dynasty's decision to forcibly assimilate Arab traders helped to break up trade links. The Arab world itself was also in decline. There is no way to accurately measure the region's share of the global economy. However, the Arab world was hard hit by regular outbreaks of plague. Indeed, Cairo suffered eight episodes in the 1600s alone. The Arab textile producers also faced growing competition from imported European cloth from as early as the 1700s. But it was the rise of the European sea powers and the switching of most Asian trade to the African Cape route that delivered the decisive blow to the Arab economies.[9]

Today, it is like watching history in reverse. Trade along the Silk Road has returned. There are Chinese traders in Damascus. There are Arab traders in Yiwu. Even if the traders are not using the same land routes across Central Asia, the ports in Dubai are certainly bustling with activity. The changes are welcomed in the Arab world. The rise of China and the resurrection of the Silk Road appear to roll back the dark periods of Ottoman Rule and advent of European sea trade. The symmetry between events today and these centuries ago are compelling. So, it is no wonder that Arabs talk almost reverentially of the Silk Road in their dialogue with the Chinese. The Silk Road is symbolic of an era when the region was at its peak and there are signs that the Arab world has taken the first steps toward recapturing its historical role.

If so, Syria has the most to gain. The country faces two radically different paths. The first path is depressingly familiar. Today, the Syrian regime is an international pariah. It has yet to sign a peace treaty with Israel. It is accused of sponsoring political assassinations in Lebanon. It hosts leaders from Hamas and Hizbollah. This is a path that leads to economic stagnation. The second path, by contrast, is more optimistic. It is a Syria that again emerges as the region's trading hub. It is a Syria symbolized by traders, such as Abdul Midani, who from their offices in the old city of Damascus buy and sell goods with the rest of the world. It is events after 2001 that have made these two paths clearer permitting the country to remain unchanged or recover its historical legacy.

* * *

In July 2004, President Bush spoke of an Axis of Evil during his State of the Union Address. It was a bold declaration made in the aftermath of September 11. Iran, Iraq, and North Korea were the original members of the Axis of Evil. But Under Secretary of State John Bolton added Syria to the list the following year.[10] Washington imposed economic and political sanctions in 2004 later tightening them.[11] Although the European Commission signed a Partnership Agreement with Syria in 2004, they said it was "difficult to imagine deepening our relations" given the current political circumstances.[12] Relations with America and Europe remained frosty a few years later, especially after accusations of Syrian involvement in the assassination of former Lebanese President Rafiq Hariri. It was as if the country had fallen off the map.

But many Chinese traders disagreed with the West's assessment. Instead, they have labeled Syria a "cohesive force" (*ning jiu li*) for the Arab world.[13] It was their personal view, rather than official Chinese policy. But the expression recognizes the important historical role Syria has played as a terminal point for the Silk Road and as a trading hub for the region. These traders are willing to bet that Syria will continue to play this role despite the economic and political sanctions imposed by America and Europe. They assume that the underlying tides of history are too powerful for the sanctions imposed by a foreign government. Indeed, China itself is rising on much the same historical tide that has buoyed Syria. The number of Chinese traders walking the streets of Damascus continues to grow even as Washington tries to wall the country off from the rest of the world.

Syria's status as a "cohesive force" is aided by its relative stability. This is no small achievement. The country suffers from the same sectarian divisions between Sunni, Shi'a, Christian, and Kurd that afflict Iraq and Lebanon. The country also shares borders with Iraq to the east, Lebanon to the west, and Israel to the south. An intrusive security apparatus helps keep the peace. And, although the Syrian government has openly defied America and Israel in past decades, it has avoided inciting armed conflict. This strategy is now paying off handsomely. Chinese traders refer frequently to Syria's "stability" as a reason to base their operations in the country.[14] How long the country will remain stable is debatable. But at least for now the rise of China is helping to ignite memories of the country's historical role as a trading hub.

The Adra Free Zone is a poster child for the chance that Syria may choose to take the second, more optimistic, path before it. The industrial park enjoys duty-free status and is a major transshipment hub for the region. Zhou Dongyun has recognized the value of the Adra Free Zone as a commercial hub. Her newly constructed China City is especially popular among visiting Iraqi officials. Its two-storey exhibition halls sell everything from office equipment to factory equipment. Chinese traders are also

using the Adra Free Zone to sell to the broader region, in particular Lebanon, as reconstruction efforts after the 2006 war have
spurred demand for construction materials. The industrial park is
playing a similar role to the open-air squares in the old city of
Damascus that once hosted traders arriving along the Silk Road.

As I left the Adra Free Zone, I was reminded of the other path
Syria might yet take. Across the road from the industrial park
lies an armed camp belonging to a Palestinian militant group.
An ageing concrete wall topped by barbed wire ringed the camp.
There were guards napping in watchtowers; their automatic rifles
propped casually against wooden chairs. I laughed and pointed
the sight out to a friend. He looked embarrassed. "This is the
old Syria. The Adra Free Zone is the new Syria," he said. He
might be right and the Syrian government is increasingly focused
on economics rather than politics. The bustling scenes in the
Adra Free Zone certainly contrast starkly with the Palestinian
guards napping in their chairs. More importantly, whereas
America is focused on the armed camp, China is focused on the
industrial park.

There is reason for hope. The Syrian regime may continue
to butt heads with Western governments, but the changes taking place have created opportunities for individual traders. It is
difficult to observe their activities, not least because they hide
them from the Syrian regime itself. Take the story of one trader
who, from a small street-level office in the old city of Damascus,
buys and sells container loads of coffee and sugar while they are
still at sea, using nothing more than a phone and a Swiss bank
account. It is individuals like him who are hoping to ride the
new tide of economic reform. This is refreshing for Syria. The
bustling scenes in the Adra Free Zone may yet be a better guide
to the future than the sleeping guards in the Palestinian Armed
Camp. However, a historical legacy is not enough to spur economic growth.

Syria needs to repeat the China miracle. The regime certainly hopes for the same rapid growth and social stability. Who
wouldn't? Large parts of the Arab world want much the same. In
October 2007, a Pew Survey indicated that a median 52 percent
of people from Egypt, Jordan, Kuwait, Lebanon, Morocco, and
Palestine rated a stable economy as more important than political

freedom.[15] Yet a stable economy isn't easy for the poorer Arab economies. The first steps of economic reform are often the most challenging and can result in social instability. It is hard to exaggerate the importance of this fear of social instability in a region that is watching Iraq being engulfed in sectarian flames. It makes sense that the China growth model has emerged as a contender to America and Europe's growth models, especially as the latter are blamed for a damaging global financial crisis and economic recession.

The appointment of a Chinese academic, Lin Yifu, as Chief Economist for the World Bank underscored the growing influence of the China model. Lin was the World Bank's first chief economist from a developing country. His appointment validated not only the model itself, but was also recognition of China's power to inspire other economies to travel down the same path. Lin was quoted by the *Wall Street Journal* as saying that he thought the World Bank should spend more time designing policies tailored to specific countries. "If the World Bank wants to help the developing countries or the transitional economies, they need to come to the countries to work with the government and research institutions."[16] Lin was advocating a more hands-on approach to economic reform, in effect, the China growth model.

The Syrian leadership is already hooked. Shi Yanchan, a former Chinese ambassador to Syria, speaks of a growing number of senior Syrian leaders who traveled to China in the late 1990s, before China had even caught the attention of the world's financial markets.[17] Former Vice President Abdul Halim Khaddam, for instance, was a regular visitor. Shi recalls with some pride that the Chinese embassy's national day celebrations, held in October 2001, attracted an unusually large number of senior Syrian officials, including the influential Regional Assistant Secretary of the Baath Party. When the current President Bashar Assad visited China in 2004, Syrian officials spoke of introducing the "China experiment" (*al tajriba al siniya*) and learning from the Chinese experience of economic reforms in the past two decades.[18]

I spoke with an official at the Syrian embassy in Beijing who claimed that China regularly invited groups of Syrian academics and officials to study in Beijing. The invitees attended seminars arranged by a variety of state organizations, including the central bank, state ministries, and the state research agencies. The trips generally last several months and were funded by Beijing. It wasn't just Syrian academics and officials who attended, but also academics and officials from a wide group of developing countries. The Chinese themselves were receiving tremendous amounts of technical support from the International Monetary Fund and World Bank, as well as foreign governments. They were then repackaging the advice for the developing world.

In this way the China model has helped spur economic reforms in Syria. It makes sense that the Syrian regime might try to replicate the success of the Chinese Communist Party. The ruling Assad family and its supporters have maintained their grip on power since the late 1970s. The China model provides a way to pursue economic reforms while avoiding painful social upheavals. The ascent of President Bashar Assad to power in 2003, after the death of his father, has also helped removed obstacles to economic reforms. A sluggish economy and rising unemployment rate had left the Syrian government with few alternatives. But it was the China model that emboldened the regime to take the final step. It was economic reform, but with Chinese, rather than Western, characteristics.

Syria has gradually moved forward. It has liberalized its banking sector, permitting private banks to open branches. Already, the major Lebanese banks have built gleaming new branch offices in the dusty city. The government introduced new legislation to attract foreign investors. The Syrian Central Bank cut interest rates in 2003, for the first time in 22 years, later permitting banks greater flexibility to set their own deposit and lending rates.[19] It is now possible to change money freely on the street without worrying about a long, prison sentence. A stock market is also planned, although it had yet to open by early 2008. Meanwhile, Dubai's Emaar is developing a residential project called the "Eighth Gate" worth nearly $500 million outside Damascus. It is just one of the many residential construction projects across Syria.

However, a story I heard convinced me that economic reform was real. The Syrian Minister of Economic Affairs held a meeting in February 2007 to discuss the latest Chinese-style five-year economic plan. Investors from the private sector were invited to attend. They were reportedly stunned at what took place. The Minister delivered a presentation using Microsoft PowerPoint slides and invited the private sector's participation in the planned investment projects, including a highway to the Turkish border. He was surprisingly honest in his assessment. "If we can finish even a quarter of the latest five-year plan it will represent an improvement." It wasn't until the investors left the building that what had happened really hit them. The presentation was held in the same building that regularly hosted the Baath Party's senior leadership. It was also the same building in which political opponents vanished. A private investor who attended the meeting recalls, "We used to look the other way in fear when driving past this building." How things have changed.

The Chinese are also playing a more direct role. The household electrical goods manufacturer, Haier, is so far the largest Chinese investor in the country. Its Syrian factories produce 50,000 washing machines and 50,000 microwave ovens annually.[20] This is tiny compared to what the company's factories produce back in China, but it was still enough to capture 20 percent of the Syrian market. Haier has an aggressive marketing campaign and advertisements for its products are plastered on billboards all over Damascus. Syria is also only the beginning, as the company has ambitions to export to the neighboring Arab markets. Haier is applying the same business strategy it has used in China during the 1990s, producing both for export and for local consumption as rising income growth spurs demand for household electrical goods.

But Chinese companies were making a bigger contribution in construction. It isn't hard to see why. Syria's infrastructure dates back to the eighties when the country still had significant oil reserves and the Soviet Union was providing financial support. But it has aged badly since then and there are few Syrian construction companies able to build large infrastructure projects. The Chinese construction companies, by contrast, have no such problem. They fed on a glut of spending since the early 1990s as the Chinese authorities pumped money into large infrastructure projects, in particular ports, roads, and utilities. It is common for Chinese construction companies to build cheaper and faster than their American and European competitors. The Sichuan Machinery Import and Export Company, which built a $180 million hydroelectric facility in the north of Syria, is just one of many Chinese companies operating in the country.[21]

The Chinese telecoms company Huawei is especially active. The company itself is controversial. It is accused by some of patent theft and maintaining links to the military.[22] But it has also successfully sold its services abroad, focusing mainly on developing economies where its experience at constructing cheap telecoms infrastructure is in demand. In February 2007, the company held its regional conference in Damascus. Its employees from across the Arab world flew into the Syrian capital. I had heard about the conference from a Syrian friend who had helped to arrange their accommodation and transport. It was his first genuine contact with a group of Chinese businesspeople. "Are they always so excited?" he asked. "They rushed about shouting at each other. It was impossible to keep them together. But they were happy to be here," he recalled with a smile.

There was good reason the company's employees were so happy. Huawei had recently captured a large share of the Syrian market at the expense of its competitors, Ericsson and Siemens, by offering a similar product at a much cheaper price.

There are many similarities between the Syrian economy today and the Chinese economy in the 1980s, and many of the lessons learnt by China are immediately applicable in Syria. Critics may argue the China model supports rogue regimes, yet the China model is also built on the reforms, which were recommended by the International Monetary Fund and World Bank. And China is arguably doing a better job in selling the same reforms. Consider a Syrian official who visited Beijing in the 1990s and returns for a second visit today. His experience of the city's transformation, whether it's soaring skyscrapers or ten-lane freeways, is a better advertisement for economic reform than any claim the multilateral institutions can make. But most importantly, the China model stresses social stability and it is hard to exaggerate the importance of this for a country like Syria.

This doesn't mean Syria will succeed. Indeed, the Syrian regime has ignored a cardinal rule of the China model. It has failed to separate economics from politics, in particular foreign politics. It hosts political activists such as Khalid Mishal, the chief political officer for the Palestinian group Hamas. It also stands accused of aiding Islamic militants traveling to Iraq. But most importantly it has failed to sign a peace treaty with Israel. The Chief of the Syrian Economic Society, Issam Za'im, admitted that the country had suffered because of its refusal to sign such an agreement, arguing, in a March 2004 article, but that the country has little choice when faced by the threat of the "Zionist enemy" (al 'aduw al sahyuni).[23] The Syrian Economic Society is at the forefront in debating economic reform. Za'im is a former Minister of State Planning, and his views are reflective of many in the senior leadership.

China has no such problem. Today Japanese manufacturers are free to invest in China even as Beijing criticizes Tokyo about visits to the Yasukuni Shrine where Japanese war criminals are interred. Taiwanese manufacturers build factories in the mainland Chinese province of Fujian not far from the same military arsenals that target Taiwan. But it is not entirely fair to compare the two situations. After all, China is no longer at war with Japan and shares kinship with Taiwan. Nonetheless, China has benefited by embracing its North Asia neighbors, specifically Japan, Korea, and Taiwan. The three countries have invested nearly $300 billion in China during the past decade while also transferring years of managerial and technological expertise to China.[24] Syria is not yet close to repeating China's experience of the past two decades, albeit it may benefit from the rise of an "Islamic Corridor" and the tendency for Arab investors to invest in the Arab economies.

Indeed, China itself may struggle to separate economics from politics in the Arab world. So far the Chinese government has deliberately emphasized economics at the expense of politics. Take, for instance, President Hu Jintao's address to the Saudi Arabian National Consultative Council in April 2006. I watched a live broadcast from my hotel in Dubai while escaping the midday heat. President Hu mentioned the words "harmonious" 22 times and "cooperation" 13 times in a speech of no more than 3,000 words. He made no mention of Iraq even though the conflict raged next door.[25] A Chinese journalist who worked in the region later told me that Beijing had instructed the state media to report only on economic relations, rather than political relations.

It helps that China has little historical baggage in the Arab world. While researching for this book, I came across hundreds of references to the Silk Road (si chou zhi lu) in the

Chinese-language media. The Silk Road represents China's last substantial engagement with Syria before trade along the route faded in the 1600s. That isn't true of Europe, which invaded the Arab world during the Crusades and later ruled it as colonial powers. It also isn't true of the United States, which had armed Israel and twice invaded Iraq. China recognizes it has arrived in the Arab world with a clean record and it isn't about to waste that opportunity by embroiling itself in the region's politics unless there is a clear strategic imperative. So far, no such clear strategic imperative exists, so China maintains its steadfastly neutral line.

*   *   *

However, the Chinese car manufacturers already face political challenges in Syria. An Iranian state car manufacturer has recently constructed a factory near the Adra Free Zone. The first cars were due to roll off the factory line in 2008. It was a joint investment between the two countries and everyone in Damascus was talking about it. "This is the first real Syrian car," said one friend. The Chinese car manufacturers have ambitions to win a contract to replace the Syrian army's ageing automobile fleet. Xie He, a major Chinese investor, described the contract as "hunter's bait" (*yi kuai you ren de dan gao*).[26] But I wonder how successful they will be, given the tightening political cooperation between Damascus and Tehran, especially at a time when Syria and Iran feel vulnerable to the large American military presence in Iraq. It isn't always enough to offer the lowest price to win business in the Arab world. It is also important to offer political support, especially against a larger and better funded opponent like America.

The Chinese government may also find that Chinese companies are inadvertently targeted. Take the Chinese Harbor Construction Company which was building a port in the northern Lebanese city of Tripoli in July 2006.[27] After the first Israeli strike on Beirut International Airport its employees decided to "hold firm." But Israeli warplanes later struck at a project managed by the Chinese Irrigation and Hydroelectric Company. Manager Fu Xinrui feared his own site was now a target, so a group of employees first walked around the construction site taking pictures as proof of their work. Later they boarded eight vans. Embassy officials attached Chinese flags to the top of the vehicles to ward off Israeli warplanes. Another Chinese company, the Skylion company, had earlier been diverted east through the mountains after the Israeli navy bombed the road. So, Zhang Tianquan, a former police officer, flagged down oncoming traffic to enquire if the north route was safe. It was. Eighteen hours later the convoy finally arrived in Damascus, exhausted, but alive.

The experience of the Chinese Harbor Construction Company is instructive. It underscores the risks that more Chinese companies in the Middle East will periodically find themselves in the crossfire. The risks are even higher if Chinese companies successfully focus on winning infrastructure contracts. It isn't clear how the Chinese government might respond if its citizens are indirectly, or even directly, targeted. If employees from the Chinese Harbor Construction Company were killed in the strikes, might the Chinese government have taken a different stance toward the war? Might it have forgotten its own cardinal rule of separating economics from politics, especially if the event resulted in a popular outcry from the Chinese public itself?

There are other problems. It is easy to see why the China model might appeal to the Syria regime. Syria has few alternatives. It has yet to enter the World Trade Organization. It has yet to enter a free trade agreement with the European Union. It faces sanctions imposed by Washington. Individual traders also fall foul of tighter global standards, in part sponsored by American regulators, aimed at curbing financial transactions related to terrorist financing. I recall a conversation with a Syrian trader who was a regular visitor to China. "I can't even set up a bank account in Hong Kong. I've tried several banks, but I'm refused when they see my Syrian passport." Might it be that the China model has less relevance for those parts of the Arab world already integrated with the global economy and enjoying strong relations with America and Europe? To test this idea I turned to Egypt.

*   *   *

Egypt has long competed with Syria for influence in the Arab world. The expression "No war without Egypt, no peace without

Syria" is testimony to the historical importance of the two countries. But there the similarities end. Egypt has signed a peace
agreement with Israel. It has warm relations with all the Western
capitals. It has been a member of the World Trade Organization
for many years and has worked hard to establish a free market economy. In short, Egypt has become a full member of the
global economy, whereas this will likely take Syria far longer.
So it isn't clear if Egypt has any need for China. If not, is the
pull of the China model limited to countries such as Syria which
are refused entry to the global economy because of their political stance?

Cairo is big. It claims 16 million inhabitants. Not surprisingly
the city's infrastructure is stretched. Traffic jams appear out of
nowhere and the outer suburbs periodically lack electricity. The
authorities have continued to build, but struggle to keep apace
as thousands of new arrivals migrate to the city daily. I arrived
disheveled, as my flight had been delayed in Dubai for 24 hours.
My luggage was lost, permanently, so I spent the afternoon shopping. In the mall across from my hotel I bought several cotton
shirts. Egypt's textile industry has grown rapidly, fueled by an
ample supply of cheap labor and world-famous cotton, and the
country draws comparisons with China. And I thought the shirts
I purchased not much different in price to those manufactured
by the big Chinese textile manufacturers in China's Pearl River
Delta.

I was lucky enough to meet Fikry Tadros. Fikry understands
China. He worked in Beijing as the Egyptian commercial
attaché between 1997 and 2000. Today he lives in Cairo and is
General Manager for an Egyptian firm importing pharmaceuti-
cals from China. We met in Cairo in the office of the Egyptian
Businessmen's Association, which lies in the southern suburb
of Giza. From the sixteenth floor it has a view of the pyramids.
They loom over the southern suburbs. Maybe the pyramids are
an inspiration to the city's officials, but I would find it hard to
live in their shadow. Who wants to be compared to the accomplishments of the Pharaohs 4,000 years earlier? Fikry and I
spent a moment contemplating the last remaining ancient wonder before sitting down on a worn leather couch and turning to
the topic of China.

Fikry had arrived in Beijing too early. Trade with Egypt was still in its infancy. "It was only after 2000 that trade relations really started to grow," he recalls. And the reason? The Egyptian economy was motoring ahead, fueled by a cocktail of rising oil prices and increased tourism. China was also working to build trade relations. Fikry recounted dozens of Chinese trade missions to Egypt in the past few years. As a result, Chinese exports to Egypt grew fast, from $875 million to $5,100 million, between 2001 and 2009.[28] Investment, especially in the textiles sector, is also growing, albeit the absolute levels are still small at around $57 million.[29] Chinese textiles manufacturers are using Egypt's export quotas to the European Union and United States as way to escape their country's own quota restrictions. They also see the country as a springboard to Africa.

These links also extend beyond trade. Fikry spoke of the growing number of Egyptian students studying agriculture in Beijing. It is just another aspect of the China model. Egypt is applying the lessons learnt by China to feed a large, but still relatively poor, population. The agricultural technologies may be less advanced than in the West, but they are suitable for a developing country. Likewise, Huawei, the Chinese telecoms company, has a large presence in Egypt. Again the technologies may be less advanced, but Huawei understands how to price its services for a developing country. It also understands how to build a telecoms infrastructure in a challenging environment, having cut its teeth in the poorest Chinese provinces and having built similar infrastructure in Afghanistan, Egypt, and Pakistan.

Yet Fikry has mixed feelings about the China model. "Many of the Egyptian elite were Western-educated. They still have strong ties with America. We still look to the West to import our technology. We still look to the West for aid and loans. The China model is perhaps more important for those Arab countries, in particular Iran and Syria, who are unable to trade with the West. China is very clever, very long-sighted, in developing these relations." If he is right then it might be premature to worry about the China model. The model is more appropriate for countries worried about social instability and unable to access Western financing and technologies. This suggests the China model is ultimately a more pragmatic alternative for countries such as Syria, rather than Egypt.

But then I prompted Fikry about September 11. "Yes. September 11 changed a great deal in Egypt," he said. "The West made the mistake of linking terrorism to Islam. The Egyptian elites feel cheated. They haven't turned away from the West...," he paused searching for right word. "...but they are less enthusiastic about the West." Fikry later drove me back to my hotel. It was a slow journey and I had plenty of time to think about Fikry's remarks. Egypt is a proud country. It is the birthplace of Arab nationalism. It hosts the Arab League. It considers itself the leader of the Arab world. Yet the number of Egyptians receiving visas to the English-speaking countries has fallen since 2001, not just for traders but also for professionals.[30] This is a rejection that must be difficult for such a proud country, so perhaps the China model does offer an alternative.

Simon Kitchen, the English economist working for the Egyptian investment bank EFG-Hermes, agrees. He has watched the country evolve from a sleepy backwater to take its place in the global economy. He had this to say: "China is a role model. It has succeeded by itself. It has inspired countries with a colonial history, such as Egypt. It's similar to when Japan defeated Russia in the early 1900s." Japan later emerged a global economic and military power. Likewise, it may take years, or even decades, before we can fully understand the success of the China growth model and its importance as a point of inspiration for the developing world, in particular, the Arab world.

*   *   *

Ironically, the greatest risk to the successful export of the China growth model to the Arab world is China itself. So far, a majority of Arabs view China's growing economy as having a positive impact on the Arab world, according to a Pew Survey in 2007.[31] But this may change. The China model is not the only policy driving economic relations between the Arab world and China. There is a more important policy, at least from a Chinese perspective. It is called "Go Global" (*zou chu qu*). This policy lies at the heart of China's economic interactions with the Arab world. It also potentially has a far less equitable outcome for the Arab economies and individual Arab traders.

It is Go Global that has really shaken the global economy. The policy was already part of the Chinese domestic policy debate in the late 1990s, but it gained considerable traction after the country's entry to the WTO. The senior leadership realized it had to spur its domestic sector to look for opportunities abroad and make the most of WTO entry. The policy partly achieved official status in 2002 when it was reviewed by the then Commerce Minister Shi Guangsheng in the Communist Party journal *Seek Truth*.[32] Even so, it still barely registered among investment bank analysts at the time, as it was too vague an idea to capture attention. But Go Global was to later explain a great deal about how China managed its foreign economic relations, in particular how it managed its relations with the Arab world.

The Go Global policy appeared to confirm the West's worst fears. It was as if China had ambitions to take over the world. When the Chinese oil company CNOOC attempted to purchase an American oil company Unocal in 2005, its actions sparked fears that China wanted to lock up the world's oil exports. When Chinese clothing manufacturers grabbed a majority share of the American market, their actions stirred concerns for the health of the developed world's textile industry. Meanwhile there were Chinese traders spilling into the world's markets, from the shiny exhibition halls of Dallas, Texas to the dusty street stalls of Lagos, Nigeria. The gates were open and China had finally marched out from behind its fortress walls. Not surprisingly, there was much wailing and gnashing of teeth in the mainstream media as the world tried to withstand the impact.

Yet Go Global is more a reflexive response to risks at home, rather than an intentional strategy to dominate global markets. The Chinese government worries that the country's shortage of raw materials such as oil and iron ore leaves it hostage to foreign raw material producers. For instance, it worries that any disruption to oil supplies will throw millions of manufacturing workers out on to the streets, so it has encouraged domestic oil companies to buy up foreign oil assets, such as CNOOC's failed bid for Unocal. Meanwhile, entry to the World Trade Organization has opened up the domestic market to foreign competition. But the Chinese leadership fears that domestic companies will struggle to compete, so it has encouraged domestic companies to acquire more advanced foreign competitors, such as Lenovo's successful purchase of the IBM Notebook PC division in 2004.

Most of all, the Chinese leadership is worried about fierce competition at home. In the early 1990s Chinese manufacturers were largely competing with foreign manufacturers for market share. But eventually Chinese manufacturers started to dominate market share in a growing number of product lines, such as microwave ovens. This meant their competitor was no longer based in St. Louis, Missouri, but in Wenzhou, Zhejiang. The problem is that everyone enjoys the same cost structure of cheap labor, subsidized utilities, and a stable currency. A fierce price war erupted as a result. The introduction of B2B websites such as Alibaba.com markedly improved market efficiencies and pushed prices even lower. The solution was to encourage manufacturers to tap new foreign markets. The opportunities were mainly limited to markets in the developing world as markets in the developed world were already saturated.

This relentless downward pressure on prices is a common theme I hear as I travel through the Arab world. Take one Chinese trader I met in Dubai selling gifts. I asked him how business was. "It was fine. But it's been getting tough since the other Chinese traders arrived," he said, pointing at a shop across the street. Likewise, the managers of China City in Syria's Adra Free Zone permit just two representatives from each industry to display in the exhibition halls in order to discourage competition. The conclusion? When Chinese manufacturers choose to Go Global, they aren't so much advancing into foreign markets, but fleeing domestic markets. Moreover, the private sector is often at the vanguard of changes in behavior, with the government only later legitimizing their actions and providing official support.

That said, the Chinese government still supports the private sector, mainly through its embassies. China has embassies in all the Arab countries, as do the other major powers, such as the United Kingdom and the United States.[33] Each embassy has an economic affairs bureau which promotes investment and trade between China and the host country. The bureau operates as part of the embassy, but is ultimately responsible to the Ministry of Commerce. It's an arrangement that isn't all that different from most embassies of the developed world. The bureaus are active.

For instance, it was the economic affairs bureau attached to the Chinese embassy in Damascus that helped arrange the International Chinese Car Exhibition in 2006.

These bureaus also support individual traders, mainly through websites ultimately hosted by the Ministry of Commerce. Each of the websites contains specific information about a host country, identifying new market opportunities or noting changes to tariff regulations. The quality varies. But in the case of Syria, I found the Chinese-language material more useful than the Arabic-language material posted on websites run by the Syrian government itself. I later spoke with Yusuf, a Syrian trader in Yiwu, about these websites. He had migrated to China a decade earlier as a 17-year-old to avoid military duty. Yusuf spoke good Chinese and was well connected with the local business community. He claimed that the local traders used the websites heavily in order to tap new markets. I later heard confirmation from local Chinese traders both in Yiwu and abroad that the websites were indeed popular.

Their most popular feature is the chat forums. Traders can post questions to the bureaus. The answers are later posted in discussion forums for everyone to read. Most postings relate to traders trying to contact Syrian buyers for their goods. Others ask questions about market conditions and trade regulations. A few even beg for assistance in resolving cases where buyers had not settled payments. The usefulness of the chat forums varies from country to country, but the quality of responses is often impressive. It helps that working in an economic affairs bureau isn't a dead end job. Xie Zhongmei, for instance, was head of the bureau in Damascus between 2002 and 2004, and after her return to Beijing was promoted to a senior position in the West Asia Division at the Ministry of Commerce. There is an incentive to do a good job.

And their efforts are appreciated. "First, we want to thank you for your hard work in foreign countries," said a chemicals manufacturer in his posting to the chat forum. "You have suffered so many years abroad," began a kitchen utensils supplier. "We express our sympathy for you who have had to work so hard in foreign countries," said a shipping agent. I still find it strange that despite the number of Chinese traveling abroad for trade there are few who appear to really enjoy it. I started asking Chinese traders whether they enjoyed Arabic food, or whether they lived alongside Arabs. Most didn't. Most ate Chinese food. Most lived in small Chinese communities near their workplace. Again, only the intensity of competition in their domestic markets has forced them to seek out opportunities in foreign markets.

There is a good possibility that Go Global may spoil interest in the China model. Syria, for instance, is chasing the same rapid growth and social stability as China. It may instead face a flood of Chinese manufacturers fleeing their domestic market. The Chinese government must strike a careful balance in the Arab world, not permitting the negative implications of Go Global to overwhelm the Arab economies. Otherwise, the Arab governments may turn less receptive to the China model. So far, there is no sign Arab governments are turning away from China. For instance, the Chinese traders are filling gaps in the Syrian economy, especially in the automobile, utilities, and telecoms industries. But the Syrians are equally proud of their own manufacturers and would react negatively to a sudden flood of imported Chinese goods. The same is true of Egypt and the other less developed Arab economies. China must tread carefully.

It is still too early to judge the outcome. Relations between China and the Arab world have only just started to flourish. On the positive side, the Chinese government is sensitive to any change in sentiment toward the country. Its Economic Affairs Bureaus will certainly help to gauge the impact of Chinese traders on local Arab economies. The Arab governments are meanwhile receptive to what they hear in Beijing. However, the relationship has yet to be seriously stress-tested and tensions between the China growth model and Go Global are a useful reminder that relations between the Arab world and China are still delicately poised. It is more likely that events in the coming decade will surprise observers rather than confirm their expectations. The speed at which change is taking place, both in the Arab world and China, only makes the potential for a shock even greater.

CHAPTER 5

Young Women and the Future of the Arab World

When former Syrian Vice President Abdul Halim Khaddam, traveling to China in 2001, stopped in the southern city of Shenzhen, what he saw amazed him. The city is a pinup for China's remarkable economic success. The Chinese government granted Shenzhen special economic privileges in the early 1980s, permitting it to trade freely with the rest of the world. The results were explosive. Hong Kong investors poured billions of dollars into the city, relocating their factories across the border to take advantage of the cheaper labor costs. From a sleepy fishing village, Shenzhen grew into a mighty metropolis of more than eight million people, attracting migrants from all over the country. Khaddam reportedly praised the wisdom of former paramount leader Deng Xiaoping,[1] who was largely responsible for the economic reforms that had benefited Shenzhen. It is not hard to imagine the Syrian Vice President hoping to repeat the same miracle in Syria.

What he didn't know was that young women between 15 and 29 years of age accounted for over 30 percent of Shenzhen's eight million population.[2] Most were unmarried and living hundreds of kilometers away from their family home. Khaddam would have been shocked. Being a good Sunni Muslim, his daughters were unlikely to have worked until after they were married. I couldn't help but think that if he had known the city's demographics he might not have so readily praised Deng. It's certainly unlikely he would have wanted to replicate the exact same growth model in Syria. Yet Shenzhen wouldn't have grown so rapidly in the past two decades without these young women. Their willingness to migrate to the coastal provinces and work in the export manufacturing and services sectors was vital to unlocking China's vast economic potential in the past two decades.

Jane Zhou is typical of many of the young women in Shenzhen. She works as a sales representative for Green Technologies, the electronics company that sells electronic versions of the Quran. I was intrigued after reading one of their advertisements and booked an appointment to visit their office. It was situated in the city's suburbs, surrounded by a collection of factories, dormitories, office blocks, and a Volkswagen dealership. A guard waved me through the gates and I caught the lift to the tenth floor. It was a poky office and computer wires snaked across the floor. Jane and her two colleagues stood up quickly after I entered. We shook hands and they offered me a seat at a small meeting table. After a few pleasantries Jane pulled out an electronic Quran from its green packaging and started to demonstrate its functions.

Jane was from Guangxi province to the west of Shenzhen, a ten-hour bus trip or a one-hour flight from the city. She had graduated in foreign languages from a university in Guilin, a major city in the province. Most of her classmates went to work as tour guides. The province is famous for its landscapes and overrun by tourists. "But I'm too lazy to work as a tour guide," Jane explained, "I don't like to walk." So instead she'd made the trip to Shenzhen with her boyfriend. They used one of the more popular employment websites to find a job. It wasn't so difficult as long as you had a degree and spoke English. This was her first job and she hadn't been with Green Technologies all that long. But she liked the company and thought the boss was nice, "even if he is from Guangzhou and is very local." She and her colleagues often ate together or played ping-pong after work. It was a good life.

I asked to see the factory. Jane agreed. It was a short walk from the office. The factory is typical of the tens of thousands of similar factories in Shenzhen. It was located in a nondescript ten-storey building with small windows. We caught a large service lift to the seventh floor. A female guard sat inside the lift behind a desk with a portable fan to keep her cool. Green Technologies was just one of more than a dozen manufacturers occupying the building and rented a large space on the upper floor. As we entered, I saw several dozen young women seated behind workbenches in three neat rows. They were hunched over, focused intently on their work, assembling the electronic Qurans from small component parts. Several young men in blue overalls sat at the ends of the three rows touching the finished products with electrical charges to test if they worked.

The factory manager walked over, shook my hand, and offered to take me on a tour of the factory floor. It was a decent place, clean, well lit, with plenty of safety signs attached to the walls. There were certainly worse places to work in the city. Large wire cages occupied half the floor and were used to secure the electronic parts from theft. The other half was occupied by the young women in their neat rows. They barely acknowledged our presence as we observed them assembling small component parts. Most of the women, like Jane, were from Guangxi province. Later, when we left the complex, Jane pointed out the dormitories to me. They were easy to spot. The women lived six to a room and, pressed for space, had hung their washing outside the window. The same scenes are repeated across Shenzhen.

After returning to the office, I purchased a dozen Qurans. I made to leave, but Jane was worried I wouldn't find my way back to Hong Kong. She was determined to escort me safely to the border post. So, we caught the city's newly built underground railway together, chatting the whole time. I finally waved goodbye at the customs hall. I thought nothing of it at the time. But the journey said a great deal about the freedom enjoyed by young women in China. Indeed, Jane is no exception. Young women have made the most of China's booming economy. Many work in factories similar to those in Shenzhen, while others serve food in small restaurants, sell clothing in retail stores, audit books for accounting firms, or have started companies now worth millions of dollars. It is hard to imagine China's economy without them.

The importance of young women was made clear in 2004 when stories of labor shortages in the major export manufacturing regions began to emerge. The shortages were especially intense in Shenzhen and its neighboring cities. This was bad news. The region produces over 30 percent of the country's total exports. The Ministry of Labor confirmed the shortages. It estimated that the city of Shenzhen alone was suffering from a shortage of 100,000 workers.[3] It was a stunning figure. The American economy was adding just 170,000 workers a month the same year. It seemed impossible. Was China's endless supply of labor running dry? The shortages grew worse in the following years. Foreign manufacturers I spoke with during this period talked of having to increase their wages and benefits programs to attract labor.

What had changed? First, the manufacturing sector had grown too fast. Its demand for young women was unquenchable. Second, and more importantly, the services sector was also hiring young women aggressively. As I traveled around the interior cities it was a common sight to see shop windows displaying help wanted signs. If you are a Chinese female, aged between 18 and 25, taller than 150 cm and speak Mandarin, it isn't hard to find work today. All of a sudden, the largely coastal factory owners had to struggle to attract young women from the interior provinces to work in their factories because working conditions and salaries were better in the services sector. And, of course, if you wanted to find a husband, it was wiser to stay in your home province rather than travel thousands of miles to a strange city.

Young Chinese women were also trying their luck in the Arab world. They are a major driver of trade flows between the Arab countries and China. There is no data, but, as I traveled through the Arab world and met Chinese traders in Cairo, Dubai, and Damascus it was clear that the vast majority are women. There are few comparisons. For instance, it is rare to see Western women working in the Arab world. The largest number work in Dubai where the foreign population accounts for around 80 percent of the total population and social restrictions are far less onerous. Even in the Arab world's less conservative countries such as Egypt, Jordan, or Morocco job opportunities are scarce and largely limited to multilateral organizations, such as the United Nations or relief agencies. Young Chinese women, by contrast, have spread across the region, lured by the opportunity to make more money abroad.

I later learnt what it meant to be a female Chinese trader in the Arab world. Fog had inexplicably shut the airport in Dubai and my plane was diverted to Doha. We sat on the tarmac for five hours waiting for the weather to clear. But the time wasn't wasted. I was seated next to two female Chinese traders who, after observing me reading a Chinese-language newspaper, struck up a conversation. The first trader sold lighting fixtures. She had factories in Guangdong and Vietnam. She had also traded in the Arab world for more than ten years, making over a dozen trips annually. So I put the question to her, "What is it like for women to trade in this region?" "Not easy," she replied. "Dubai and Kuwait are okay. Egypt and Syria are harder. Saudi Arabia is almost impossible. But it's good money. The region is booming."

The second trader sold electronics. She was on her way to Riyadh. I hadn't seen many Chinese traders, either men or women, in Riyadh. "How do you sell your goods?" I asked. "I meet my customers through the internet," she replied. "We later arrange to meet in Riyadh at my hotel. But I always cover my face with this," she explained, pulling out a black hijab from a bag stuffed under the seat in front of her. "Still," she sniffed, "The men don't treat me with respect. It's hard work." Her neighbor was also traveling to Riyadh, but for the first time. "Are you afraid?" I joked. She smiled, "Yes." We chatted further until we were finally allowed to leave the aircraft. I wished them luck as we waded down the aisle through a mess of spilled rubbish and airline blankets.

China values its women traders. Indeed, a Chinese-language newspaper describes them as "Female Heroes" (*nu zhong hao jie*).[4] In this case it was referring to the female Chinese traders in Dubai who occupy a building near Al Nasser Square. After reading the article I visited the building. I arrived just after lunch when it had yet to open, so I sat outside and waited. It wasn't long before the traders arrived. It was an odd contrast. The area is still relatively conservative. Most of the shopkeepers in the district are Arab, Indian, or Pakistani and are conservatively dressed. Not so the female Chinese traders. I was taken aback when the first women arrived. They wore short skirts and sleeveless tops. It was no different from a street scene in Yiwu. Perhaps their refusal to defer to local customs explains their success. It certainly didn't stop them from hiring Pakistani assistants.

Most of the female Chinese traders are found in a small four-storey shopping complex. A large sign was strung from the top storey. It had "China City" printed across it in bold red letters. I stopped at a shop on the first floor that sold women's clothing. The shop owner was from Zhejiang province. We chatted for a while. "How is business," I asked? "Okay," she replied. But she said it was easy to sell women's clothing in Dubai. Many women felt uncomfortable buying underwear and they preferred to be

served by a woman. In fact, most of the shops in the complex
sold women's clothing. Like the China City in Syria's Adra Free
Zone, the Chinese in Dubai's Al Nasser Square had also decided
to group together. But here there wasn't a man in sight. The shopping complex was entirely run by female traders.

*   *   *

The contrast with the Arab world is stark. Unemployment rates
for young women are multiples higher than the rates for young
men. In Egypt, for instance, over 40 percent of young women
are unemployed versus 20 percent for young men. The national
unemployment rate is just 9 percent. The same is true in most
other Arab countries. This raises an interesting question. Is it
possible for the Arab world to grow at the same rates as China
if young Arab women remain on the sidelines of the economy?
After all, young women are the magic ingredient of the China
growth model and the recent relative shortages of young women
are also a reason the economy perhaps is not growing as fast as it
would like.

Syria is a useful comparison. The Syrian leadership is a great
admirer of China's economic success. Syria is also less socially
conservative than the Arab Gulf countries. It isn't Lebanon.
But it is common to see women walking down the street wearing makeup, their heads uncovered. The Syrian government is
also socialist in origin and discriminates positively in favor of
women. As a result, women make up a large share of public sector employees. Indeed, walk into a Syrian bank today and the
majority of employees are likely to be women. Yet the unemployment rates for young women are 36 percent versus 16 percent for
young men.[5] If Syria's young women face challenges, then the
challenges faced by young Arab women, especially in the more
socially conservative Arab countries, are likely even greater.

Syria is also a useful comparison for the potential economic
loss. The former Syrian Vice President had nothing but praise
in 2001 for Shenzhen's rapid development. In 2001, Syria and
Shenzhen were similar sized economies at around $25 billion.
By 2007, although Syria's economy had grown to $37 billion,
Shenzhen's had left it far behind, at $89 billion.[6] The fact that

young women make up over 30 percent of Shenzhen's work-force helps explain the difference. Shenzhen's neon-lit economy is built on the type of light manufacturing and services sectors that rely heavily on young women. Syria's less dynamic economy, by contrast, is struggling to kick-start its own light manufacturing and service sectors while huge numbers of young women are unemployed.

So, why are young women so underemployed? There are important cultural reasons. Many are unmarried and are discouraged from mixing freely with single young men at the workplace. In many cases, they are even restricted by law from working at specific times or in certain occupations.[7] It isn't until after young women are married that they are likely to be allowed to work outside the home. This presents a problem. It isn't easy for a mother to leave her children with a relative while she works. The average Arab family has three children,[8] and the responsibility for caring for those forces many mothers, especially young mothers, to stay at home.

Is this likely to change? I decided to find out. Syria was the best place to start my journey. I decided to bring with me the box of electronic Qurans I had purchased in Shenzhen. I wanted to know how the average Syrian might feel if young Syrian women started producing the same devices on factory lines, especially if it meant Syria's economy achieving Shenzhen's rates of economic growth. I also brought with me pictures I had taken of the factory in Shenzhen and its neat row of young women from Guangxi province. A friend in Damascus arranged for me to meet Jamil Majid, an Islamic scholar who was also a fan of China. He had written extensively comparing Islamic thought to various Chinese philosophies. I thought he was a good person to start with.

Jamil was also a part-time dentist. He offered subsidized services in the afternoon to his local neighborhood. We met in his waiting room one day. It was early in the afternoon, an hour before his first clients were scheduled to arrive. Jamil was enthusiastic about the electronic Quran. "It's a great idea," he said. "They are already selling similar versions here in Damascus. But Korean-made, I think. Eighty dollars. It's good value." Jamil was even impressed by the recorded recitations. "The Imams are mainly from Saudi Arabia. They are all famous. Who would have thought the Chinese could be so clever?" Jane Zhou and Green Technologies would have been pleased. Perhaps there was a market for their product in Syria, after all. Jamil and I continued to chat for a while about the merits of the device.

Then I explained to Jamil how the electronic Quran was constructed. I described my visit to the factory floor in Shenzhen. I described the young women who lived far away from their families. Yet Jamil wasn't that bothered. "What's so wrong with that? It's no different to young women living in the dormitories in Damascus University. Everyone is working together under the same roof even if they are far from home." It wasn't exactly the answer I had expected. I later put the same question to other Islamic scholars and received similar answers. Perhaps the China model wasn't so unrealistic. Maybe there is a chance for young Arab women to work in light industry. I doubt young Arab women are likely to enjoy the same freedom as Jane Zhou, but even a small amount of change will make a difference.

I then turned to an expert. Nader Fergany is the lead author of the *Arab Human Development Reports*, written between 2002 and 2005. The reports, sponsored by the United Nations, raised the bar for analysis of the Arab world. They tackled taboo topics, such as the media and politics. They also relied heavily on statistical data, rather than opinion, to support their arguments. They even laid blame for the problems in the Arab world on the Arab world itself, rather than on foreign powers. However, it was the fourth and final report, entitled *Towards the Rise of Women in the Arab World*, that attracted the greatest opposition. Nader recalls that even supporters of his first three reports hesitated after learning the subject of the fourth report. "Is this something you really want to write about?" a colleague asked. The role of women was apparently a bigger taboo subject than either media or political freedoms.

I had a meal with Fergany in an old suburb of Cairo. We weren't able to park near the restaurant and so had to walk a short distance. Along the way we passed Sayyida Zeinab Mosque. The mosque is popular among women. It is claimed to be the burial place of Sayyida Zeinab, who was the granddaughter of the Prophet Mohammed and one of Islam's most famous women. It is perhaps no coincidence that one of Cairo's earliest girl schools is located nearby. We finally reached the restaurant after entering a small back alley. The restaurant was famous for its beef and goat kebabs and its Whisky Baladi, a fiery nonalcoholic drink that is made from the juice of spicy radishes and other vegetables. "I hope you have a strong stomach," Fergany said, laughing. He ordered bread and several kebabs and we started to talk.

Fergany knows China. He has visited the country frequently since the early 1970s. He had written an article comparing its developmental experience with that of the Arab world, titled "From Red Book to Yellow Book." I spoke to him about the importance of young women to the Chinese economy. I asked about the possibility the Arab world might eventually permit its young women to work in light industry, like the Chinese women do in Shenzhen. Fergany paused, before replying with a question of his own. "But what changed in China? I mean, this was a country in which foot-binding was once a common practice. Now, females, young or old, are free to work in almost any occupation. If the status of women changed in China why can't it change in the Arab world? But a 'Cultural Revolution' might be needed here as well."

It was a fair point. A century ago, the life of a Chinese woman was hard. Foot-binding was the worst of many practices. The binding process began between the ages of four and seven years and continued until the foot was reduced to a doll-like three inches. Women lost their mobility and were generally unable to travel outside except in a sedan. Female infanticide was also rife. Young women might even be bought and sold in markets by their husbands and parents. For many women the only way out of their misery was suicide.[9] Yet times were already changing in the early 1900s. The last Emperor attempted to outlaw foot binding. Women silk spinners in Guangdong province formed a collective, refused to marry and organized for higher wages and shorter hours.[10] Later, the Nationalists created a Women's Department to address sexual equality.

However, it was the rise of the Chinese Communist Party that was the major turning point. Mao Zedong was keenly aware of sexual equality in his early years. He wrote nine essays on the subject, inspired by the death of a Miss Chao, who had slit her throat on her wedding day rather than enter an arranged marriage.[11] The Communist Party later viewed women as potential allies in their attempt to bring about the transformation of society. In 1950, a new Marriage law shattered the old traditional family structure.[12] The new law gave a wife equal status to her husband. It also gave a wife the right to choose her occupation. Women were also encouraged to speak about their experiences at what were called "speak bitterness" sessions.[13] The changes did not result in full equality. But they laid the foundations for today's rapid economic growth.

There are many reasons cited for China's economic success. I believe the role played by young women ranks among the most important. As we observe the rise of two historic powers, it is intriguing that one is male-centric whereas the other is more egalitarian. Moreover, one has the lowest rates of women working in the workforce while the other has some of the highest. Whether the Arab economies choose to follow the China growth model will therefore potentially have a large impact on the number of women in the workforce. Less clear, however, is whether the Arab world is ready, or even wants, to embark on the same path as China did during the early 1900s and undertake the type of change that will similarly draw Arab women into the workplace.

* * *

There are signs of change. *The Arab Human Development Report* notes that the share of women with jobs rose 19 percentage points between 1990 and 2003. The absolute share is still small at just 33 percent, among the lowest in the developing world. Moreover, the increase is partly explained by robust economic growth after the sluggishness of the early 1990s. Arab women are typically the first to lose their jobs during a period of slow growth, according to Nader Fergany,[14] so the share of women working was starting from a relatively low level, making initial gains relatively easy. Nonetheless, Al Jazeera's heavily made up female anchors are just one sign that the situation is indeed changing.

The public mood certainly favors change. *The Arab Human Development Report* noted that 91 percent of respondents, in Egypt, Jordan, Lebanon, and Morocco believe women should have an equal right to work. Moreover, 78 percent of respondents believe that women should have the right to equal work conditions.[15] The latter is perhaps the more important figure. The fact that Arab women are banned from working during certain hours or in certain occupations is a prime cause of high unemployment. If the respondents believe this is unfair then unemployment might just fall. The survey suggests that Jamil Majid, the Islamic scholar and part-time dentist I met in Damascus, in fact represents a larger wedge of the population that indeed welcomes women in the workplace.

The number of Arab female entrepreneurs is also on the rise.[16] This is a welcome development, as female-owned businesses tend to employ more women than male-owned firms.[17] Arab women are especially active in the services trade.[18] However, they share few similarities with Jane Zhou. Most Arab female entrepreneurs are aged above 35, married, and have at least two children.[19] Sure, they are trading with the rest of the world, but they are using mobile phones and the Internet to place orders. Indeed, I have never met any Arab women in Yiwu. But this doesn't mean there aren't any Arab Female Heroes comparable to the Chinese Female Heroes who have launched their careers thousands of miles from home selling women's clothing in Dubai.

However, there must also be more fundamental economic change. Michael Ross, an Associate Professor at the University of California, argues that oil explains the high rates of female Arab unemployment.[20] Oil production is a relatively easy way to make money. As a result the oil sector tends to squeeze out light manufacturers, such as clothing and household goods manufacturers. The problem for women is that they are more likely to find work in a clothing factory than in an oil refinery. This is not the only challenge. Ross also argues that women have less reason to work in oil-rich states. Oil-rich governments like Kuwait tend to make large cash payments to households or subsidize utility and housing costs. If so, a single, usually male, income is often enough to feed and house a family.

Morocco is an example of what happens when the non-oil sector grows. In the early 1970s, the Moroccan government started to promote its textile exports to Europe. It made sense. Morocco is just a short boat trip to Spain. Moroccan workers were also much cheaper to employ than European workers. The Moroccan government initially intended to use the textile industry as a way to reduce unemployment for men. But the plan didn't work as expected. Yes, the country's textile exports to Europe boomed. However, the textile industry deliberately employed unmarried women. One explanation is that unmarried women earn less than unmarried men making them more attractive employees. Regardless, by 1980, women accounted for 75 percent of the industry's total employees.[21]

The Arab Gulf countries show what happens when the oil sector dominates. Female unemployment rates are a high 30 percent in Qatar and 39 percent in Saudi Arabia, for instance.[22] Social attitudes no doubt play a role. But if Ross is correct, then it is a bias toward oil production that plays a big role in raising female unemployment rates. It certainly helps explain why female unemployment rates are far lower in Morocco than they are in Qatar and Saudi Arabia.[23] A change in the public mood and the growing number of Arab Female Heroes is an important development, but in order for the change to be sustained, Arab governments must pursue more fundamental economic reform and wean themselves off their reliance on oil by developing their non-oil manufacturing and services sectors.

China may help by encouraging Arab governments to pursue such reforms. However, it is also already leading by example in the Arab world. The arrival of female Chinese traders, in their sleeveless tops, has certainly grabbed attention. The Chinese government also appoints female ambassadors to the Arab world. China's former ambassador to Syria, Zhou Xiuhua, is a good example. She was reportedly well connected and a competent Arabic speaker. Zhou was also the second female Chinese ambassador to Syria since the mid-1990s. It would be wrong to overstate the importance of this. Nonetheless, the prominence of Chinese women in the Arab world might act as a source of social change just as the China growth model serves as a force for economic change.

*   *   *

The problems resulting from unemployment are not restricted to young women, of course. More young Arabs are in work today as economic growth has accelerated since the rise in oil prices. But, unemployment rates for young Arab men are nonetheless high – for instance, in Egypt (21 percent), Syria (16 percent), and Jordan (28 percent).[24] Walk around the streets of Cairo or Damascus during the day and it isn't hard to spot young men killing time in coffee shops. The problem is that the Arab world is in the grips of a demographic bulge. Nearly 64 percent of the Arab world is aged less than 29 years.[25] This is equivalent to 170 million people, or roughly the United States, labor force. It is a major headache for Arab governments. They must find 1.8 million jobs every year simply to keep up with the rise in the youth population before they can worry about reducing the unemployment rate itself.

Many are frustrated by the fact that having connections, or *wasta*, is often more important than education in finding a job. Young men must rely on the assistance of family members or pay a middleman to find a permanent job. This is especially true for countries, such as Egypt and Syria, with large public sectors. Indeed, 54 percent of Syrian youth claim to find their job through family connections.[26] The result is that young men can't get a job without good connections. But when they have to pay a middleman, it is expensive. Egyptian newspapers claim that an Egyptian youth must pay a bribe of $5,500 to find a position in the petroleum sector, $3,670 in the electricity sector, and $1,830 for a job in the Ministry of Religious Charities.[27]

Young Arabs who do not have sufficient *wasta* must wait long periods before finding a full-time job. Arab economists call this "waithood." It describes the situation of young men who are still living at home and working in part-time jobs while searching for full-time jobs. Unfortunately, many delay marriage until they can find a permanent full-time job. Yet a failure to marry can put young Arabs in a position of limbo. The challenge is trying to prevent young people from feeling excluded from society.[28] "Marriage and forming a family in Arab Muslim countries is a must," says Azza Korayem, a sociologist with the National Center for Social and Criminal Studies in Egypt. "Those who don't get married, whether they are men or women, become sort of isolated."[29]

It doesn't help that marriage is expensive in the Arab world. Diane Singerman, an Associate Professor at American University, published a fascinating study in late 2007 indicating that between 2000 and 2004 the average cost of marriage in Egypt was $5,900. This is big money, equivalent to six times the average national wage.[30] By this benchmark, it would cost the average American $230,000 or the average Briton $310,000 to marry in their own country.[31] It is a staggering amount of money for a young groom. So while there are a growing number of young Arabs who deliberately choose to marry later, for many it is the prohibitive cost that forces them to do so.

Why is marriage so expensive? Housing and furniture each account for around 30 percent of the total cost. A bride's family will negotiate hard in order "to create a well-financed, comfortable, and impressive home." Indeed, a couple will generally only move into their new house or refurbished room after all the furniture and accessories are in place. In this respect, the rise of China has ironically helped by producing cheaper household goods. But other costs have risen simultaneously, especially medical and transport costs, making it even more difficult to afford marriage. Egypt is no exception. The cost of marriage is even higher elsewhere. It is estimated at $43,000 in Saudi Arabia. Less is spent on housing, owing to the greater opportunities to rent rather than buy an apartment. However, more is spent on the dowry, celebration, and honeymoon.

The cost of marriage is a common worry. I recall Syrian male friends complaining that Iraqi refugees have pushed home prices higher in Damascus. Syria was host to an estimated one million Iraqi refugees after 2005 as the civil strife in Iraq worsened.[32] A sizeable number of the refugees were relatively wealthy and were renting houses in Damascus and other cities. My friends would wring their hands in frustration, as we chatted while drinking mint tea at home, or eating a dish of chicken and cashew nuts on the rare occasion I dragged them to the old city's only Chinese restaurant. They knew that rising home prices meant they would have to delay their marriage plans for several more years. In the meantime they would have to continue living with their parents.

The Arab governments are worried enough to finance mass weddings. In Egypt, for instance, it is common to stage weddings of upward of 200 couples. One mass wedding held in the small coastal city of Idku married 65 couples in an open-air stadium. Each couple was allowed to invite dozens of family members and friends. The local governor attended while a television personality served as the master of ceremonies.[33] The Palestinian organization Hamas is also a supporter of mass weddings. In August 2004, the organization married 60 Palestinian couples in a refugee camp in Syria and provided each couple with $1,500 in a mixture of cash and household appliances. It wasn't the first event either. In 2005, the organization had married 226 couples in the Palestinian city of Nablus.[34] Mass weddings are now common across the Arab world, even in wealthier countries such as Saudi Arabia.

Arab governments have meanwhile tried to find other ways to distract their idle young men. Syria has a solution: conscription. Young Syrian men generally serve two years in the army. This helps to keep them off the streets. Not all serve in the army. A lucky few can use their connections to avoid serving. The only alternative is to flee the country. One young Syrian trader I met in Yiwu had migrated to China in order to avoid conscription in the army. It wasn't an easy choice, but he thought three years learning to speak Chinese and building commercial relationships was more profitable than three years camped on the Syrian border with Iraq. Moreover, "with the money I earn in China I can build enough *wasta* to avoid the army permanently and even get married," he said.

As James Wolfensohn, a former President of the World Bank, said, "if they [young Arabs] are frustrated and are unable to find work and build their families, there will be unrest, dissension and very possibly violence."[35] Wolfensohn was also a special envoy to Gaza on behalf the United States, European Union, Russia, and the United Nations. He has since set up a Washington-based think-tank focusing on youth exclusion in the Arab world. A failure to provide jobs for Arab youth may indeed result in greater social instability. It may also result in greater religious identification as young Arabs attempt to find solace and purpose. Already, tension between the Arab world and the West is partly built on religious lines. The West therefore has a stake in the Arab world's ability to generate sufficient jobs and income growth in the coming years.

The rise of China may help. China was an important reason for the tripling in oil prices since 2004 and the Arab countries are making the most of the windfall to create jobs. Take the King Abdullah Economic City in Saudi Arabia. This ambitious project is intended to generate 500,000 new jobs[36] and help reduce a 15 percent unemployment rate for male youths.[37] The project would have been difficult before 2004, as the country was burdened by debt.[38] Today, the debt is largely paid off as a result of surging oil prices. If the International Energy Agency is right, China's thirst for oil will help to ensure oil prices remain above $60 a barrel during the next two decades, making it easier for Arab governments to afford the type of capital projects that will draw young men out of coffee shops and put them to work in factories and offices.

Trade flows between China, the Arab world, and Africa are helping the Arab Gulf economies to build service sectors and reduce their reliance on oil. This means jobs for young Arabs as baggage handlers, taxi drivers, and accountants. Take Dubai. Its ports are among the world's largest as it handles cargo arriving from Asia. The city is also building a new airport that when completed will rank as the world's largest, capable of handling 120 million passengers a year.[39] The existing airport already serves as a hub for the millions of passengers traveling between Asia, Europe, Africa, and, of course, the Middle East. Dubai's financial sector is also servicing trade and investment flows between all three continents. Dubai's neighbors Bahrain and Qatar are now trying to repeat the same successes.

China has also had a more individual impact. Take Mohammed Nasser, the Palestinian trader I had met in Yiwu. Mohammed had already lived in Yiwu for several years, but he planned to stay for several more to earn enough money to return to Palestine and marry. He was born in Gaza, but the recent troubles made it almost impossible to earn enough money at home. Unemployment in Gaza was 29 percent.[40] But Yiwu offered Mohammed new hope. His business of selling leather belts to the booming Saudi Arabian market was turning a good profit. Mohammed had two Chinese employees, a four-room office and a four-foot long fish tank. There was little chance he could have owned the same back in Gaza.

Tourism also offers opportunities. Tourism receipts are important for a number of Arab countries, in particular Egypt, Jordan, Morocco, Tunisia, and Syria. It is increasingly common to hear Chinese spoken at tourist sites, not just by Chinese tourists, but also by the Arab vendors who are trying to sell them souvenirs. The vendors in Cairo's bazaars might know just a few words, but the fact they have taken time to learn them is an indication of the growing purchasing power of Chinese tourists. In Egypt, the number of Chinese tourists doubled to 74,000 between 2005 and 2007,[41] while the Chinese government signed an agreement with the Syrian government in August 2007 opening the way for Chinese tourists to travel to the country.[42]

Yet it is not all good news. A flood of cheap Chinese imports may force local factories to close, or discourage new factories from opening. Remember the Egyptian I met on the plane to Yiwu. His shoe factory in Cairo is now empty; instead, he imports from China, shuttling between Cairo and Yiwu three times a year. Not all Arab countries are affected, but Egypt is the most exposed. It is often called "the China of the Arab world" because of its large labor force and cheap wages. However, Syria and Morocco are also at risk. So far, complaints have been muted. But there is a risk that a growing flood of cheap Chinese imports will result in job losses rather than jobs growth. The Chinese government must strike a careful balance between pursuing its policy of Go Global and assisting Arab governments to reform their economies.

Food prices also matter. Admittedly, household goods prices have fallen as a result of cheap Chinese imports, but Chinese households are spending their rapid income gains on more food, such as meat and soybeans. This is bad news for Arab households. The Arab region is the world's largest importer of food. For instance, the Arab world and Iran together account for nearly 26 percent of the world's total wheat imports.[43] Luckily, China produces most of its own wheat. But when it doesn't, it turns to the global wheat market. Its imports can push global wheat prices markedly higher. If wheat prices rise, so does the cost of the flat bread available all across the Arab world. In 2008, there were riots in Cairo as the cost of flat bread spiraled higher.

Although it is difficult to forecast food prices, there are promising signs that the Arab world's light manufacturing sector may yet find room to grow in spite of China.

In 2008, there were signs that Chinese exports were less competitive as a result of rising wage and material costs. A stronger currency was also taking its toll. There were stories of foreign investors opening factories in Vietnam, instead of in China. Meanwhile the Chinese government is encouraging factories to produce more profitable goods such as automobiles and notebook PCs, as less profitable goods such as toys and textiles tend to pollute, consume scarce resources, and create bottlenecks at already busy transport hubs. Its efforts have been successful. So there is a good chance that the Arab world will find it easier to compete with China's cheap consumer goods exports. The rapidly growing Chinese domestic market even offers opportunities itself. It might be that Arab traders eventually travel to Yiwu in order to sell products, rather than buy them.

The Arab world is also fortunately positioned next to one of the world's largest consumer markets. Europe's \$294 billion imports from China in 2009 were larger than its imports from America. More remarkably, China's trade with Europe increased by \$240 billion between 2000 and 2009, a figure equivalent to twice Egypt's annual GDP.[44] This is instructive for the Arab world. If Chinese factories are indeed priced out of the global market for such goods as toys and textiles, then Arab manufacturers will find an opportunity to replace them. Arab factory owners already enjoy a few advantages relative to their Chinese competitors. For instance, the Euro-Mediterranean free trade area expands on earlier agreements and aims to create a matrix of free trade agreements between the European Union and the Middle East countries.

And so the Arab world is delicately poised. Its large youth population is a potential "demographic dividend." East Asia enjoyed the same demographic dividend between 1965 and 1990. However, Asian governments harnessed their youth putting them to work in export factories in Hong Kong and construction sites in Bangkok thus laying the foundations for today's "Asian Miracle." The Arab world is similarly positioned. Yet, the outcome is not guaranteed. Latin America is also halfway through its own demographic dividend, but has failed to capitalize on it as a result of poor policy decisions.[45] There is still no indication as to whether the Arab economies will follow the East Asian path or the more disappointing Latin American path.

What is clear, however, is that the rise of China will play an important role in determining whether the Arab world can make the most of its demographic dividend. Observing changes in young female unemployment is a useful way to measure the success of Arab governments in reorienting their economies away from oil and toward the non-oil sectors, especially the light manufacturing sectors. The Arab world isn't likely to build its own version of neon-lit Shenzhen and its thousands of dormitory factories. But there may be a halfway house that accommodates the Arab world's social distinctiveness, especially with regard to the status of women, while also supporting the type of economic reforms that promise to put the Arab economies on a more China-like growth trajectory.

America and Europe have a great deal at stake in the outcome. If China's rise spurs economic growth in the Arab world, youth unemployment will fall. However, if youth unemployment rises there is a risk that frustrated young Arabs will weaken social stability. Arab governments may in turn use religion to anchor their legitimacy among Arab youth. The growing importance of religion to daily political life matters for Western governments. It is through religion that grievances with the West's foreign policies, especially in Iraq and Palestine, are often voiced. A rise in unemployment thus risks alienating Arab youth from America and Europe. The rise of China is not an isolated event for the West, but is felt as far as the West's relationship with the Arab world's large, and potentially unemployed, youth population.

CHAPTER 6

The New Public Relations War: "Al Jazeera" in China

Al Jazeera's Beijing office occupies the upper floor of an apartment block near Tiananmen Square. I arranged to meet the bureau chief, Ezzat Shahrour, one winter and had rashly decided to walk from my hotel, along Jianguomenwai Dajie. The morning traffic had already turned the overnight snowfall into a dark slush and my face was bitterly cold by the time I arrived at the apartment block. Shahrour was from the northern Syrian city of Aleppo, which was obvious the moment his secretary opened the door for me. His office was crammed with the furniture Aleppo is famous for. It is beautiful, made of handcrafted rose and walnut wood, and inlaid with mother of pearl. I have similar pieces in my own apartment. It wasn't hard to imagine that such furniture had also found its way to China centuries earlier along the Silk Road.

Shahrour had lived in Beijing for over a decade, starting as an official at the Palestinian Embassy before joining Al Jazeera. He had reasons to be proud of his work at the station. Shahrour has done a great deal toward raising the profile of China in the Arab world. His greatest success was a special program on China using equipment borrowed from CCTV, the Chinese state broadcaster. The special, called "Eye on China" was broadcast over several days and ran for nearly three hours. It was tremendously popular and Al Jazeera later produced similar features on other countries. The feedback from the Chinese Embassies in the Arab world was also positive. He later sent me a DVD copy through the mail and I spent an evening watching several episodes – it wasn't what the West typically associates with Al Jazeera.

The Al Jazeera anchor in Doha introduced the special by saying "ni hao," using the Chinese word for hello. The special then cut away to an anchor in Beijing seated in a Chinese pavilion overlooking a lake. During the next three hours he interviewed officials from the Foreign Ministry, Chinese Radio International, and Cultural Ministry. All the officials spoke in Arabic. The anchor also interviewed two students about China's one-child policy. The anchor asked what it felt like to be an only child. One of the students replied, in Arabic, "I don't feel any different. There is nothing remarkable." There were also a series of stories on Chinese Muslims. The footage included images of Muslims praying in mosques and welcoming visiting Arab Imams. The special ended with a story on Yiwu, interviewing one of the many Arab traders in the city's exhibition halls.

Al Jazeera's "Eye on China" is symbolic of the role the media is playing in the rise of the Arab world. It is not immediately apparent. Attention is instead focused on exports, oil prices, and the Arab wealth funds. But the media is an equally important force in global rebalancing. Al Jazeera first issued its challenge to the West during its reporting of the Afghanistan War. It confirmed its status as a new media power during the Iraq War. But Al Jazeera's influence extends further. It has achieved more than simply shaking up how events are reported in the Arab world. It has also opened up direct lines of communication between the Arab capitals and Beijing. In the West we often assume that developing countries must rely on the Western media to broadcast their voice to the world. Not anymore. The rise of Al Jazeera and the Arab news stations is a major new influence on the way global public opinion is formed.

Take Al Jazeera's bureau in Beijing. Today the average Arab household can watch news from Beijing as easily as they already watch news from Brussels or Washington. It was a simple but dramatic step toward lifting China's profile in the Arab world. Not surprisingly the Chinese government has made increasing use of the station to reach out to Arab households. I asked Shahrour when he first noticed a change in attitude from the Chinese authorities. "After September 11," he replied with a grimace. "But the real change was after 2004, as oil prices started to rise." The Chinese government started to worry about its growing dependence on the large Arab oil producers. All of a sudden Shahrour found Chinese officials ready to speak on Al Jazeera. It was a remarkable change for a country typically wary of the foreign media, preferring to "speak little, do more."

Al Jazeera claims to be the first foreign broadcaster to receive a live interview with a Chinese official.[1] I couldn't verify the claim, but I did watch the interview later. The General Director for the West Asia Division of the Foreign Ministry, Zhai Jun, had appeared on "No Limits" (*bila hudoud*) in November 2006, a program that grills its guests similar in style to the BBC's *HARDtalk*.

Zhai's performance was impressive. He spoke in Arabic for over an hour. The interview had started friendly enough as the program's host, Ahmed Mansour, asked Zhai about China and the military threat it presented to the United States. But then it got heated. Mansour first asked why China, as a member of the United Nations Security Council, hadn't used its veto to prevent the Iraq war. Zhai avoided the question. Later, Zhai claimed China's relations with Israel were no different to its relations with any Arab country, only for Mansour to rebut, "But they are different. Israel exchanges military technologies with China. That doesn't happen with the Arab states." Now Zhai started to look uncomfortable as he fidgeted slightly in his chair. Regardless, he continued to debate with Mansour. He even took questions from dial-in callers during the final ten minutes.

It wasn't the last time Zhai appeared on the news station, so the Chinese government must have considered his interview a success. It was almost impossible for the Chinese government to speak directly to the Arab street a decade ago. Not anymore. Aside from a few diplomats and Arabic-language specialists, I imagine there are few who recognize that China is using Al Jazeera to raise its profile in the Arab world. Al Jazeera's Beijing bureau is a reminder of how important public relations are today. Now the Chinese government can directly lobby the average Arab household in Amman, Cairo, Dubai, or any of the Arab cities. It has struck an important blow in an increasingly global public relations war.

It is a war America is struggling to win. Take Iraq. The American government is engaged in efforts to spin its achievements to a skeptical Iraqi population. Yet, while American companies are among the best in the world at selling their products, the American government lags far behind. A Pew Survey in June 2007 showed that 67 percent of Palestinians had favorable impressions of U.S. science and technology, whereas just 15 percent had favorable impressions of the U.S. government itself.[2] European governments have not always performed much better. The challenge for America has grown greater, not smaller, in the past few years. The Arab news stations have contributed to these poor ratings by broadcasting their own views and images to the average Arab household.

I thought their success was best captured by a poster in Shahrour's office. He pointed to it as we left with a smile on his face. The poster was made up of a montage of shots but in the bottom right corner, written in bold white letters, was the statement, "If everyone watches CNN, what does CNN watch?" I laughed. The answer was Al Jazeera. It summed up everything the Arab news station has accomplished in the past decade. Al Jazeera stood up to CNN in its own backyard and won. It was able to break the Western media's monopoly on how events in the Arab world are reported. Its greatest prize is its ability to help set the region's agenda through its use of powerful images, such as Iraqi militants battling American tanks on street corners.

Al Jazeera hasn't just broken the grip of the Western media, it has also inspired others to try the same. In the past it had seemed impossible to take on the financial might of the Western media. Take CNN, for example. Its annual expenditures are estimated at more than half a billion dollars.[3] That's a lot of money for a small developing country, even assuming it has the technical expertise to set up a news station. Of course, Al Jazeera has wealthy backers. But it has also demonstrated that the Western media's monopoly can be broken, especially when it is operating outside its home territory, such as in the Arab world. It makes sense that a developing country might want to create its own Al Jazeera. The Western media is, after all, reporting for a Western audience. It ultimately pursues a Western agenda.

China is an especially keen student. Al Jazeera's Director General had visited Beijing on several occasions. His visits were initially met with skepticism, but when he eventually met with the Chinese Foreign Minister, the minister reportedly praised the station, applauding the way it had stood up to Western governments.[4] China has long chafed at the power of the Western media, with good reason. Although the government still censors its domestic media, there is a desire for the Chinese media to set its own agenda when reporting foreign affairs. Yet today, many Chinese-language reports on foreign affairs are translated from the English-language media. It is not an ideal situation. Sun Bigan, the Chinese special representative to the Middle East and a veteran diplomat, described the problem in an interview to a Chinese-language magazine in 2003.

"I think the Chinese media has not done enough. Through timely and effective reporting of the Gulf War and the U.S.–Iraq War, CNN and Al Jazeera established their influence in the world media. If the Chinese media wants to expand its influence, we can't overlook the Middle East. It has always been the focus of the world." He continued, "When reporting issues in relation to the Islamic world, we need to have a firm understanding. For instance, the Chinese government is against terrorism of all forms. But we are also against linking terrorism with specific countries or regions. Some people from the West think that terrorism is related to Islamic religion. But this is not the truth."[5]

The Chinese state news agency, Xinhua, agrees. In 2006, Xinhua's President Tian Congming publicly declared his intent to seek "basic replacement of the competition."[6] In this instance, Tian was targeting foreign financial news providers, such as Bloomberg and Reuters. His ambition was also limited to the Chinese domestic market. The news agency had benefited from the imposition of new regulations the same year requiring foreign financial news providers to sell their financial products through Xinhua.[7] But comparisons with Al Jazeera are not unwarranted. After all, Al Jazeera had changed the way the Western media reported political news in the Arab world. Might Xinhua likewise change the way the Western media reports economic news in China?

Xinhua also has global ambitions. It is just one of the many Chinese state news agencies with foreign bureaus. The People's Daily and the Guangming Daily also have reporters based throughout the Arab world. However, Xinhua's operations are grander in scale. The People's Daily, for instance, has just a few reporters in a few Arab capitals, whereas Xinhua operates bureaus in 17 Arab states. Its headquarters is in Cairo. A newly built eleven-storey building is home to an estimated

30 reporters, not including local staff, who publish in Chinese, Arabic, and English, for distribution through the Middle East and Africa. The building is a statement of intent. Indeed, when it was opened in November 2005, a representative from the Egyptian Ministry of Information praised the news agency, saying Xinhua, compared to the Western media, was "more just, objective, and comprehensive."[8]

Is Xinhua the next Al Jazeera? Not quite. Xinhua still faces a number of large obstacles, most importantly, the restrictions it faces when reporting the news. I asked Ezzat Shahrour his opinion. "My friends at Xinhua tell me Al Jazeera was lucky. They say if it wasn't for the war in Afghanistan we wouldn't have achieved such success. But this wasn't it," he recalled with a shake of his head. "It was the fact that we made the most of our privileged access in Afghanistan, also, the fact that we weren't afraid to report the news. I tell my friends in Xinhua that they enjoy the same privileged access in North Korea at a time when the world is hungry for news. They should use North Korea to build their reputation, in the same way we used Afghanistan." It was a fair point. If Xinhua sheds even a small crack of light on events in North Korea it would go a long way to establishing its credibility and fulfilling its global ambitions.

This isn't likely to happen immediately. The Chinese government still keeps a tight leash on Xinhua. For instance, the news agency produces two types of reports. The first is for public release. The second is considered too sensitive for public release. It deals with such issues as corruption and social unrest in stories that more closely resemble investigative journalism found elsewhere in the world. Xinhua's editors still welcome this kind of reporting, but they mark it for "internal reference" and dispatch it to the senior Communist Party leadership.[9] It is likely that Xinhua is in fact writing incisive reports on events in North Korea, but such reports are unfortunately intended for a select audience and are unlikely to be released so long as the leadership is using them to maintain its grip on events at home and abroad.

The upshot is that China will struggle to produce its own version of Al Jazeera for the time being. The Chinese government enjoys too much control over its domestic media. But the accomplishment of Al Jazeera in its battle with the Western media has nonetheless revealed a desire in China, and in other developing countries, to wrest their agendas away from the Western media. This is the real Al Jazeera effect. It has ensured that the days of CNN's monopoly over 24-hour news are finished. It is as important to global rebalancing as are the Egyptian traders buying hardware in Yiwu, Zhong Dongyun's "China City" on the outskirts of Damascus, the rise in oil prices to near $150, or the Arab wealth funds and their gleaming corporate headquarters.

*   *   *

The West is responding. But the results are so far mixed. In February 2004, the Board of Broadcasting Governors, an independent agency of the U.S. government, launched Al Hurra, an Arabic-language satellite television station broadcasting 24 hours per day from its base in Virginia. Al Hurra aimed to "support the board's antiterror broadcasting initiatives in the Middle East and counter terrorist media campaigns by providing accurate reporting and analysis of the news and by explaining American policies."[10] The board had launched Radio Sawa, an Arabic-language radio station, a few years earlier. It also mandated the Middle East Broadcasting Networks to manage the two stations on its behalf. The stations were controversial from their inception. Most damningly, the stations replaced the Voice of America's Arabic service and in doing so created a legion of disgruntled former employees.

Al Hurra certainly isn't going to win viewers as an advocate of an "independent view." Arabs typically view all media agencies, even Al Jazeera, as political vehicles. Historically, Arab governments tightly controlled their domestic media. Even today, private media agencies are typically owned by Arab tycoons with a political agenda. Al Jazeera is no exception – in the late 1990s, it was accused of pro-Israeli bias after permitting Israelis to speak on the program.[11] As a nonnative Arabic speaker, it is challenging to read Arabic-language newspapers. It is not enough to simply read a newspaper, you also have to know the political views of its owner to appreciate the bias in the reporting. The problem for Al Hurra is that the vested interests of the owners of Al Jazeera, or the Arab newspapers, such as Al Safir and Al Hayat, are at least closer to those of the average Arab household than Al Hurra and its ultimate paymaster, the American government.

Al Hurra doesn't face competition from just the Arab news stations. The BBC started its own Arabic-language channel in 2008.[12] The British state broadcaster had attempted to start an Arabic-language television channel in the early 1990s, but aborted the project after disagreements with the Saudi Arabian government. Ironically, 120 of Al Jazeera's original staff were hired from a joint Saudi-BBC channel that failed in the late 1990s after a series of political disputes.[13] The second incarnation of the BBC's Arabic-language news station appears less encumbered and better positioned to exploit the institution's 60 years of experience in radio broadcasting to the region. France 24 also started its own Arabic-language channel in 2007.[14] Yet, Al Hurra, the BBC, and France 24, face an increasingly crowded space in the Arab world. They may struggle to succeed.

The best response I have read was in a study on U.S. diplomacy led by former American ambassador Edward Djerejian, commissioned by the House Appropriations Committee and published in 2003. It revealed "a high level of skepticism" in the Middle East toward any sort of state-owned television. It argued that the funds would be better spent contracting American public and private firms to produce high-quality programming that could be then distributed through existing channels in the region, such as Al Jazeera.[15] A similar comment might have been directed at the BBC. The broadcaster already has a long history of producing such high-quality programming. Indeed, an editorial in Al Sharq Al Awsat cited statistical research that a large majority of Arabs favored the BBC producing independent Arabic-language programs.[16]

The Chinese government is already on the right path. Its decision to lend Al Jazeera television equipment was smart thinking. It didn't have editorial control over the final product, but Al Jazeera's three-hour documentary spent much of its time exploring historical relations between the Arab world and China. The remainder of the time was left to exploring China itself. The Chinese government effectively enjoyed a free ride from one of the Arab world's most popular satellite television stations. It is reasonable to assume that the number of Arab households watching the documentary was far greater than the number who watched Al Hurra the same week. Ironically the Chinese had used the power of market forces to stage a major public relations coup. It should be an important lesson for Western governments.

*   *   *

Al Jazeera isn't the only challenge. The Chinese government excels in its more old-school techniques. Its ability to "stay on message" helps explain why it achieves higher ratings in the Arab world. For instance, 43 percent of Jordanians had a favorable view of China in June 2007, whereas just 20 percent had a favorable view of America.[17] China's tight control of the domestic media is a major advantage. It uses "blow wind meetings" (*chui feng hui*) to guide the major newspapers on how to report events in the region. For instance, a number of Chinese reporters I have spoken with claim they are guided through the "blow wind meetings" to focus on China's economic, rather than political, ties with the Arab world. This makes the domestic media a powerful public relations arm for the Chinese government.

Xinhua is in the vanguard. There are few Arab journalists living in China itself. So the agency translates its articles into Arabic for publication in the Arab world. In doing so it enjoys great scope to "spin" its message. Indeed, in 2006, Xinhua signed an agreement with Egypt's *October Weekly* to provide Arabic-language articles for the newspaper.[18] For the moment, *October Weekly* is mainly buying Xinhua's reporting of Chinese domestic affairs, but it may one day buy its reporting of foreign affairs. Meanwhile, Xinhua is also reporting on China's activities in the Arab world. Its reports are later translated into Arabic and English. Ironically, its reports now serve as a major source of information on China's activities in the Arab world, of course, after the message has first been appropriately spun.

The Chinese state news agencies are also more directly targeting their Arab audience. I realized this while searching for Arabic-language articles on the Chinese International Car Exhibition held in Syria in June 2006. I did find an Arabic-language article, but was taken aback at how extensively it reported the event. So, I decided to check the source. A news agency called Chinese Radio

International had posted the article. It is the Chinese version of Voice of America, broadcasting and publishing in over forty languages. In this instance the agency's Arabic-language department had published the article for release in the Arab world. Chinese Radio International was originally established in the 1950s as part of the Chinese Communist Party's efforts to strengthen political ties with the rest of the world, but it has since evolved as a result of market reforms. It is now equally effective at building economic ties.

The state media agencies have also played important roles in educating Chinese traders about the opportunities in the Arab world. The major trade industry newspapers regularly send reporters abroad to report on market conditions in the Arab economies. They are an invaluable resource. Take, for instance, the *International Business Daily*. The paper was established in 1985 by the Ministry of Commerce, which has since funded its operations. It was in the *International Business Daily* that I originally stumbled across details of the Chinese International Car Exhibition in Syria. Their reporter was invited to attend the tour alongside reporters from the *Xinhua Economic News* and other papers. He waxed poetical about veiled Syrian women waving to the tour from their balconies,[19] but he also reported extensively on market conditions for the automobile sector. No doubt, his articles were read by Chinese car manufactures back home.

The efforts of the state media agencies aren't always intentional. By simply increasing their coverage of foreign affairs, for instance, they have encouraged traders to find new markets. Take Wang, the foreign trade manager for the Jia Xing clothing company in Yiwu. In August 2006, he had heard from the company's office in Dubai that there were severe shortages of consumer goods in Lebanon as a result of the conflict, so Wang watched the war on CCTV, the state television broadcaster, ready to ship goods the moment hostilities concluded.[20] The news portals of Sina.com and the documentaries of Phoenix Television likewise help Chinese traders to identify new markets. I once asked a Chinese trader at Dubai's Dragon Mart, "Why Dubai?" She claimed to have seen a Chinese-language documentary on the Arab world and thought to herself, "This looks like an opportunity."

It seems that Western governments are losing the public relations war. Attention to public relations has slipped since the fall of the Soviet Union. In the mid-1990s after the collapse of the USSR, for instance, the American government abandoned many of its public relations weapons. This included the fateful decision to disband the United States Information Agency in 1999, which was perhaps the nearest equivalent America had to an official Information Ministry. What use was an Information Ministry now that the Soviet Union no longer existed? Yet the events of September 2001 and the rising economic challenge from China are a reminder that winning the Cold War wasn't the end of history. There is another public relations battle to be fought. Moreover, Western governments face multiple, and increasingly sophisticated, opponents.

*   *   *

Arab governments are also guilty of the same mistakes made by Western governments. They have failed to engage the Chinese domestic media to the detriment of relations between the Arab world and China. Ma Xiaolin is a former Chief Correspondent for the Chinese state news agency Xinhua. An Arabic speaker, Ma worked in Gaza and Kuwait during his years with Xinhua, later leaving to work as editor-in-chief for the news magazine the *Globe*. He is rightly considered a "Middle East expert" (*zhong dong tong*) and well qualified to speak on the issue of media relations between China and the Arab world. In 2004 he wrote an article examining Chinese press coverage of Arab affairs[21] and was strongly critical of the failure of Arab governments to lobby Chinese journalists.

Israel has not made the same mistakes. Ma claims that Chinese reporters assigned to Israel are typically invited to the Israeli embassy for a briefing before their departure. Ma never received a similar invitation from the Kuwaiti embassy. He only received an invitation to the Palestinian embassy after he had completed a three-year rotation in Gaza and had returned to Beijing. It was all too little, too late. Ma also writes that the Israeli government invites many senior Chinese scholars and newspaper editors to visit Israel. As a result, there is a growing faction of Chinese scholars and newspaper editors that increasingly favor Israel. They are known as the Israeli faction (*qin yi pai*).

Ma's article reminded me of a conversation I had earlier with Chen Keqin, a reporter at the official *Guangming Daily*. He had spent several years studying Arabic in Syria in the 1960s sponsored by the Chinese government. He had later worked more than twenty years in the Arab world and his Arabic was excellent. But Chen had more recently developed an interest in Israel, where he had spent the past few years working in Jerusalem. In 1995, relations between China and Israel were established, but it took several years before the *Guangming Daily* received permission from the Chinese government to set up an Israeli bureau. When it did, in 1997, Chen was duly dispatched. And, despite his long history in the Arab world, Chen grew to "appreciate" Israel as well as the Arab world.

He is not alone. The rise of the Internet and the growing number of Chinese bloggers have changed the way Arab issues are debated in the domestic Chinese media. Take Ma Xiaolin, who later set up a website for bloggers called Abundant United Community. Ma's experience reporting the daily battles between Palestinian youth and the Israeli military had left an indelible impression on him. He wanted to create a website to encourage the "exchange of ideas." I had earlier found an article in the *Arab World Journal*, a Chinese-language journal dedicated to Arab affairs, written by Shun Chunjie, a former Chinese ambassador to Syria. It was while trying to make contact with Shun that I stumbled across his blog on the Abundant United Community as well as a series of articles written by Ma on the Arab world.

As Ma argues, public sentiment toward the Arab world has shifted in recent years. It is the rise of the Chinese blogger, and blog sites such as Abundant United Community, which is partly responsible. The Chinese blogger does not attend "blow wind meetings" and is not responsible to the senior editors at Xinhua. The Chinese blogger is therefore more inclined to argue an independent view in foreign affairs. This is a marked change from past practice. From the late 1950s, the Chinese government was a supporter of socialist causes in the Arab world, recognizing pan-Arab nationalist governments in Egypt, Syria, and Yemen as "anti-imperialist." Its stance meant China was more inclined to positioning itself on the side of the Arab states rather than Israel. But this is changing as a result of reforms and, in particular, the rise of the Chinese blogger.

Today there are concerns about Islamic militancy that didn't exist a decade ago. It is difficult to gauge the true extent of this concern. But as fighting between Hizbollah and Israel was escalating in July 2006, I followed a chat room managed by Sina. com, a major Chinese news portal. My initial impression was that a majority of the chat room's participants sided with Lebanon against Israel. Many were angry that the Israeli bombing had caused the deaths of so many young women and children. But exclude this, and the debate started to look more balanced. There were even a few specific concerns about Islamic militancy, which had perhaps escaped the censors. Now a chat room isn't the best place to track public sentiment, not least because of censorship, but I can't help thinking that Ma is right, and that attitudes toward the Arab world are less favorable than in the past.

This doesn't mean that interest in the Arab world is fading. In fact it is quite the reverse. Sina.com created a special home page for the Lebanon war, no different than those created by the BBC and CNN, including the latest news, interactive maps, biographies of the key players, timelines of earlier conflicts, and editorials by academics. Now, Sina.com isn't just any website. It is a world leader. In terms of daily hits, it ranked number 21 in the world in October 2008, far ahead of the CNN at 46 and BBC at 48.[22] Admittedly, it isn't a place for investigative journalism and it relies too heavily on translations of English-language articles when reporting foreign affairs. But the fact Sina.com allocated considerable resources to reporting of the Lebanon war signals China's rising, not falling, interest in the Arab world.

I saw evidence of this shift shortly afterward in Damascus. My plane had just taxied to its gate at Damascus International Airport when a Chinese camera crew suddenly leapt out from behind the last row of seats. I hadn't noticed them during the flight. But with camera in hand they lined up a Syrian passenger still struggling to collect his luggage from the overhead compartment. He looked shocked, but he stopped, smiled, and answered their questions even as the other passengers filed off the plane. I later introduced myself to the reporter, who was surprised to hear

Chinese spoken and we struck up a brief conversation in the aisle of the plane. His name was Tao Lu. His team was on assignment for Phoenix Television to cover the war. Tao and I swapped cards and we promised to meet up later in Damascus.

Phoenix Television plays an unusual role in the Chinese media. It broadcasts in Mandarin Chinese for a largely mainland Chinese audience. Based in Hong Kong, the station enjoys greater liberties in what it reports. Phoenix Television's CEO, Liu Changele, is a former People's Liberation Army Colonel who reportedly has strong ties to the mainland government. Since its establishment in 1996 Phoenix Television has learnt how to tread carefully with the mainland censors, while still pushing the limits of media freedom. Most importantly, at least for Tao, the station has a strong interest in foreign affairs. It claims to be the only mainland Chinese station to have provided live coverage of the September 11 attacks. Phoenix is a good model for what an ordinary mainland Chinese news network might look like in the future.

In the event, I didn't have a chance to meet Tao in Damascus, but we did meet later in Hong Kong. We arranged for a meal in Kowloon after work. Tao had just returned from a trip to Cuba. He was jet-lagged, but pleased at having obtained an interview with the Cuban Vice Foreign Minister. "Not even CNN had managed that," he said. Tao was Phoenix Television's international reporter. He had originally worked at the Chinese Foreign Ministry as a translator. Tao had covered stories in Cuba, Iran, Syria, and Turkmenistan since joining Phoenix Television. He had also interviewed the former U.S. Defense Secretary, Donald Rumsfeld. I met Tao in a restaurant with commanding views of Hong Kong Island and its neon-lit skyscrapers. The restaurant was famous for its northern style of Chinese cooking. While we waited for the food to arrive I asked Tao about his trip to Syria.

Tao had stayed in Damascus while his colleagues traveled on to Beirut. It was a productive week. The Chinese ambassador to Syria had arranged meetings with a number of senior Syrian officials, even representatives from Hamas and Hizbollah. The ambassador had good connections and knew how to pull the right levers. Tao had also hired a cameraman in Syria who was, by chance, a brother-in-law of the Syrian Vice President, a coincidence that led to Tao's interview with the Vice President himself. Tao remarked later at his amazement at how well the Vice President had conducted himself in front of a camera given that such interviews are unusual in Syria.

The arrival of Phoenix Television and the other Chinese media in the Arab world helps to break the monopoly of the Western media. The problem is that Chinese viewers aren't entirely enthralled about what they are watching. The events of 2001 and the rise of Islamic militancy have created fears about the Arab world among the Chinese public. The failure of Arab governments to lobby the Chinese media also works against Arab interests, especially if the Israeli government continues to lobby China's "Israeli faction." So, although the Arab world has achieved remarkable success with the Arab news stations, and is likewise benefiting from the arrival of the Chinese media in the Arab countries, it still has considerable work to do selling itself to the Chinese public.

*   *   *

America and Europe must fight a better public relations battle. It isn't enough to attract investment from the Arab wealth funds, send Airbus executives to lobby Emirates Airlines, or import more oil from Saudi Arabia. This helps to cement economic relations with the Arab world. But it won't necessarily win friends. Western governments must learn to make use of the Arab news stations to communicate with the average Arab household. They must also make use of the "old-school" techniques applied so successfully by China in order to spin a positive image in the Arab world. It is this mixture of the new and the old that makes the West's public relations battle in the Arab world so challenging.

The U.S. Government Accountability Office, in 2007, argued a similar point in front of Washington politicians. It recommended the State Department adopt a "campaign-style approach," advising it to define a core message, identify and segment target audiences, and use audience research to inform and redefine the efforts as needed.[23] They didn't specifically recommend using the Arab news stations or adopt a Chinese-style "blow wind" approach, but the implication is there. How else is the State

Department to reach a mass Arab audience? Its suggestions are no different from those a marketing executive might pitch to a company's CEO, effectively advising the State Department to take a more commercial approach in its public diplomacy efforts.

The Pew Surveys have shown a sharp rise in the number of Arabs who feel hostile toward America in recent years.[24] Of course, America has tough policy options in the Arab world. It can't be expected to keep everyone happy. But the U.S. Group on Public Diplomacy had this to say: "We have failed to listen and failed to persuade. We have not taken the time to understand our audience, and we have not bothered to help them understand us. We cannot afford such shortcomings." Europe has also suffered as a result of perceived bias against Islamic interests, especially as tensions with large Islamic populations grow.

China is clearly succeeding where the West is not. It helps that the Chinese government still has a variety of information agencies, such as the Central Propaganda Department, and that Xinhua reports directly to the State Council. The structure might resemble a relic of the Cold War. But in the near two decades since the fall of the Berlin Wall, these agencies have deployed the domestic media in support of China's efforts to strengthen relations, not just with the Arab world, but the entire developing world. Ironically, in an age when Western governments are increasingly skilled in selling their message to the Western media, it is the Chinese government that is more proactively using the media to sell its message to the Arab people.

*   *   *

America and Europe must also listen to the Arab media. Today Arab investors are major players in the world's financial markets. First, the Arab world's $1,400 billion in foreign assets is a source of liquidity for global markets. Indeed, the Arab wealth funds played a useful role in stabilizing America's financial system during the sub-prime mortgage crisis. Second, oil prices are at record highs, in part due to China. The Arab world is also expected to account for a growing share of the world's oil production. Information about the Arab world is thus important for investors trading oil futures, betting on political uncertainty, or even forecasting more mundane things such as inflation, consumer demand, and profit margins, all of which influence the price of financial assets. The average trading desk thus has an insatiable appetite for news.

The trading floor I worked on in Hong Kong was no different. Large plasma television screens hung every 20 feet along its walls. Each was tuned permanently to a 24-hour news channel and offered a check on the health of the world at any point in time. Traders sat behind computer screens stacked three high and three wide. At least one terminal spewed out news from the major media agencies in a constant stream of terse headlines. "Fed's Bernanke warns on inflation," "U.K. December housing prices fall," "Bank of Japan's Fukui worries about a strong Yen." Nothing escapes your attention on a trading floor. It is like looking down on the entire world from a thousand feet. Walk off the floor, cut the information flow, and the world suddenly contracts. Addicted, most traders use their Blackberrys like umbilical cords to prevent complete separation.

In July 2006, I watched the initial stages of the Lebanon War from the floor. The large plasma television screens displayed the first Israeli strikes on Beirut International Airport. Little puffs of smoke hung above the tarmac marking where the missiles had struck. The war started small, but escalated fast. It wasn't long before images of fleeing Lebanese refugees were plastered on the large screens. Oil rose nearly $10 a barrel, while investors sought safe haven assets, such as the Swiss Franc. The U.S. Federal Reserve also added to the uncertainty, as it considered pausing after 17 consecutive interest rate hikes. From the trading floor we were observing the world from a thousand feet. Nothing could escape us. Could it?

*   *   *

A week later I arrived in Damascus. The airport was empty. Where were the refugees? A friend met me in the arrivals hall and we drove back toward the city. The war was still raging to the West, a few hours drive from Damascus, but it hadn't shaken the city from its lethargic pace. Indeed, the fierce summer heat had reduced the city to its usual crawl. This was the Damascus

I remembered, a city almost entirely cut off from the financial markets. The Internet is increasingly pervasive, but even so, it is possible to walk the streets, soaking in the atmosphere of the old city, and pretending the outside world has vanished at least temporarily.

But I was shocked to see Hizbollah flags hanging from shop windows, a striking splash of yellow against a backdrop of dusty streets and gray buildings. It was a bold statement of support that would have been impossible a year earlier. The Syrian regime doesn't tolerate challenges to its rule, especially from a religious movement based in a neighboring country. In the 1980s the regime fought a costly battle against Islamists, resulting in thousands dead and parts of the city of Hama flattened, and it continues to maintain tight control over the country's Islamist movements. Its control is unpopular but is also credited by many as contributing to the country's relative stability, even as its neighbors have fallen apart. So the flags were a shock. And it wasn't just the flags, it was also the posters with pictures of Sheikh Nasrallah, the spiritual leader of Hizbollah.

Yet the Western media made no mention of the flags. It didn't help that Syria still maintains strict controls on both domestic and foreign media. But I thought the flags a pertinent symbol of how the war had mobilized the Arab street and, at least temporarily, bridged the differences between the Shiite and Sunni factions. A number of Sunni governments, including Egypt and Saudi Arabia, were forced to backpedal when they realized that they had misjudged the mood of the general population. Saudi Arabia had even labeled Hizbollah's actions as "dangerous adventurism." The Sunnis I spoke with in Syria were also fiercely critical of Egypt and Saudi Arabia. It appeared that the Syrian regime had made a smart decision to ignore the Hizbollah flags and let the street vent its anger. It was a sign of the extent to which opposition toward America and Israel had the capacity to unite Arab public opinion.

I later listened to Friday prayers, invited by a friend. We met at the bus station near President's Bridge. It was a 30-minute trip to the mosque in one of the city's ubiquitous small minibuses. The bus was full of mainly young men looking uninterestedly out of the windows. Two young girls sat in the front wearing jeans and gaudy plastic jewelry. The windows were open and a breeze helped take the edge off the Damascus heat. After 20 minutes we arrived on the outskirts of the city. The area is known as "the countryside" (*al reef*). Perhaps a few decades earlier it did have orange groves, but an expanding city was now feeding at its edges and it had an unplanned feel to it, with double-storey residences and shops thrown up alongside what were once rural tracks. We jostled alongside other minibuses, eventually pulling up outside the mosque.

The mosque itself was nothing special. A dusty four-storey building built out of concrete breezeblocks with a minaret attached. The Imam was speaking on the first floor. The mosque was full, so we waited outside listening to his sermon. He was speaking in literary Arabic. That was a problem. My literary Arabic was ok for political discussions, but religious discussions were a stretch. I nudged Tayseer occasionally for help with a phrase. The Imam spoke for 30 minutes before prayers began. He spoke about the war in Lebanon before launching into a broader criticism of Israel and the United States. But this was just a small part of his sermon, as he shortly moved on to talk about the Islamic community itself. The Syrian regime keeps a close watch on the Imams and their sermons. But even so I had expected a more fiery delivery.

As the prayers concluded the congregation slowly poured from the building. Hundreds of men were suddenly crammed into the small space outside the front of the building beneath the fierce summer sun. But most were resigned to the heat and chatted amiably. This wasn't like the scenes often portrayed in the media. There was no call for action against America and Israel. It felt like another ordinary day. It's unfair to extrapolate this experience across the entire country. But what struck me was how different the calm atmosphere outside the mosque was compared to the panicked atmosphere on the trading desks back in Hong Kong and, most likely, in London and New York. In spite of the large plasma television screens, the news terminals, and the instant messaging, it wasn't clear if those desks were receiving the right information.

The trading desks aren't at fault. But the experience was instructive. The desks are hungry for information. Traders typically spend thousands of dollars a month to plug themselves into the best possible news feeds. They are responding to headlines from dozens of media agencies every day. But the discrepancy between what the traders were reading on their news terminals or watching on their plasma TV screens and the events in Damascus suggest that the information was still skewed. A trader who bets on bad information generally loses. A government that bets on bad information loses a lot more than just money. But there is good news. The rise of Arab news stations has created a new opportunity to view the Arab world and hear the voice of the Arab street. It is an opportunity worth taking.

CHAPTER 7

Arabic and the Language of Globalization

My hotel concierge put me in touch with Ma Guoming. I had earlier tried contacting a number of translation companies, but it was peak season in Yiwu city. Their Arabic translators were busy. I thought the hotel concierge might be able to help, as the hotel was full of foreign traders. He could, but said to expect a fee of 500 yuan for the day. I agreed. So he made a few calls and finally found a translator for me. Together we caught a taxi to meet Ma. It was cold and, as we pulled up the curbside, Ma was breathing steam, his hands stuffed deep into his jacket pockets. He opened the passenger door and climbed quickly in. I introduced myself, and we chatted a short while in Arabic. Then I asked a price. "Two hundred yuan ($30). For the day," he said, replying in Chinese. There was complete silence in the front seat. Finally the concierge turned to me. "Good price," he said as a sickly grin spread across his face.

The concierge had spoken with Ma earlier and had said to charge the foreigner 500 yuan. He intended to split the 500 yuan two ways. It was the only reason he had caught the taxi with me. But Ma didn't want to cheat me. He was a Muslim born in Xinjiang province, which covers most of the country's northwest and includes large stretches of the Silk Road. Ma had studied theology for ten years in Xinjiang with the aim of finding work as an Imam, or Islamic cleric. He started his studies at a local college before finishing at an Islamic school in the provincial capital Urumqi. He never did find work as an Imam – the competition was too fierce – but he did graduate speaking excellent Arabic. It wasn't the most useful skill in the late 1990s, but that all changed after 2004 as the number of Arab traders in Yiwu surged.

I have to admit I was initially skeptical about Ma. I shouldn't have worried. Ma was a trained theologian and his formal Arabic was superb. He also understood colloquial Egyptian and Syrian. He was about 40 years old. His padded winter jacket emphasized an already stocky frame. Thin, wire-framed glasses hung tenaciously to his broad, ruddy face. Ma was a Muslim and born nearly 3,000 kilometers to the west. But he looked no different from the rest of Yiwu's Chinese population. The same is true of the majority of the 10 million Hui Chinese scattered throughout the country. Ma's only odd habit was to stop and grasp my arm firmly in order to emphasize a point. It is a habit common with Arab men and was the only thing that visibly marked Ma out from the rest of the population.

I had hired Ma to find out what it is like for an Arab trader in Yiwu. So for the next few hours we spoke only Arabic with each other. He took me to the stores most popular with his clients. The first was a jewelry stall selling fake gold necklaces adorned with religious images of the Kaaba and the Quran. Prices were ludicrously cheap – a bag of 10 necklaces sold for less than 20 cents. I was planning to travel to Damascus later in the year and wanted to find out what they might sell for in the city, so I purchased several bags. I asked Ma in Arabic which of the necklaces were most popular among Syrians. "I don't know," the stall vendor replied in Chinese. "Arabs are all the same." Ma translated and winked at me. For the next few hours he and I haggled our way through endless rows of stalls full of Islamic ornaments, Arabic silverware, plastic Pyramids, headscarves, and water pipes.

English is the world's language. Many Arab and Chinese traders prefer to speak in English with each other rather than rely on a translator. But not all. Yiwu's translation business is booming as a result. Estimates put the number of Arabic translators working in the city at 1,000.[1] The Hui Chinese account for the majority of translators. Descendents of the early Silk Road traders, the Muslim minority have studied Arabic mainly in Islamic schools. Not just the small mosques, but also at the ten institutes officially registered to train Imams and Islamic scholars.[2] The Chinese Islamic Union estimates there were just two Arabic-language institutions operating in the country during the early 1980s, but the number has since expanded to over 100 institutions with an estimated 10,000 students.[3]

The city of Linxia is typical. A two-hour flight from Yiwu, the city lies at the start of the vast deserts and lofty mountains that stretch west across Central Asia. It also lies near the Silk Road and likely received Arab traders a thousand years ago. Today, the city's main street is cluttered with signs advertising Arabic-language classes. A small number of mosques have even hung advertisements outside their front doors.[4] It is here that many future translators learn Arabic before migrating to the coastal provinces and China's export factories. The schools are an example of how the Hui have responded to the economic reforms of the past 20 years and have found a niche for themselves in a market economy.

The Hui are also testimony to the grassroots change that underpins the strengthening relations between the Arab world and China. They are not part of a grand strategy formulated by the Chinese government. Instead, thousands of mainly young and often poor Chinese Muslims have recognized an opportunity to create a better life for themselves. Freed by the economic reforms of the past two decades, the Hui have turned their religion into a source of employment. It is too easy to attribute the rise of trade flows between the Arab world and China to the fact China sells cheap consumer goods. However, it is the Hui, driven by a mixture of religion and poverty, who also play an important role in attracting Arab traders to Yiwu and other Chinese cities. Like the Arab traders, the Hui are also fine threads in the new Silk Road tapestry.

Yet, the Hui Chinese are only part of the story. The majority Han Chinese are also studying Arabic. There is no official figure on the number of students, but the employment search engines require job seekers to register their ethnic group. I found over a thousand Arabic translators looking for work on one popular site. Nearly a third registered as Han Chinese. Many had studied in Beijing. The Foreign Language University in Beijing is especially popular. It is an incubator for future Chinese diplomats. Its Arabic-language department is housed in a small building designed to look like a mosque. Its green dome contrasts starkly with the buildings surrounding it. I once visited in winter when the dome was capped by snow, an odd sight compared to the dust and heat of the Arab world. The institute is producing hundreds of Arab translators, just like the private institutes in Linxia and the training colleges in Wuzhong.

However, the Han Chinese, especially those studying at the elite language institutions in Beijing, are more likely to work in government, such as for the Foreign Ministry and the Chinese Academy of Social Sciences. In January 2006, when the King of Saudi Arabia visited Beijing, his delegation was amazed at the fluency of their hosts. "The teachers are all Chinese there, yet their Arabic is fluent. They don't even talk slang," recalled Sultan Attar, a Saudi Arabian banker.[5] I have heard of similar stories from other Arab officials and businesspeople who talk of their surprise, and pleasure, at meeting Arabic-speaking Chinese officials in Beijing. The meetings are part of the same public relations battle the Chinese government is pursuing in the Arab world through Al Jazeera.

Indeed, Al Jazeera's three-hour long documentary "Eye on China" was unusual for the number of Arabic-speaking officials it interviewed. In a telling comparison, the Arab news station later produced similar documentaries on Iran and Turkey. "We had to translate. Neither the Iranian nor the Turkish government produced the same number of officials prepared to speak Arabic," said Al Jazeera's Beijing bureau chief. Yet Iran and Turkey are direct neighbors of the Arab world. Zhai Jun's appearance on Al Jazeera's "No Limits" was another example. Zhai, by speaking in Arabic, demonstrated his empathy for the Arab people. He likely elicited the same positive response from his Arab viewers as did his colleagues from their Arab guests in Beijing.

The Chinese government has long recognized the importance of language to its public relations efforts. Arabic language has been taught in Chinese universities since 1943.[6] The Chinese Communist Party sent language students to study in Arab capitals such as Damascus in the early 1960s.[7] Mohamed Maamouri, an Arabic-language professor now at the University of Pennsylvania, visited Beijing in the early 1980s and likewise recalls meeting with a number of Arabic-speaking academics and officials even then.[8] The Chinese government has long put a priority on language studies. The number of Arabic-speaking officials isn't a result of the events after September 2001. Its focus is now paying off as the government attempts to build relations with Arab governments.

It is tempting to view relations between the Arab world and China as one dimensional. The Arab world is hungry for China's consumer goods while China is thirsty for the Arab world's oil. Yet, relations between the two are built on broader foundations. Chapter 6 discussed the importance of media. This chapter focuses on the importance of language. I imagine few are familiar with China's rising ranks of Arab speakers. It is a pity. Sure, many Arabs and Chinese will continue to speak English with each other. But the Arabic-speaking translators in Yiwu are part of a grassroots change that is binding the Arab world to China. The Arabic-speaking officials in Beijing are meanwhile part of a deliberate government strategy to build bridges with the Arab world. Language is the hidden glue to relations.

How different is it in the West, especially in the English-speaking countries. The events of 2001 and the subsequent invasion of Iraq revealed a shortage of Arabic-speaking officials. Neither was it clear if Western governments put the same premium on using Arabic-speaking officials as did the Chinese government.

Abderrahim Foukara is Al Jazeera's Washington bureau chief. A Moroccan, Foukara completed his PhD in the United Kingdom and has a delightful English accent. We spoke one night by phone. I had called to ask about the number of Arabic-speaking American officials who are interviewed regularly on Al Jazeera. "None," he replied. It was incredulous. America is faced with a major strategic challenge in the Arab world. Its occupation of Iraq alone is likely to last years. Yet it didn't have a single official regularly speaking in Arabic on Al Jazeera. I had only shortly finished watching "Eye on China." The contrast between its parade of Chinese Arabic-speaking officials and the situation in Washington was stark.

"There was one," Foukara recalls. "His name was Alberto Fernandez." I asked him whether Fernandez had made a difference. "He did," Foukara recalled. "It had a very powerful impact. Not only did he speak Arabic, but he was also fluent in the nuances of the culture and this served him extremely well when reaching out to his audience." Fernandez was Director of Public Diplomacy for the State Department's Bureau of Near

Eastern Affairs. A skilled Arabic speaker, he had spent years living in Egypt, Iraq, Jordan, Kuwait, Syria, and the UAE and had conducted dozens of interviews in Arabic. Just like Zhai from the Chinese Foreign Ministry, Fernandez was prepared to appear on Al Jazeera, make a few jokes, even get angry.

But in 2006, Fernandez stirred up a firestorm. He was quoted on Al Jazeera as saying:

> History will decide how the US record in Iraq will be. God willing, we tried to do the best. But, I think that there is ample room for severe criticism. This is because undoubtedly, there was US arrogance and stupidity in Iraq.

The State Department claimed Fernandez was misquoted, although the BBC Monitoring service later confirmed he did in fact use the words arrogance and stupidity.[9] It was an unfortunate comment. Critics attacked Fernandez for sympathizing with Al Qaeda. His supporters claimed he was simply reaching out to his audience. Fernandez initially received the support of senior officials in the State Department, according to colleagues, and remained in his position for a number of months. But he eventually stood down and was appointed Charge d'Affaires to Sudan in June 2007. Fernandez was sidelined even as Arab opinion turned increasingly against America. It is hard to imagine that Zhai Jun is exposed to the same type of scrutiny in Beijing when he speaks on the Arab news stations. Indeed, the Beijing rumor mill was speculating on Zhai's promotion in 2008.

The Fernandez affair sent a damaging signal to other Arabic-speaking American officials: "Stay on message. Make a mistake and it's a potential career killer." There are few officials prepared to step up and replace Fernandez. It is too easy to use a poorly chosen expression when faced by a hostile interviewer. The State Department is now producing daily briefing sheets for all its diplomats in the Arab world.[10] These sheets help diplomats to stay on the message. The problem is that, in this increasingly flat world, the message is ultimately intended, not for an Arab audience in Riyadh, but for an American audience in Atlanta, and so the message is likely to reinforce Arab bias toward America.

Moreover, the original problem remains. There simply aren't that many Western officials who can speak Arabic fluently. The same combination of grassroots change and government strategy evident in China is not immediately apparent in America and Europe. The problem is especially acute for the American government. In August 2006, Jess Ford from the U.S. Government Accountability Office reported to the Senate Committee on Foreign Relations on this shortfall. His office noted that 37 percent of language-designated positions in the Middle East were filled by staff without the necessary language skills.[11] He wasn't the first to worry. The Iraq Study Group, a ten-person panel led by former Secretary of State James Baker and former U.S. Congressman Lee Hamilton and charged with assessing the situation in Iraq, had this to say:

> All our efforts in Iraq, military and civilian, are handicapped by Americans' lack of language and cultural understanding. Our embassy of 1,000 has 33 Arabic speakers, just 6 of whom are at the level of fluency. In a conflict that demands effective and efficient communication with Iraqis, we are often at a disadvantage. There are still too few Arabic language-proficient military and civilian officers in Iraq to the detriment of the US mission.[12]

It's not all bad news. The number of Westerners studying Arabic is on the rise. The American Language Association shows an increase in the number of students between 2002 and 2006, from 10,584 to 23,974.[13] The U.S government has made a considerable effort to advance Arabic-language studies through its National Security Language Initiative, which has allocated money to establishing foreign language programs in schools and to hiring more foreign language teachers.[14] It has also allocated money to support foreign language students wanting to study abroad. It's too early to judge the success of the initiative, but the rise in the number of students studying Arabic is certainly encouraging.

I heard similarly encouraging news in Egypt. I spoke with Dr. Zeinab Taha, Director of the Arabic Language Institute at the American University of Cairo. The university's campus was built in the early 1900s. It now looks out of place against the chaotic traffic in Midan Tahrir Square. But inside, its white walls and brown wood paneling is an oasis of calm. The institute is one of the most popular places to study Arabic, and the number of applications has tripled in the past five years. "There are too many applications. We can no longer accept everyone," Dr. Taha says. She conservatively estimates the total number of foreign students studying Arabic in the American University in Cairo at around 700, or twice the number from five years ago. There are probably another 500 students in the city's other language institutions. It is an impressive increase from just a few years ago.

"It used to be mainly postgraduates who were trying to polish up their language skills before starting a career. But the number of undergraduates applying to study Arabic has also jumped," Dr. Taha says. The biggest increases have been recorded in the Study Abroad program, which generally lasts a year. I hadn't expected this. It is common for American undergraduates to spend 12 months in Beijing studying Chinese in order to strengthen their resumes. If Dr. Taha is correct, American undergraduates are traveling to Cairo for the same reason. It is an encouraging change. It suggests American employers are searching for Arabic-speaking graduates in the same way they are looking for Chinese-speaking graduates. Market forces are working. The supply of Arab specialists is responding to the increase in demand.

I heard similar stories from a friend of mine, Mohammed Iskandar, who runs a language college in Damascus. He had also observed a jump in the number of students, and he noticed a change in what students wanted. "The American students now want to learn a specific colloquial dialect. I get requests to learn colloquial Syrian or colloquial Palestinian. This never happened before. The Europeans still want to learn the written language, with maybe a few lessons in the colloquial language." The change makes sense. Funding for Arab specialists has increased since September 11 and the Iraq War. It is likely many of the students intend to find jobs in the State Department or security services. Again, the supply of Arab specialists is responding to an increase in demand.

Yet I wonder if this is enough. The State Department classifies Arabic as a "super-hard" language. A speaker is rated on their ability to speak according to five levels, with "1" the lowest and

"5" the highest and usually assigned only to native speakers. The important difference is between levels "3" and "4." A level "3" can talk one-on-one, but will struggle, for instance, to participate in a heated debate with a group of people at a restaurant. Ideally, the State Department wants lots of level "4" Arabic speakers who can stand in front of an Al Jazeera camera and explain American policy to Arab households. In 2004, the last year for which complete figures are available, the State Department had 200 level "3"s, but just 27 level "4"s.[15] In 2007, the Baghdad Embassy had just ten officials rated at level "3" or above suggesting improvement was slow.[16]

So, although the rising number of Arabic-language students is encouraging, it isn't enough unless it translates into a larger crop of level "4" Arabic speakers.

There are many challenges. First, American officials are reluctant to live in the Arab world for extended periods. In May 2006, the Government Accountability Office estimated that the average tour for a public diplomacy official was 2.7 years. However, in a Muslim country it was just 2.1 years. Moreover, it was less than one year in a country considered a security risk.[17] No surprise, but fifteen of the twenty countries considered a security risk are Muslim countries. Iraq, for instance, is a security risk, which means family members are not allowed to travel with officials to the post. But who wants to live away from their family for more than a year? The problem is that it takes more than a one-year tour to turn a level "3" speaker into a level "4" speaker. Indeed, the Government Accountability Office advises that "shorter tours contribute to insufficient language skills and limit officers' ability to cultivate personal relationships."

Second, who really wants to be a level "4" Arabic speaker? To judge by events of the past decade, chances are high you will spend an extended part of your career in a war zone, such as Iraq. This might appeal to some, but not all. In November 2007, the Secretary of State Condoleezza Rice threatened to force officials to serve a tour in the Arab world in response to a shortage of volunteers. No doubt, Arabic speakers were at the top of her list. How many potential level "4"s did this put off? There is also the challenge of operating in a hostile environment. A Pew Survey released in June 2007 indicated that just 20 percent of people in Egypt, Jordan, Morocco, and Palestine have positive feelings toward America.[18] For an official who has to spend years living and studying in the region, it cannot be fun defending America's often controversial policies.

*　*　*

Of course, Arabic isn't the only language classified as "super-hard." The U.S. State Department also considers Chinese as "super-hard," in addition to Korean and Japanese. Surely the classification implies there is a similar shortage of Chinese speakers? Not so. I first studied Arabic in Jordan in the early 1990s, later continuing my studies in Syria and Lebanon. I learnt Chinese nearly a decade later. I have since met dozens of foreigners who speak fluent Chinese, but only a handful who speak fluent Arabic. Why is this? First, it is easier for many foreigners, especially female, to live in China and study the language. Second, China's recent rapid growth has created far more employment opportunities. However, after probing deeper I found a more intriguing and powerful explanation. It was a chance meeting with four young Chinese students in the Syrian capital of Damascus that first alerted me to the explanation.

The four were students at the Abu Noor Institute, which is famous for catering to foreign religious students from Asia and Africa. While walking through the wealthy Damascus suburb of Hamra I had stumbled across the students unpacking small toys from boxes for display along the sidewalk. It was a way to earn money during the summer vacation and their relatives sent a new shipment over each month. I introduced myself and, taken aback to hear a foreigner speaking Chinese in Syria, they invited me for a meal at their house. They lived in the old suburb of Salihiyya, a beautiful part of the city – a maze of small streets hugging the lower slopes of Mount Qassioun. Arab refugees had first populated Salihiyya in the eleventh century after fleeing Crusader massacres in Jerusalem. Rental prices are cheap as the streets are dangerously steep.

I arrived the following day and was met at the front door by one of the students, Li. It was hot and he was wearing nothing but a pair of shorts and a plastic flower-print apron. It was an odd sight, but Li was an excellent cook. While I waited for his dishes of dan dan noodles and fish-flavored pork, I chatted with his three housemates. We spent most of our time trying to get my Hong Kong mobile phone to play Chinese pop songs. Three of the students, Li, Yu, and Rong, were from the northern province of Inner Mongolia. The fourth, Su, was from the central province of Henan. They had yet to return home. "Syrian visas are difficult to get," Li explained. "I had to apply in Bangkok. A friend of mine owns a restaurant next to the Syrian embassy. He knew the staff there and helped with the application." But the four weren't in a rush to go home. "Everyone in China worships money (*bai qian zhu yi*)," they complained.

We initially used a mixture of both Arabic and Chinese. But their Arabic was still poor, so we finally switched to Chinese. I asked about their studies. "We started learning formal Arabic. Everyone told us you could speak the formal language on the street. But you can't. Now we've started to learn the colloquial language. But it's even more difficult. There are too many ways to say the same thing," Li said, smacking his palm on the table in disgust. He had a valid point. The challenge for students is that formal Arabic often differs radically from the many varieties of colloquial Arabic. A student must learn both formal and informal Arabic to be fully functional in Arab society. This is a major commitment. Not surprisingly, most opt to study a single variety, typically formal Arabic.

What is formal Arabic? It is the language used for public speaking. Al Jazeera's anchors speak formal Arabic, for example, even if they prefer to speak colloquial Arabic at home. Why the difference? Arabic is the vehicle of Islam. It is the language used by the Quran. It is the language used to tell the stories and sayings of the prophet. All Muslims, irrespective of whether they are Egyptian, Iranian, or American, are assumed to have a functional literacy in the language, if only to be able to read the Quran. This makes the Quran, in effect, the ultimate Arabic grammar book. It sets the rules for the language. Muslim scholars have not surprisingly resisted change in the language as a result. The upshot is that formal Arabic, or *fusha*, is now radically different to the colloquial Arabic spoken in the home and on the streets.

A story related by an English professor, Neil Parkinson, neatly captures the problem.[19] Parkinson writes of an Egyptian friend who was passionate about *fusha*. His friend decided his family would communicate with each other exclusively in *fusha* in order to learn to speak the language fluently. One day Parkinson boarded a busy bus with his friend and his friend's young daughter. But the father and daughter became separated in the ensuing crush of passengers. They yelled out to each other in *fusha* to try and reestablish contact only for the entire bus to break out into laughter. It was strange for the passengers to hear the formal language used in such an informal setting. This is the dilemma of formal Arabic. It might be the language used by Al Jazeera's anchors or a Muslim scholar, but it is not the language used in everyday conversation.

The result is that *fusha* exists in a twilight world. Arabs view it as the real Arabic language, yet they typically don't use it. Instead, Arabs use a variety of colloquial dialects, such as Iraqi, Moroccan, or Syrian Arabic. "Many Arabs do not even consider the colloquial dialects a language," says Dr Taha. It is like English speakers claiming that the language of Shakespeare, or sixteenth-century Britain, is the real English language. Sure, they might speak British, American, or Australian English at home and on the streets, but it is the language of Shakespeare that is used in formal situations. And so, while colloquial Arabic is used by 300 million Arabs every day, the majority does not recognize it as the true Arabic language.

Yet, *fusha* is an important foundation of the new Silk Road. Its resistance to change has strengthened the linkages between the global Islamic communities. *Fusha* is a part of the shared experience of being Muslim regardless of nationality. It permits Fadi, the Syrian stall vendor in Damascus, to share a classical heritage with Ma, the Chinese translator in Yiwu. This is a powerful glue in an increasingly globalized world. Mainly Islamic communities in Asia, the Middle East, and East Africa are restoring trade links established a thousand years ago. Arab investors are likewise investing along an "Islamic Corridor." A country that has plenty of *fusha* speakers also likely has all the ingredients attractive to an Islamic investor, such as mosques and Halal food. *Fusha* is an old world tool that is also thriving in the new world.

The Hui Chinese can testify to the link. The Hui have steadfastly resisted total assimilation with the majority Han, even when faced with the Ming Dynasty's policy of "sinification." Chinese historians attribute their resilience to the tendency for the Hui to live within walking distance of a mosque where they can pray and study Arabic. It is called "a large dispersion, but a small focus" (*da fen san xiao ji zhong*).[20] By dispersing, but remaining focused, the Hui have managed to retain their identity throughout the centuries in spite of the pressures. The same is true today as Arabic-language studies continue to draw the Hui together in the small Islamic schools across the country and have left the community prepared for the arrival of Arab traders.

The Chinese government has recognized the power of *fusha*. It has tolerated, even promoted, the study of Arabic by the Hui and the Han Chinese. It has actively hired Arabic-speaking graduates to work in the country's ministries and research institutions. The challenge for America and Europe is to likewise recognize the importance of *fusha* as a glue for the Arab world, and to encourage more officials to speak to the Arab media without fear of public opinion at home. The early signs are encouraging as Western students, especially American students, respond to the rising demand for Arabic speakers. But this isn't enough unless a rising group of skilled linguists are spending extended periods in the Arab world demonstrating empathy for Arab culture and building relations with the average Arab household.

* * *

Mohamed Maamouri established the first Chinese Language Degree program in Africa while working at the University of Tunis in the early 1980s. He was later invited by Chinese officials to visit Beijing. It was in the early years of economic reform, not long after the end of the Cultural Revolution and the death of Chairman Mao. Maamouri also spent several months traveling around the country. His interest in Chinese had begun as a student in London. "I was sitting in a Chinese restaurant and noticed two Chinese waiters were writing notes to communicate with each other. I asked why and it turned out they both spoke a different dialect." Not so three decades later. Today, the waiters are likely to use *putonghua* to communicate. It is the differences in language that help distinguish between a rising Arab world and a rising China.

Putonghua, unlike *fusha*, is widely spoken at home, in the office, and on the street. Yet in the early 1900s China faced the same challenges as the Arab world. What changed? The Chinese government aggressively pursued language reform over decades. Today, a majority of Chinese can communicate in *putonghua,* as well as their own regional dialects. The four Chinese students I met in Damascus were no exception. They each spoke a regional dialect, but they spoke *putonghua* together to communicate and it didn't feel unnatural. This is good news for a foreign language student. It is enough to speak *putonghua*; forget about the colloquial dialects. So why was language reform possible in China, but not in the Arab world? The role of religion is an easy answer. But it was the Chinese Communist Party that changed the Chinese language forever.

In 1912, the last Qing emperor fell. The Chinese nationalists, who deposed him, also tried to scrub away the worst excesses of the discriminatory imperial system. They targeted the formal language in the belief it discriminated between the masses and the educated elite. It did. Only the educated elite had the money and time to learn the language. So the nationalists replaced it with a version more commonly spoken on the streets in North China. It was a monumental act. In a brush stroke they enfranchised a huge share of the population. There was still a difference between the formal and colloquial languages, at least outside of North China. But the new version of the formal language, later named *putonghua*, was far easier to learn. The nationalists didn't know it at the time, but they had unwittingly assisted the rise of the Chinese Communist Party, which, drawing its support from the newly enfranchised masses, took control of the country in 1949.

The party accelerated the pace of language reform in order to consolidate its grip. It targeted the rural areas. The rural population was an important prop to the Chinese Communist Party, yet was also more likely to speak a dialect and suffer from illiteracy. Chairman Mao Zedong recognized the problem. After all, he was born and started his political career in Hunan province. Today the province is still relatively poor. In 1949, the Chairman famously

stated that "Language must be close to the masses. We must realize that the masses are the inexhaustible and abundant resource
of the revolutionary culture." And so, party workers championed
putonghua in the same way the imperial state had championed its
more complex precursor. Indeed, just ten days after the creation
of the People's Republic China the party established a national
organization for language reform in Beijing.[21]

The organization faced a daunting challenge. First was the
complexity of the written language. Party workers argued that
illiterate Chinese adults usually took five years to learn 2,000
basic characters. Not so in Vietnam. Indeed, Vietnamese adults
took just 100 hours to learn to read popular literature after their
written language, once modeled on Chinese, was now changed
to an alphabet. What was the point of producing propaganda
material if the illiterate masses couldn't read it? So the Ministry
of Education introduced a simplified list of 1,500 of the most
commonly used characters in the early 1950s. A delegate to the
conference from the Communist Army claimed that cadets in
military school could master 500 simplified characters in two-
thirds of the time used to learn the same traditional characters.[22]
A powerful change indeed.

It wasn't just the written language. The spoken language was
also causing problems for party workers who tried to mobilize
support for government campaigns. The party workers, who visited homes and factories, complained of the difficulty in communicating in the local dialect. The Chinese Nationalist Party
had already designated the dialect spoken in North China as the
national standard, but lacked the funds to effectively promote its
use. The Chinese Communist Party did not, and promoted its
use in school and at official functions. It worked. In 2004, a survey of 140,000 people indicated that 53 percent of the population could speak *putonghua*. Its use is also growing, especially
among the better-educated, younger population – among people
aged between 60 and 69, only 31 percent can speak the language,
whereas among people aged between 15 and 29, the figure is considerably higher, at 70 percent.[23]

It is too easy to attribute China's rapid growth to cheap labor
and a cheap currency. What about language reform? Ironically
the Chinese Communist Party laid an important foundation for

today's market economy. Today, Ma Guoming can travel thousands of miles from his village in Xinjiang to work in the city of Yiwu as an Arabic translator using *putonghua* to communicate with the local Chinese residents. Language reform is an important component of the China model. It is why over 400 million workers,[24] or nearly three times the size of the American workforce, can travel anywhere across the country in search of employment. It is a change that even the European Union, where labor is still relatively immobile, would envy. It is the remarkable flexibility of China's labor market that helps underpin the country's double-digit growth rates.

It is this flexibility that helps to explain China's success in the Arab world. The ability to draw on the brightest officials from across a country larger than the European Union and put them to work in Beijing or any of the Arab capitals is an important competitive advantage. Likewise, the ability to draw on the business skills of Yiwu's residents and combine them with the language skills of the Hui community's translators is a similarly important competitive advantage. As we witness the rise of two, once historic powers, language clarifies an important difference between them. China, or more specifically the Chinese Communist Party, has chosen internal unity and has used language to bind a large country together. The Arab world, by contrast, has opted for external unity and has used the language to bind together a large Islamic community.

The Chinese government is also trying to export its success. It is trying to encourage more Arabs to speak Chinese. Take Rada, who works in the Chinese Economic Affairs Bureau in Cairo. She had studied Chinese for a year in Beijing; her studies sponsored by the Chinese and Egyptian governments. Nonetheless, it is still early days. "They aren't many like me. Not yet, at least," Rada says. Most Arabs still prefer to speak English or hire a translator while in China. The Arab world has no equivalent for institutions such as the Beijing Foreign Studies University, which has produced 60,000 graduates since it was opened in the 1940s.[25] It is symbolic of the importance the Chinese government attributes to foreign languages.

I have looked for Chinese language schools in the Middle East, but found only a few. Fang Zheng is typical. He was a teacher at

the only Chinese language institute in Damascus. The institute
is sponsored by the embassy, but still had less than a few dozen
students in early 2007. Fang was a native of the central northern
Shaanxi province. He was, not surprisingly, Hui Chinese. A student at the Abu Noor Institute, the embassy had decided to draft
Fang and put him to work as a Chinese language teacher. I asked
how the school was progressing. "It's still slow," said Fang. "Most
Syrians still prefer to learn English. But we're gradually attracting more students, especially from the wealthier families, also
especially from the families already trading with China."

More recently, the Chinese government has also sponsored
Chinese language departments in Cairo and Lebanon called
"Confucius Institutes."[26] It is a good start. It might be that Arab
traders will one day no longer have need of Yiwu's translators.
But for the time being, the Arab world will face similar challenges
to the West in developing its pool of foreign language speakers.
Luckily, the Arabic-speaking Hui translators and Han officials
have offered a helping hand, and it is more likely the Arab world
will continue to rely on the linkages that are forged between
mainly Islamic communities partly through their use of *fusha,*
in contrast to the more strategic approach taken by the Chinese
government.

*   *   *

The success of English owed initially to the reach of the British
Empire. Its more recent gains owe to America's cultural and economic dominance. But times are changing. The rise of the East
has issued a challenge to the English-speaking world. Sure, students across the Arab world and China are learning English.
But speaking English is not enough, as recent events have demonstrated. Military intelligence analysts are studying Arabic.
Investment bankers are studying Chinese. Encouragingly, the number of Western students studying Arabic and Chinese is rising.[27]
However, the importance the Arab world and China place on their
own languages also helps to explain how these two historic powers
are likely to engage, not just with each other but also with the rest
of the world.

How should the West respond? Language study is a good start. The large number of Western students in Beijing testifies to the importance of the Chinese language. The rising number of Westerns students in Cairo and other Arab capitals likewise testifies to the growing importance of Arabic. But there are challenges. The first is turning more level "3" speakers into level "4" speakers, to use the U.S. State Department's terminology. This requires years of study living in a foreign country. But is there any incentive? Perhaps not. Before the sub-prime mortgage crisis hit, Western economies had experienced their strongest period of almost uninterrupted growth since the 1970s.[28] I wonder how many students were deterred from studying abroad by the rich pickings at home.

As a result, China enjoys a head start. Its developing country status means language studies open doors to a new life for the average Chinese citizen. Take the Hui Chinese who are studying Arabic in part because it offers a way to escape the grinding poverty of the western provinces. The experience of the students at the Beijing Language University is likewise instructive. Competition for government posts is fierce. Many students hope that their studies will help them win an opportunity to work abroad. This mixture of competition and opportunity creates greater incentives to study Arabic. The power of market forces is evident. The same market forces are a disincentive in America and Europe where opportunities in the domestic economy are greater than those abroad.

CHAPTER 8

Implications for the West: A New Center of Gravity

The events related in this book are the early tremors of a historic global rebalancing. However, it is not governments and multinational corporations but rather thousands of individual Arab and Chinese traders that represent the first tremors of change. It is a change occurring at the grassroots level. The distinction is important. Who notices the activities of an Arab trader in Yiwu or a Chinese trader in Damascus? It isn't obvious how their activities have a meaningful impact on life in America and Europe. But these traders are symbolic of more powerful tides that are reshaping the global economy. The challenge is in trying to identify the forces at work as the center of gravity starts to shift away from the West toward the East.

There are an estimated 200,000 Arab traders who visit Yiwu every year.[1] There are tens of thousands more in other Chinese cities such as Beijing and Guangzhou. They are the reason Arab cities, from Cairo to Dubai, are flooded with Chinese goods. The Arab traders aren't alone. There are also tens of thousands of Chinese traders in the Arab world. The number of Chinese traveling abroad rose from 10.5 million to 47.7 million between 2000 and 2009.[2] The Chinese government recognizes that finding employment for its large population is crucial to the country's health. This means finding jobs, if not at home, then abroad. It is the stories of these individuals that best explain the changes taking place.

The tides of change were already building before 2001. Consider Adam, a Chinese classmate of mine at the University of Jordan in the early 1990s. Adam's father was an ambitious man with plans to trade with the Arab states and had sent his son to Jordan to learn Arabic. Adam was from Zhejiang province, his hometown was likely not far from Yiwu. But I didn't realize the importance of Adam's background at the time. After all, China was still a minor player. Its GDP was just $400 billion in 1991, ranking it between Brazil and Australia. Today, its GDP is $5,000 billion and trade flows with the Arab world have surged.

However, the tides of change have gathered tremendous force since 2001. It was the events of September 11, China's entry into the World Trade Organization in December 2001, and the surge in oil prices in 2004 that accelerated the pace of change. The West's financial and economic crisis is the latest, but not the last, event in this great global rebalancing. Yet the Western media is largely silent about the growth of trade flows between the Arab world and China. This isn't surprising. The events are taking place on the other side of the world and largely in a foreign language. America and Europe are also rightly distracted by wars in Afghanistan and Iraq, risks of terrorism at home, and a flood of cheap Chinese imports that has undermined the average households' job security.

The risk is not an economic challenge, but a social challenge. China overtook the United Kingdom in 2002 and Germany in 2006 as a larger exporter to the Arab world.[3] It then overtook America in 2008. But does this matter? After all, the large share of its trade is in small consumer goods, such as the ornaments, hammers, and clocks which typically sell for less than a few dollars in Yiwu's exhibition halls. This doesn't have a large statistical impact on economic growth, at least not in the West. Moreover, even if American and British exporters lose market share in the Arab world to China, the economic losses will be small relative to those already suffered from the flood of cheap Chinese exports which have produced large factory closures and job losses in America and Europe.

However, the flow of goods between the Arab world and China is accompanied by a similar flow of people. Yiwu's streets are bustling with Egyptian, Syrian, and Yemeni traders. There are Chinese women arriving at Dubai's airport to fly onward to meet clients in Saudi Arabia. Traders in the old city of Damascus set up small offices in Shanghai to trade cotton. Not so in the West. Large Western companies, like Carrefour and Wal-Mart, are mainly responsible for buying Chinese goods and importing them for sale in the Western economies. Indeed, there is altogether less reason for Western traders to live abroad today. After all, the Western economies have grown robustly in the past two decades, and housing, medical, and schooling standards are typically higher at home.

It wasn't always this way. In his book *Colossus*, Niall Ferguson writes of the number of Britons who lived abroad in the early 1900s. There were around 168,000 living in India in 1931,[4] at a time when the British population was just 46 million, versus 60 million today. What explains these large numbers? First, Britain still possessed one of the world's largest empires. But second and more importantly, many Britons saw greater opportunities abroad than at home. The Irish and Scots made up a disproportionate share of these colonies. Many of Hong Kong's largest companies, such as Jardine Matheson, were established by Scottish entrepreneurs who left their home country and never returned. They left because employment opportunities were limited in Britain's damp and slow-growing northern regions.

Where are the Irish and Scots today? Back home. Scotland's unemployment rate was only 5 percent in 2008. And the few who are unemployed are protected by welfare payments, so incentives to travel abroad for work are less. Moreover, Scottish companies are increasingly global and there is less reason to travel abroad to trade with foreign countries. For instance, the Royal Bank of Scotland is one of the world's largest banks with offices throughout China and the Middle East. It also employs 3,250 people in its Edinburgh headquarters.[5] Many are engaged in the bank's operations in China and the Middle East via email, phone, and videoconference, traveling only periodically to visit local foreign offices.

Today, the Irish and Scots have been replaced by the Arabs and Chinese. The fall in trade barriers has created opportunities for them to make money. Most of the Arab world entered the World Trade Organization after 1990, or is currently negotiating to enter. China entered in 2001.[6] Average incomes are also relatively low, so the incentives to trade are greater. There are also more specific challenges. For instance, Syrian traders are exploiting the still high margins that make it profitable to fly several times a year to Yiwu to purchase goods for sale in Damascus, whereas Chinese traders, by contrast, are fleeing the intense competition at home to try and capture the same high margins abroad. The result is an echo of events over a century earlier.

The Irish and the Scots are no doubt happy to have left their poverty behind. Yet this comes at a cost. It seems like there are fewer Westerners who are prepared to live decades, or even a lifetime abroad, relative to the size of today's population. It is popular to talk of a "Flat World" today. Yet, while the world is flat, it is also shallow. Low-cost airfares and high-speed communications permit more Westerners to travel abroad for shorter periods. And although the West is more familiar with the East, its depth of understanding is possibly more superficial than a century earlier. There is an expression "You don't know a man until you've worked beside him." I wonder if the West has lost its ability to learn about the Arab world and China if only because there are fewer Westerners prepared to spend the years living abroad to acquire "local knowledge."

The experience of the Irish and Scots is instructive. They often lived abroad for years, if not a lifetime. Many spoke the local language. Extended periods abroad are the best way to obtain fluency in a language, especially in one of the "super-hard" languages. A reluctance to commit to extended periods in the Arab world may explain why the U.S. State Department has struggled to find enough Arabic speakers. The British Foreign Office has had fewer problems, partly because many of its best Arabic speakers are the legacy of the British Empire. I recall attending a conference in Cairo in the late 1990s and listening to a British speaker who introduced himself to the audience in Arabic. It drew a muttering of admiration from the audience. The speaker? A former British colonel who had served years in Oman.

If the West is to engage with the rise of the Arab world it must acquire local knowledge. It must learn from the example of the Irish and Scots. The intelligence community's collective failure in Iraq underscores the importance of local knowledge. This relates to both language skills and the cultural understanding acquired by studying in a foreign country. As an American intelligence analyst told the Iraq Study Group, "We rely too much on others to bring information to us, and too often don't understand what is reported because we do not understand the context of what we are told." The group later advised that "The Defense Department and the intelligence community have not invested sufficient people and resources to understand the political and military threat to American men and women in the armed forces."

It is encouraging to see a rise in the number of American students studying Arabic in Cairo and Damascus. But if their studies are for no longer than six months they will struggle to develop the language skills to transition from what the State Department classifies as level "3" speakers to level "4" speakers. Indeed, the State Department's problem attracting diplomats to bid for hardship posts is revealing. In 2005, posts in Europe received an average 15 bids per position. By contrast, posts in Africa, the Middle East, and South Asia received just four to five bids per position, while sixty seven positions in Africa and the Middle East received no bids at all.[7] In short, there are no modern equivalents to the Irish and Scots who once staffed the British Colonial Service. This is a problem.

Yet what are the advantages for Arabic speakers? In 2008, a U.S. State Department Officer with a Master's and five years experience earned around $54,000.[8] It was possible to increase the amount modestly depending on the posting and skills. Yet to acquire fluent Arabic skills means living in the Arab world for at least three years, more likely longer. And it doesn't end there. A large number of posts in the Arab world are "unattended," implying a person cannot travel with a family. Moreover, an officer having spent years in the region must then defend the policies of a typically unpopular Washington administration. The alternative? A $200,000 job at an American investment bank hungry to make money in a region flush with cash and growing at 6.4 percent a year. Today, market forces rule.

It isn't hard to find critics of America's public relations efforts in the Arab world. Former Secretary of Defense, Donald Rumsfeld, wrote that after the merger of the United States Information Agency (USIA) into the State Department, "the country lost what had been a valuable institution capable of communicating America's message to international audiences powerfully and repeatedly."[9] But it was his successor who had the strongest criticisms to make. Robert Gates said, "Most people are familiar with cutbacks in the military and intelligence," but, "what is not as well-known, and arguably even more shortsighted, was the gutting of America's ability to engage, assist, and communicate with other parts of the world – the 'soft power,' which had been so important throughout the Cold War." He was damning of the decision to freeze hiring of new Foreign Service officers and disband the USIA.[10]

If America and Europe are looking for a benchmark, why not look to China's activities in the Arab world? Chinese Radio International regularly produces Arabic-language stories for publication in the Arab press. Likewise, Xinhua produces Arabic and English language articles for publication in Arab newspapers, such as Egypt's *October* weekly. A good start would be to rebuild the USIA. There are signs of change. Karen Hughes, Undersecretary of State for Diplomacy and Public Affairs, implemented 75 percent of what the Advisory Group on Public Diplomacy in the Arab and Muslim World recommended, according to Edward Djerejian, who chaired the group.[11] A rapid response unit was set up to counter negative reporting toward America. An informal ban on American officials appearing on Al Jazeera was lifted. A regional spokesman's office was also set up in Dubai to handle queries from the Arab media.[12]

However, it will take time to produce results. Like the Irish and the Scots who lived for years in Africa and India, it takes time to acquire the local knowledge that is necessary to succeed in a foreign country. As Edward Djerejian says, "There has been a change. The U.S. State Department has increased spending and is heading in the right direction. But the effort needs to be accelerated. We need more than numbers. We need sustainability. We have to prepare the ground for the United States to engage the next generation of Arab leaders. This might not help us today, but it will help us in the coming decades." Western governments must shake off the vagaries of the electoral cycle and spend years, not months, lobbying the Arab street. It is still not clear whether they have the stomach for the fight.

A new American President may help. The developing world will find it easier to identify with Barack Hussein Obama than it did with any of his predecessors. The fact that Obama's middle name is a common Arabic name is itself a public relations coup in the Arab world. His election may help to shift attitudes toward the Arab world. However, Obama's policies, especially his security policies, are still untested. Moreover, his election doesn't imply that the American government will radically reform its public relations in the developing world, it only hints at the chance of change. Neither does it imply that more Americans will seek to acquire the local knowledge that comes from living abroad. This is the sort of change that takes years.

*   *   *

The price of oil is important to this book. Oil at $80 a barrel, rather than $30 a barrel, means billions in dollars of extra revenue for the Arab world. But are prices likely to remain high? The assumption I have made is that China has changed the oil balance equation, if not permanently then at least for a lengthy period. The rise of other oil thirsty economies, such as India, makes this outcome even more likely. A similar assumption is made by the International Energy Agency and many industry analysts. However, not all agree, arguing that there is a risk that oil prices will again fall to their earlier lows. Indeed, oil prices were falling in late 2008 as the world's economy slowed. If so, the Arab world will find it harder to purchase Chinese DVD players or American companies.

Would this spell the end of the new Silk Road? No. Admittedly, the strength of trade flows between the Arab world and China will fluctuate in line with oil prices. However, the changes at work are not linked purely to the price of oil. The door between the Arab world and China, which was shut for centuries, is now open again. It will remain open even if oil prices fall to $30 a barrel. The events explored in this book are the result of deep underlying currents impervious to short-term fluctuations in oil prices. Three factors are particularly important to the durability of this story over the coming decades. First is the rise of the China growth model and its emphasis on rapid growth and stability. Second is the rise of the Arab wealth funds. And, third is the importance of geography, in particular the rise of an "Islamic Corridor."

*   *   *

The China growth model, built on the principle of rapid growth with social stability, has issued a robust challenge to the Western model. Why? It is believable. An Arab leader visiting China is visibly struck by the country's rapid development. Think of Egyptian President Hosni Mubarak who visited China nine times since 1983. In that time the Chinese economy grew tenfold, from $300 billion to $3,000 billion. Or think of Syrian Vice-President Abdul Khaddam who watched Shenzhen's economy surge ahead of Syria's since 2001.[13] So forget the International Monetary Fund and the World Bank. What China offers is especially relevant to countries taking their first steps toward a market economy. Moreover, a global financial crisis and economic recession has more recently weakened the faith of many in America and Europe's growth models.

Is the China model a threat to the West? Not necessarily. The China model is built on foundations similar to the Western model, in particular the pursuit of a market-based economy and higher living standards. The Chinese government has relied heavily on advice from Washington-based institutions in its pursuit of these aims. China is then repackaging this advice for distribution to the developing world. So Syrian officials attending seminars in Beijing are receiving similar advice to what the World Bank and International Monetary Fund might have offered. More importantly, the Chinese government is doing a better job of wrapping the package: a Syrian official who walks out of a seminar room onto the streets of Beijing is immediately struck by how economic reforms have changed the Chinese capital. In this way, China is acting as a cheerleader for economic reform in the Arab world.

And economics matters. I almost always feel safe in the Arab world. But the few times I have felt unsafe is in the presence of large groups of young unemployed men. This is true in all parts of the world. But in the Arab world, it is especially difficult for a young man to find work. He must first accumulate sufficient *wasta*, or build the right connections. In the meantime, he exists in a twilight world, unmarried, living at home, and waiting to enter adulthood. There is the risk he feels alienated from the government as a result of his frustrations. I have often wondered if the troubles in the Arab world could be at least partly resolved through higher employment. If the China model can promise this, it should be welcomed by America and Europe.

Politics also matters. The China model has captivated Arab governments in two ways. First, it promises rapid growth without regime change. There is a tendency for the West to link economic reform to political reform, so many Arab officials view economic reform as a Trojan Horse for political reform. The experience of China may convince them otherwise. It certainly has in Syria. Thus the grip of China model will fluctuate in line with the degree of social stability in the Arab world. Today, in Iraq, Lebanon, and Palestine, there is less stability relative to a decade ago, so it is no wonder Arab governments are looking at China's accomplishments with envy.

Second, the China model also promises independence from the West. Egypt for instance has benefited enormously from Western aid and advice, and yet President Hosni Mubarak is an admirer of China. In Egypt, I have heard officials praise the way China has periodically defied the West. Of course, Egypt is a friend of the West. But the fact that Britain effectively ruled Egypt between 1882 and 1936 is a sore point for a proud country. The Egyptian leadership must at times wish for the same independence to occasionally defy the West and assert the country's economic and historical primacy in the region.

How should the West respond? The natural place to start is through a more aggressive promotion of its own brand of economic reform, for instance, educating Arab officials about American and European growth models. True, the Western model might not be as applicable to the Arab situation, but it will nonetheless appeal to those officials who do one day hope for a more liberal society. Western governments must encourage Arab officials and students to visit the West. This is already happening through the International Visitors Program, a U.S. State Department initiative. The Bureau of Educational and Cultural Affairs estimates that some 200 current and former heads of state and about 1,500 Cabinet-level ministers have attended this program.[14] This is a good start, but the extension of these programs is vital to building bridges with the Arab world.

American universities in the Arab world are also a powerful, but often overlooked, force. The American University of Beirut, the Lebanese American University, and the American University of Cairo are three widely respected institutions. They have maintained their independence from American foreign policy responding more to local issues rather than to the latest thinking in Washington. Nor are they the only American institutions in the region. A number of American universities have set up satellite campuses in the Arab world in the past five years, including Georgetown University, George Mason University, and Carnegie Mellon University. The appeal of an American-style degree is so great that a large number of local institutions award joint degrees with American institutions.[15]

As the Advisory Group on Public Diplomacy, a body commissioned by the U.S. Congress in 2003 to report on U.S. public diplomacy in the Arab and Muslim world, said, "Even today, when Arabs and Muslims harbor an extremely negative opinion of the United States, they maintain a positive view of American education." It added, "Because they have been nurtured in the American liberal-education tradition, graduates of these universities are typically open-minded and thoughtful interlocutors with whom Americans can work to address common concerns."[16] Supporting American universities in the Arab world is a relatively cheap yet effective form of public diplomacy. The results may take years, if not decades, to emerge. Yet today many of America's friends in the region received an American education. There may be even more in the future.

* * *

The rise in the price of oil, of course, set the scene for the rise of the Arab wealth funds. But now for many Arab oil producers, the price of oil is increasingly irrelevant. They have swapped oil income for corporate income. Today, the earnings performance of the Dow Jones is almost as relevant as international oil prices to the economic health of the average Arab oil producing country. At the top of the list are Kuwait, Qatar, and the United Arab Emirates. Together their foreign assets are estimated at over $1,000 billion, yet their national population is around 3.1 million people. This comes to about $320,000 per resident. Assume a 5-percent return a year and these foreign assets represent a healthy income stream. The United Arab Emirates, in particular, increasingly looks more like a large holding company and less like a large oil producer. It has arguably already secured its post-oil future.

The Arab wealth funds will remain major players in the world's financial markets; indeed their importance will grow in the next decade. Oil fell in late 2008, but the Arab oil producers are still largely posting trade surpluses. The annual income streams from more than $1,400 billion worth of existing assets must also be reinvested. It is also unlikely that Kuwait and the UAE, in particular, will dip into their funds to finance spending. Kuwait is so far the only major historical exception to the rule after it used its fund to help finance the country's post–Iraq War reconstruction. The International Monetary Fund has estimated that the world's wealth funds are likely to be worth $10,000 billion in 2012, of which the Arab wealth funds account for a large share.[17] Moreover, the Arab wealth funds are part of a shrinking pool of potential investors as a result of the recent financial crisis.

America and Europe will have to learn to live with Arab investors as major players in the world's financial markets. What are the risks? There is a fear that the funds are more interested in power than money. In January 2008, the Arab wealth funds were grilled during a panel discussion held at the World Economic Forum in Davos. Former U.S. Treasury Secretary Lawrence Summers worried about the risks that a fund might invest in a firm only to start making suggestions: it might propose to an "airline to fly to their country, want a bank to do business in their country, or want a rival to their country's national champion disabled."[18] It wouldn't be a first. Think of the way American pension funds disinvested in companies doing business in South Africa in the 1980s. Is it possible that Arab Wealth Funds will behave the same way toward, for instance, companies doing business in Israel?

This is unlikely. First, the Arab Wealth Funds are unusual. They are largely responsible to the small ruling families of the Arab Gulf countries. Many of these rulers are American educated. They also rule relatively small populations, so the Arab street in Abu Dhabi and Dubai has a less powerful grip than it does in Cairo, Damascus, and Riyadh. Neither are the Arab wealth funds a new phenomenon. The Kuwait Investment Authority, for instance, has been a large stakeholder in British Petroleum and Mercedes Benz for around two decades.[19] Moreover, if the Arab world really wanted to strike at the American economy it already has a far more effective weapon: oil. Yet, it hasn't used oil as a political weapon since the late 1970s, in spite of Israeli's occupation of Lebanon in the early 1980s, two wars between America and Iraq in 1991 and 2003, and the more recent fighting between Hizbollah and Israel.

Of course, the Arab wealth funds are a potentially more subtle tool, compared to the oil embargo. Lawrence Summers may have reason to worry if the funds do suggest an American airline fly to their country. But the Arab wealth funds recognize that Washington will be scrutinizing their activity closely. This is why they are spending so heavily on lobbyists. They also appreciate that the risks of stoking American hostility are far greater than are the benefits of adding an extra flight between New York and an Arab capital. Indeed, the Arab wealth funds would have much to lose if Washington decided to freeze their assets. This outcome might appear extreme as memories of September 11 fade, but the aftershocks of the U.S. Patriot Act, which expanded the U.S. government's powers to regulate foreign financial transactions, still ripple through the Arab world. And the Arab wealth funds recognize their status as a guest in America.

Most Western countries already have rules in place to protect against undue influence – banking, media, and telecoms sectors are often protected from majority foreign ownership. Strengthening existing regulation, rather than creating new regulation, is a useful step forward. Self-regulation will also play an important role. In late 2008, the International Monetary Fund, along with 25 wealth funds from across the world, including the Arab world, agreed on a voluntary code of conduct covering such issues as the governance, transparency, and accountability of the funds. By creating a more regulated and transparent environment, the wealth funds are less likely to stir up the same protectionism seen with China's CNOOC and with DP World's bid for American assets.

But the best advice I heard was from a Syrian diplomat in Beijing when I asked him about relations with the West. "There are good Syrians and there are bad Syrians. The difference is that China can distinguish between who is good and who is bad. The West still cannot." It is important for the West to learn how to distinguish between who is good and who is bad. This may already be happening. After the initial furor over DP World's bid for P&O, the Arab wealth funds now face fewer obstacles in purchasing American assets. But the real test may be yet to come, as another terrorist attack would again spur opposition to such sales. The challenge for the West, in particular America, is to identify between the many who are good and the few who are bad. If not, they risk sparking fear among their largest creditors, and the ramifications for financial markets will only grow in time.

America and Europe could try watching more television. But rather than CNN, try watching Al Jazeera and the other Arab satellite television stations. Admittedly, there is a bias. Most Arabs will agree with this. But the bias represents a point of view. The rise of the Arab wealth funds makes it increasingly important to understand this point of view. In a world where a few seconds delay on a major story can mean the difference between a profit and a loss I wonder how long it will be before the large plasma television screens on the trading floors of investment banks tune in to Al Jazeera, at least its English version, during a major Middle East conflict. The more aggressive hedge funds may already be doing so as they try to exploit any opportunity to beat the market.

*   *   *

The Silk Road will never match its former glory; the world has changed too much. In the 1600s, when trade last flourished along the Silk Road, America accounted for less than 1 percent of the global economy. Today, it accounts for around 20 percent.[20] Furthermore, transportation links have improved. It takes around 30 days to ship a DVD player from China to Europe.[21] It is as easy for China to trade with Brazil as trade with Syria. Surely the Silk Road has lost its relevance? Not yet. The Silk Road is about more than a trading route. It is about the historical, geographical, and religious ties that have bound the Silk Road economies together. Many of these ties lost their relevance during the past

400 years. But the rise of China, the rise in oil prices, and the events after September 11 have reinvigorated them, making the Silk Road relevant once again.

There is a compelling historical impetus to events. China's share of the global economy peaked in the 1600s.[22] It was around this same time that the Chinese Muslim Admiral, Zheng He, undertook China's last major naval expeditions. It was not long afterward that trade along the Silk Road slowed and the Ming Dynasty forced Arab traders living in China to assimilate with the local population. The reverse is true today. China is a rising economic power again. Its policy of "opening" dispenses with the practice of the previous 400 years. Arab traders have again returned to China in large numbers. The authorities build mosques to encourage more traders, while Al Jazeera's Beijing bureau is filming documentaries about Chinese Muslims.

Geography is also important to this story. Take for instance the rise of Dubai. It is playing a similar role to the Persian Gulf cities of Hormuz and Muscat in the 1600s as a link between Asia, the Middle East, and Africa.[23] It is no wonder that Emirates, based in Dubai, is among the world's fastest growing airlines.[24] It handles shipments for any city between Beijing and Johannesburg. Meanwhile, when China Construction Bank announced it would open its first three foreign branches, it chose Dubai, Doha, and London.[25] The bank plans to service Chinese companies who are planning to expand into Africa and the Middle East. The momentum of these events owes a great deal to geography. The Arab world straddles the intersection of three continents: Asia, Africa, and Europe. It is a natural beneficiary of the rise of China and the restoration of its trade links with the rest of the world.

The Arab Wealth Funds are following a similar path. They are still investing their wealth in the Western economies, but they are also investing a growing share in the economies that lie along the Islamic Corridor. This road, stretching from East Africa to China, includes most of the world's Islamic countries. Centuries ago it was also a historical trade route, not just for Arab traders but also for Asian and European traders. There is also other evidence that Islam is more recently rising as a financial force. For instance, the size of Islamic funds has doubled in five years to reach $52 billion in 2009.[26] The funds invest on the basis of

Islamic principles. The opportunities for the funds to invest in fast growing Islamic economies are also improving.

How does America fit into this picture? The rise of America has shaken the world in the past century. It created a New World and forced the Old World to look West rather than East. It was later responsible for major improvements in transportation and weakening the rationale for once-important trade routes such as the Silk Road. But the Old World is rising again. Not Europe, but China and the Arab countries. This is a challenge for America. From New York, it takes around 14 hours to fly to Beijing, Cairo, or Dubai. The rise of a New Silk Road and new Islamic Corridor is geographically challenging for America. The events are literally taking place on the other side of the world.

In 2000, trade between America and the European Union accounted for around 6.5 percent of global trade. Today, it accounts for less than 4.5 percent, as Asia and the Middle East rise again.[27] American firms must find ways to participate in the growing trade between Asia, Africa, and Europe. Yet it might be that Europe is better positioned to benefit from this trade. There are seven Arab states facing the Mediterranean making the establishment of the Euro-Mediterranean free trade area a potentially important step toward spurring trade flows within the region. Meanwhile, it takes just seven hours to fly between London and Dubai. Not surprisingly, most of the large investment banks locate their Middle East sales desks in London, not New York.

London has benefited more than most. Its financial industry has ridden the same historical tides that are buoying the Arab world. The rise in oil prices has benefited Arab investors even as the events of 2001 have encouraged investors to turn from New York to London. A growing number of Arab companies, and companies in the rest of the developing world, have meanwhile wanted to issue shares abroad. But many have avoided the United States, worried by the threat of litigation, the reach of the Securities and Exchange Commission after the Enron scandal, and onerous disclosure requirements.[28] London was the logical alternative. The city hosted a larger number of Islamic banks than New York,[29] and accounted for 34 percent of global foreign exchange trading in 2007, versus New York's 17-percent share.[30]

* * *

The threads in this book are evidence of a rebalancing in the global economy. Nonetheless, America and Europe are likely to worry most about oil security. Oil accounts for an estimated 40 percent of total trade between the Arab world and China.[31] Moreover, the oil trade will only get bigger. China accounts for nearly 40 percent of the world's annual increase in oil consumption. The Arab world accounts for around 28 percent of the world's oil supply.[32] If the International Energy Agency is right then these shares will rise in time, and oil will remain an important influence on relations between the Arab world and China. However, this is largely a mathematical relationship between the two. It doesn't immediately imply that the relationship itself will work. Indeed, there are many obstacles to stronger political, if not trade, relations.

First, China and Saudi Arabia are not easy partners. The bright lights and karaoke rooms of Beijing are a far cry from the desert dunes and private homes of Riyadh. I would expect a mutual uneasiness to persist between a conservative Islamic state and a formerly socialist but increasingly capitalist Asian state. But perhaps most importantly, China and Saudi Arabia have no shared history. Relations have only warmed in the past five years. Even today, there are few Chinese living in Saudi Arabia. There are even fewer Saudi Arabians living in China. The paucity of exchanges between peoples makes it more difficult to establish a relationship. No doubt relations will continue to strengthen, but they have a long way to go.

By contrast, America and Saudi Arabia, for better or worse, do have a shared history. America has been the dominant military power in the Middle East since World War II. It was American oil companies that helped build the Saudi Arabian oil industry. There are thousands of Americans working in Saudi Arabia today. This has left both sides with a better understanding of how the other side works. No doubt, Saudi Arabia will try to reduce its dependency on America as a result of the events after

September 11 and vice versa. But this is not the same thing as
breaking the relationship entirely.

It also isn't clear what China has to offer Saudi Arabia, aside
from buying oil and perhaps defense hardware. Saudi Arabia
doesn't need funds so long as oil prices remain at record highs
and wealthy Arab investors are ready to invest in the country. The
$25 billion Saudi Arabia has budgeted to build King Abdullah
Economic City far eclipses the economic aid China has extended
to all of Africa. So what does Saudi Arabia need? It needs technology, whether it is the technology to extract oil from an ageing
well or the technology to power the avionics in a fighter aircraft.
For now at least, America is far better suited to selling these technologies to Saudi Arabia.

How should the West respond to China's thirst for oil? It must
endeavor to reassure China about its oil security. A good start
would be to support China's membership of the International
Energy Agency, created in response to the oil shock of the 1970s.
The oil sector is notorious for its lack of transparency. The
arrival of China has made the problem even more acute. It is thus
encouraging that, in January 2007, China was invited to attend
the agency's meetings as an observer.[33] Full membership may
help the agency, and its team of over 100 analysts, better predict
China's future oil demand. This will help the rest of the world
to understand China's oil needs and ambitions. Likewise, it will
help China to understand its place in the world's oil markets.

America and Europe must also endeavor to assist China in
its efforts to promote alternative fuels and energy conservation.
In 2006, Beijing and Washington established the China–U.S.
Strategic Economic Dialogue. This group meets biannually to
discuss economic and financial issues. A participant at the first
three meetings recalls how Chinese officials were at pains to
talk about energy conservation. In September 2007, both sides
agreed for U.S. Department of Energy officials to assess 12 major
Chinese industrial firms and advise the firms on their energy
saving practices. The department would also train and equip
Chinese teams to conduct further assessments.[34] This is a good
start and should be encouraged. More efficient Chinese oil consumption potentially translates into lower oil prices for the rest of
the world.

A recent report to the U.S.–China Economic Security Review Commission also rightly argued that China's deepening economic involvement in the Arab world will spur its interest in the region's stability.[35] No doubt, China would prefer to take a passive stance toward the region. It may look to America for assistance to ensure the region's stability and also protect oil shipment routes through the Strait of Hormuz. The challenge for America is taking Chinese interests into consideration, such as Beijing's opposition to the Iraq invasion in 2003. China, unlike Japan, is likely to view American "adventurism" in the Middle East with far greater displeasure if such actions result in higher oil prices. Accordingly, America must avoid taking actions that encourage China to expand its own military force in the region, even if this is still years away.

* * *

Islam is at the heart of the forces at work. China has so far managed its relations with its Muslim population adroitly. According to official figures, its Muslim population is estimated at 20 million, or similar in size to either Syria or Saudi Arabia.[36] It would be wrong to assume China's relations with its Muslim population will wreck its relations with the Arab world. Indeed, the Chinese government has arguably used its Muslim citizens more effectively than the West to build relations with the Arab world. This might appear counterintuitive, as the Western media often reports clashes between the Muslim population and the Chinese government. However, not all Chinese Muslims are the same. The most important distinction is between the Hui and the Uyghur. Together, the two account for 18 million of an estimated 20 million Chinese Muslim population.

The Uyghur have a very different story to the Hui. Also Muslim, they identify not just through their religion, but also their territory. Uyghurs are concentrated in the western Chinese province of Xinjiang. Its capital, Urumqi, is a nearly four-hour flight from Beijing, or about the same time it takes to fly from London to Moscow. The Uyghur claim their ancestors are from the Tarim Basin. In 1760, the Qing Dynasty exerted formal control over Xinjiang, only to later lose it to Russia. The Communist

Party incorporated Xinjiang shortly after their defeat of the Nationalist Party in 1949. The Uyghur have since hoped for an independent "Turkestan" and identified with separatist causes. The Akto insurrection in April 1990 was the first of a series of violent clashes between separatists and the Chinese People's Liberation Army.

No doubt Uyghur separatists will continue to clash with the Chinese government. But Hui translators, such as Ma Guoming, will meanwhile continue to work as translators for Arab traders. Others, such as Zhai Jun, will work in the Foreign Ministry and appear on Al Jazeera. The challenge for the Chinese government is striking a balance between the Hui and the Uyghur. A report on religious freedom, written by the U.S. State Department in 2005, illustrates this balance.[37] It notes that religious freedoms are tightly controlled in areas of ethnic unrest, yet the government also permits, and in some cases subsidizes, Muslim citizens who make the Hajj to Mecca. The report also notes substantial mosque construction in areas occupied by Hui Chinese. The Chinese government has recognized ten institutes to train Imams and ten other colleges offering Islamic higher education.

This is not the same as religious freedom. But China is at least demonstrating its tolerance for Islam. For instance, newspapers reported record numbers of Chinese Muslims making the Hajj in 2009. Never mind that the total number, 12,700, is small relative to the over 2 million who make the annual pilgrimage,[38] and small relative to the size of the Chinese Muslim population. Nonetheless, the practice still sends a useful message to the Arab world. Many Arab governments face similar separatist unrest in their own countries and are thus perhaps sympathetic to the position of the Chinese government. It is not guaranteed that Arab governments will negatively respond to any perceived attack on the Uyghur population.

No doubt, an attack by foreign Muslim extremists on Chinese soil would impact relations with the Arab world. The most likely candidate is an attack on Hong Kong's financial sector. After September 11, the Arab community living in mainland China reportedly noticed an increase in surveillance. However, the number of Arab traders issued Chinese visas likewise surged. An attack on Chinese soil would provoke a harsh response. But is this likely? After all, the Chinese government has adopted a noninterventionist approach in the region, focusing on economics rather than politics. China's more intrusive security apparatus and virtual lack of immigration also reduce its vulnerabilities to an attack. It's impossible to rule the scenario out, but the odds are that relations between China and the Arab Muslim world will blossom.

*   *   *

It isn't clear if the West has fully realized the full magnitude of the change related in this book. Language barriers are a challenge. The events are as likely to be taking place in Arabic or Chinese as they are in English. Indeed, I have found the Chinese-language newspapers to contain as much information about the rise of the Arab world as the English language newspapers. The fact the changes are already evident in the pattern of global trade flows is warning enough. But so far it is only the Arab wealth funds that have really caught the West's attention through their billion dollar purchases. The thousand dollar purchases of an individual Arab trader are barely a blip on the radar screen. But add each purchase together and the sum is helping to reshape the global economy.

Two quotes underscore the importance of the forces at work. In 2006, Chinese President Hu Jintao reminded his Arab audience that "Unprecedented historical changes are taking place in the world today." He used an old Chinese expression: "We can understand why dynasties change if we use history as a mirror."[39] In 2008, David Rubenstein, founder of the Carlyle Group, an American private equity fund worth over $80 billion, agreed, saying, "We see the world economy as revolving around us, our standards our desires. But the economic center of the world is beginning to shift from Europe and America to the Middle East and Asia."[40] When the leader of the world's most populous nation and the head of one of the world's largest private equity funds start to talk of the same historic global rebalancing, it is time for the West to start listening.

Notes

1 The New Silk Road:
The Arab world rediscovers China

1. "Zhangkong zhuanye shangpin ding jiaquan, Yiwu xiao shangpin pifa zhishu jichu" (Control the right to set specialized commodity prices, Yiwu small commodities wholesale index will soon be released), *Zhejiang Baodao*, September 28, 2006.
2. *China Statistical Yearbook*, National Bureau of Statistics of China, 2009.
3. *Monthly Report – Visitor Arrival Statistics*, Hong Kong Tourism Board. Many traders transit via Hong Kong on their way to mainland China making the Hong Kong visitor arrivals data a useful proxy for visitor arrival to mainland China.
4. *Nonimmigrant Visas Issued by Nationality (Including Border Crossing Cards): Fiscal Years 1998–2009*, Report of the Visa Office, U.S. Department of State, 2010.
5. *World Economic Outlook*, International Monetary Fund (October, 2009).
6. Author's interview with Chinese Embassy officials in Cairo.
7. Author's interview with Chinese Embassy officials and Egyptian traders. See also, *Visa Wait Times*, Bureau of Consular Affairs, U.S. State Department (March, 2008). U.S. State Department figure includes wait time for interview appointment and visa processing.
8. Jason Burke, *Al-Qaeda: The True Story of Radical Islam* (London, 2007), p. 42.
9. Morris Rossabi, "The Decline of the Central Asian Caravan Trade" in James Tracy (ed.), *The Rise of Merchant Empires* (Cambridge, 1990). Rossabi argues trade developed as early as the Han Dynasty (206BC–AD200) but had dwindled to a trickle by the late Ming Dynasty (1368–1644). Also, see Frances Wood, *The Silk Road: Two Thousand Years in the Heart of Asia* (California, 2002).
10. Estimate is based on the *2000 China 5th Population Census*, National Bureau of Statistics. The census does not ask respondents to specify their religion. However, the Chinese government typically divides its "Muslim" citizens into ten ethnic categories

distinguished by common territory, language, and economy. The ten ethnic categories have a total population of 20.3 million.

11. *China: International Religious Freedom Report*, Bureau of Democracy, Human Rights, and Labor, U.S. State Department (2004). The report notes "substantial mosque construction and renovation" in areas populated by the Hui ethnic group.

12. "Constructing Conflict," *The Economist*, September 1, 2007.

13. Jonathon N. Lipman, *Familiar Strangers: A History of Muslims in Northwest China* (Seattle, 1997).

14. *Direction of Trade Statistics*, International Monetary Fund.

15. "Annual Report," *THE EMIRATES GROUP*, 2009/10.

16. "Dubai Plans Air Route To Recovery," *Middle East Economic Digest* (August 6, 2010).

17. "Mideast Airlines Face Crowded Skies, Staff Shortfalls," *Dow Jones*, January 30, 2008.

18. Ronald Skeldon, "Migration from China," *Journal of International Affairs,* 49:2 (Winter, 1996), p. 436.

19. *China Statistical Yearbook*, National Bureau of Statistics of China, 2007.

2 Chinese petrodollars and the competition for oil

1. Wallace Stegner, "Discovery! The Story of Aramco Then: Chapter 7: Damman No, 7," *Saudi Aramco World*, January/February, 1969.

2. *Saudi Arabia: Country Analysis Brief*, Energy Information Administration, U.S. Department of Energy, February, 2007. See also, *Statistical Review of World Energy*, BP, 2007.

3. Saudi Aramco is a non-listed company. However, the *Financial Times*, based on data from McKinsey, estimated its market capitalization at $781 billion at the end of 2005, whereas the market capitalization of ExxonMobil was a smaller $454 billion. See "Ft's Non-Public 150," *Financial Times* (December 14, 2006). Also, "Saudi Aramco Revealed as Biggest Group," *Financial Times* (December 14, 2006).

4. *World Energy Outlook 2007*, International Energy Agency (Paris, 2007), pp. 80 & 82. Figure for Arab world includes Iran.

5. *Direction of Trade Statistics*, International Monetary Fund, 2008. China's trade surplus rose from $32 billion to $262 billion between 2004 and 2007.

6. Author's calculations based on the "national" population of Bahrain, Kuwait, Oman, Qatar, UAE, and Saudi Arabia.

7. *Statistical Review of World Energy*, BP, 2007.

8. *World Energy Outlook 2007*, International Energy Agency (Paris, 2007), p. 123.

9. *International Energy Annual*, Energy Information Administration, U.S. Department of Energy (Washington, 2009).

10. Ibid.

11. *International Energy Outlook*, Energy Information Administration, U.S. Department of Energy (Washington, 2005).

12. *World Energy Outlook 2009*, International Energy Agency (Paris, 2009), p. 43.

13. Ibid., p. 104.

14. Ibid., p. 103.

15. *Statistical Review of World Energy*, BP, 2008. Figure is for 2007.

16. *International Energy Outlook*, Energy Information Administration, U.S. Department of Energy (Washington, 2007).

17. *General Administration of Customs of China*. Saudi Arabia accounted for 50.3 percent of China's oil imports from Arab countries in 2007.

18. *Statistical Review of World Energy*, BP, 2007. Iraq (115,000 barrels per day) ranks after Saudi Arabia (264,000 barrels per day) and Iran (115,000 barrels per day).

19. *Iraq: Country Analysis Brief*, Energy Information Administration, U.S. Department of Energy (August, 2007). Iraq's oil reserve data is based on 2-D seismic data from nearly three decades ago. More recent estimates suggest that the western and southern deserts may contain an addition of 45 to 100 billion barrels a day of recoverable oil.

20. "Iraq Revives Saddam Oil Deal with China," *Financial Times*, June 23, 2007.

21. See also, Yitzhak Shichor, "China Means Business in Iraq," *China Brief, The Jamestown Foundation*, 7:21 (November 14, 2007).

22. John Calabrese, "Saudi Arabia and China Extend Ties Beyond Oil," *China Brief, The Jamestown Foundation*, 5:20 (September 27, 2005), p. 4. See also, Henry Lee and Dan Shalmon, "Searching for Oil: China's Oil Initiatives in the Middle East," *John F. Kennedy School of Government, Harvard University*, (March, 2007), p. 16.

23. "Bush and Hu: after the Big Welcome, Hard Issues Aplenty," *Associated Press*, April 19, 2006.

24. "Hu Jintao zai Shate Alabo Wangguo Xieshang Huiyi de yanjiang" (Speech delivered by Hu Jintao to the Saudi Arabia Consultative Council), *Xinhua*, April 23, 2006.

25. "Aramco and Exxonmobil Ink Fujian Jv: Long-Pending Refining Plans Move Forward," *Platts Oilgram News,* February 27, 2007.

26. *Doing Business Report*, World Bank, 2008.

27. Energy Information Administration.

28. Richard L. Russell, "Oil-for-Missiles," *The Wall Street Journal,* January 25, 2006.

29. Author's interview.

30. "Prince Turki Discussion with Usa Today Editors and Reporters," *USA Today*, May 10, 2006.

31. *Shiyou Yanhou Baowei Zhan* (The Battle in Protecting Key Oil Routes), *Tiexeu.net*

32. Jiang Wenran, "Beijing's 'New Thinking' on Energy Security," *China Brief, The Jamestown Foundation* (April 12, 2006).

33. Ibid.

34. Li, Hongjie, "Chuyi lengzhan hou Zhongguo yu Zhongdong diqu guojia de zhuyao liyi bianhua" (Changes in Key Interests between China and the Middle Eastern Countries after the Cold War, in My Opinion), *Alabo Shijie*, (2006:5), pp. 8–9.

35. *Energy Policy Act 2005: Section 1837: National Security Review of International Energy Requirements*, U.S. Department of Energy, February, 2006, p. 16.

36. Ibid., p. 16.

37. John Wills, "Maritime China from Wang Chih to Shih Lang" in John E. Will Jr and Jonathon D. Spence (eds), *From Ming to Ch'ing: Conquest, Region, and Continuity in Seventeenth-Century China* (New Haven, 1979), p. 209.

38. Ulrich Jacoby, "Getting Together," *Finance and Development, International Monetary Fund*, June, 2007.

39. *China: Country Analysis Brief*, Energy Information Administration, U.S. Department of Energy, August, 2006.

40. Ibid.

41. "China's Overseas Investments in Oil and Gas Production," *Eurasia Group*, October 16, 2006.

42. *General Administration of Customs of China.* Data for 2008 is for period from September, 2007 to August, 2008.
43. *Energy Policy Act 2005: Section 1837: National Security Review of International Energy Requirements,* U.S. Department of Energy, February, 2006, p. 28.
44. *China's Worldwide Quest for Energy Security,* International Energy Agency (Paris, 2000), p. 74.
45. "Ethiopia Pledges to Track down Oil Workers' Killers," *The Independent,* April 26, 2007.
46. "Sinopec Vows to Keep Drilling in Africa," *The Wall Street Journal,* April 26, 2007.
47. "Captors Release 9 Chinese Oil Workers in Nigeria," *Associated Press,* February 5, 2007.
48. *Statistical Review of World Energy,* BP, 2007.
49. Morris Rossabi, "The Decline of the Central Asian Caravan Trade" in James Tracy (ed.), *The Rise of Merchant Empires* (Cambridge, 1990), p. 357. Note that trade did continue to flourish in the early years of the Ming dynasty.
50. Ibid., p. 365.
51. "Kazakhstan Threatens Investors with Nationalization," *Agence France Presse,* February 7, 2008.
52. "Kazakh-China Shipments Face Blocking Tactics," *Argus China Petroleum,* February, 2007.
53. *Statistical Review of World Energy,* BP, 2007. Daily production in Kazakhstan and Turkmenistan was equivalent to 41 percent of China's oil imports in 2006.
54. *World Energy Outlook 2008,* International Energy Agency (Paris, 2008), p. 80.
55. *Statistical Review of World Energy,* BP, 2007.
56. Ibid.
57. Ulrich Jacoby, "Getting Together," *Finance and Development, International Monetary Fund,* June, 2007.
58. "U.S. Plans New Bases in the Middle East," *Washington Post,* March 22, 2006.
59. Ibid.
60. *Military Power of the People's Republic of China,* Office of the Secretary of Defense, Department of Defense (Washington, 2006).
61. Raja Asghar, "China Promises Aid to Pakistan Port, Highway Plans," *Reuters,* May 13, 2001.

62. "The Merchant Marine: the Chinese Navy Is Growing, and Expanding Its Reach to Asia to Secure Oil and Gas Supplies," *Newsweek*, March 28, 2005.
63. "China's Footprint in Pakistan: a New Port Is a Boon Locally, a Potential Military Asset for Beijing and a Worry to the U.S.," *Los Angeles Times*, April 1, 2007.
64. "Sun Bigan: Zhanhuo zhong bu ru shiming" (Sun Bigan: Accomplished the Mission Amid the Flames of War), *Guangming Ribao*, October 1, 2005.
65. "Changing patterns in the Use of the Veto in the Security Council," *Global Policy Forum, www.globalpolicy.org*
66. "Chinese Peacekeeping Hospital Opens in Lebanon," *Xinhua,* April 16, 2007.
67. "Libanen chongjian hewu qiye canyu lichongjian de jianyi" (The Reconstruction of Lebanon and Proposals for Our Enterprise's Participation in the Lebanon Reconstruction), *Zhonguo Renmin Gongheguo Zhu Alabo Xuliya Gongheguo Dashiguan Jingji Shangwu Zanchu*, September 21, 2006.

3 The Arab wealth funds and the rise of an "Islamic Corridor"

1. Gabriele Galati and Alexandra Heath, "What Drives the Growth in Fx Activity? Interpreting the 2007 Triennial Survey," *BIS Quarterly Review* (December, 2007), p. 63.
2. "UAE May Diversify Reserves into Euros – Bloomberg Interview," *Reuters*, July 12, 2005.
3. "World Economic Outlook," *International Monetary Fund*, April, 2006, p. 80.
4. "Article IV Consultation with Saudi Arabia," *International Monetary Fund*, 2003. This puts government domestic debt at 97 percent of GDP by end-2002. Adjusting for net foreign assets would reduce the share to 75 percent. "Article IV Consultation with Turkey," *International Monetary Fund*, 2005. This puts net public debt at 76 percent of GDP by end-2001.
5. Author's calculations based on estimates by Edwin M. Truman, "Sovereign Wealth Funds: The Need for Greater Transparency and Accountability," *Peterson Institute for International Economics*, August, 2007. Also, see Gerard Lyons, "State Capitalism: The Rise

of the Sovereign Wealth Funds," *Standard Chartered and Oxford Analytica*, October 15, 2007.

6. "Pensions & Investments' 2008 Largest Money Managers," *Pensions & Investments*, May, 2008.

7. China was not the only reason for the rise in oil prices. For a more full discussion see Chapter 2.

8. "Flow of Funds Accounts for the United States," *United States Federal Reserve*.

9. Author's calculations based on estimates by Edwin M. Truman, "Sovereign Wealth Funds: The Need for Greater Transparency and Accountability," *Peterson Institute for International Economics*, August, 2007. Also, see Gerard Lyons, "State Capitalism: The Rise of the Sovereign Wealth Funds," *Standard Chartered and Oxford Analytica*, October 15, 2007. Brad Setser and Rachel Ziemba contest the $800 billion figure and argue that ADIA's external assets are likely worth less than $400 billion, especially after taking into consideration losses from the recent financial crisis. See, Brad Setser and Rachel Ziemba, "GCC Sovereign Funds: Reversal of Fortune," *Council on Foreign Relations,* January, 2009.

10. *Statistical Review of World Energy*, BP, 2007.

11. For a good historical account of Abu Dhabi see Mohammed Al Fahim, *From Rags to Riches: A Story of Abu Dhabi* (London, 1995).

12. "Emirates Prime Minister Tries to Alter the Culture of Dependence," *International Herald Tribune,* October 5, 2007. Estimates suggest the average Emirate male receives benefits worth 204,000 dirhams, or $55,000, per year.

13. Figure is based on Saudi Arabian Monetary Authority's (SAMA) net foreign assets at end-2007. Data from official SAMA website.

14. Figures include nationals only: Saudi Arabia (22 million); Kuwait (1.2 million); UAE (1.1 million), *The World Factbook,* Central Intelligence Agency, 2007

15. "Saudi Arabia's 2008 Budget," *Jadwa Investment*, December 10, 2007.

16. Kuwait Investment Authority website.

17. "Kuwait Govt Assets rise 14.3 percent On Yr to $264 Billion," *Dow Jones Newswires*, June 20, 2008.

18. "IMF Upbeat on 2008 Libya Growth, Warns on Spending," *Reuters*, November 28, 2007.

19. Data from Egyptian Central Bank website, *www.cbe.org.eg*, and Syrian Central Bank website, *www.banquecentrale.gov.sy*.
20. For more detail see Philip D. Wooldridge, "The Changing Composition of Official Reserves," *BIS Quarterly Review*, September, 2006.
21. Grant Smith, "Visa Denied: How Anti-Arab Policies Destroy US Exports, Jobs, and Higher Education," *Institute for Research: Middle Eastern Policy* (Washington, 2006).
22. "U.S. lawmakers Warn against Letting Chinese Company Take over Unocal," *Associated Press*, July 14, 2005.
23. "Arab Regional Order in the Heart of US globalization," *Al Hayat*, June 6, 2006.
24. "Small Florida Firm Sowed Seed of Port Dispute," *The Wall Street Journal*, February 28, 2006.
25. Ibid.
26. "U.S. House Votes to Block China–Unocal Deal," *Reuters*, June 30, 2005.
27. "Dubai's $600m Hub in US 'Corridor of Shame,'" *Financial Times*, January 12, 2008.
28. "Wall Street in the Desert," *Business Week*, October 8, 2007.
29. Sheri Qualters, "A Security Twist to Buying," *New Jersey Law Journal*, August 17, 2007.
30. "KIA announces participation in Citi Group and Merrill Lynch," *Press Release, Kuwait Investment Authority*.
31. "Citi to Sell $7.5 billion of equity unity trusts to the Abu Dhabi Investment Authority," *Press Release, Citigroup*, November 26, 2007.
32. "Abu Dhabi Worried by Shrinking Dollar," *International Herald Tribune*, November 29, 2007.
33. "The World's 2000 Largest Public Companies," *www.forbes.com*, March 29, 2007.
34. "Overseas Investment into UK," *Jones Lang LaSalle*, August, 2007. Figure is for 2006.
35. "The World's Billionaires," *www.forbes.com*, March, 2008.
36. "Buffett Keen on Investments Overseas," *Reuters*, May 8, 2006. Berkshire made its first acquisition of a non-U.S. based company in May, 2006 when it bought Israel's Iscar Metalworking for $5 billion. Buffett later said he saw opportunities to buy companies in the United Kingdom, Europe, and Japan.

37. *World Investment Report*, United Nations Conference on Trade and Development (Washington, 2006), p. 62.
38. "Monthly Bulletin," *Central Bank of Egypt*.
39. "Media Ties Top Sinopec Resignation to Flagship China Oil Project," *Platts Commodity News,* July 5, 2007.
40. Cityscape website.
41. Data is from EPFR Global. The figures indicate that Emerging Market equity funds (including GEM, Emerging Asian, Latin American, and Eastern European funds) had total assets worth $128.6 billion end-1999 and $775.7 billion end-2007. During this time net inflows accounted for nearly $106 billion of the difference, market gains about $407 billion, while EPFR Global added funds worth nearly $150 billion to its database during the period.
42. "The World's Successful Diasporas," *World Business*, April 3, 2007.
43. Ibid.
44. Author's calculations based on data from the UAE Central Bank's Balance of Payments data.
45. "Waiguanju zhaobing mai ma li wanyi waichu jingying guanli bozai meijie" (SAFE Is Recruiting People to Look after Its Trillion Foreign Reserves, as Operation Management Is Imperative), *Zhongguo Jingji Xinxi Wang*, December 15, 2006.
46. *Foreign Portfolio Holdings of U.S. Securities*, Treasury International Capital System, U.S. Department of Treasury. China owned $17.2 billion of U.S. treasury securities in 1994.
47. Figures are for May 2010 based on my calculations using the Treasury International Capital System, U.S. Department of Treasury. Note that the figure for the Arab world includes all "Oil exporters' holdings" of U.S. Treasury paper. It thus includes Ecuador, Venezuela, Indonesia, Iran, Algeria, Gabon, and Nigeria, in addition to the Arab countries.
48. Hillary Rodham Clinton, "Letter to Secretary Paulson and Chairman Bernanke," *http://clinton.senate.gov*, February 28, 2007
49. Mohammed Al Fahim, *From Rags to Riches: A Story of Abu Dhabi* (London, 1995), p. 32
50. "Qataris Sell OMX Stake to Gulf rival," *Financial Times*, February 14, 2008.

4 Syria learns from China while the Chinese "go global"

1. See Frances Wood, *The Silk Road: Two Thousand Years in the Heart of Asia* (California, 2002).
2. Morris Rossabi, "The Decline of the Central Asian Caravan Trade" in James Tracy (ed.), *The Rise of Merchant Empires* (Cambridge, 1990).
3. Li Jian Biao, *Zhi zhu luo yue* (Xian, 2000), p. 22. Also, see Jonathon N. Lipman, *Familiar Strangers: A History of Muslims in Northwest China* (Seattle, 1997), pp. 39–41.
4. "Zhuazhu huangjin shangji...dahao chendezhan...Xuliya ji Zhongdong diqu dui Zhongguo qiche fanxiang qianglie" (Grasp the Golden Business Opportunities...Establish a Strategic Position...Chinese Cars Are Enjoying a Strong Reaction in the Syria and Middle East Region), *Guo Ji Shang Bao*, May 29, 2006.
5. "Jiujia Zhongguo qiche pinpai jinjun Xuliya" (Nine Chinese Car Brands Advance into Syria), *Zhongguo Jingji Xinxi Wang*, March 30, 2006.
6. "Zhuazhu huangjin shangji...dahao chendezhan...Xuliya ji Zhongdong diqu dui Zhongguo qiche fanxiang qianglie" (Grasp the Golden Business Opportunities...Establish a Strategic Position...Chinese Cars Are Enjoying a Strong Reaction in the Syria and Middle East Region), *Guo Ji Shang Bao*, May 29, 2006.
7. Angus Maddison, *The World Economy: Historical Statistics* (Paris, 2003). Also, *World Economic Outlook Database*, International Monetary Fund (April, 2008).
8. Kenneth Pomeranz, *The Great Divergence: China, Europe, and the Making of the Modern World Economy* (Princeton, 2000), pp. 203 & 239.
9. Roger Owen makes a more nuanced argument. He makes the point, for instance, that European cloth imports had a "localized, irregular, and uneven" impact on the Arab textile industry. Increased European demand for cash crops even spurred production in the Arab world to the benefit of local Arab merchants. See Roger Owen, *The Middle East in the World Economy 1800–1914* (London, 2002), pp. 4–12. Also see, Peter Mansfield, *The Arabs* (London, 1992), pp. 69, 86, & 89.

10. "US Accuses Libya, Syria, and Cuba on Weapons Spread," *Reuters*, May 7, 2002.

11. *Background Note: Syria*, U.S. State Department, May, 2007.

12. Speech by Benita Ferroro-Waldner, European Commissioner for External Relations and European Neighborhood Policy, delivered to the European Parliamentary Plenary, October 25, 2006.

13. "Zhuazhu huangjin shangji...dahao chendezhan...Xuliya ji Zhongdong diqu dui Zhongguo qiche fanxiang qianglie" (Grasp the Golden Business Opportunities...Establish a Strategic Position...Chinese Cars Are Enjoying a Strong Reaction in the Syria and Middle East Region), *Guo Ji Shang Bao*, May 29, 2006.

14. Ibid.

15. "World Publics Welcome Global Trade – But Not Immigration," *The Pew Global Attitudes Projects* (October 4, 2007), p. 63.

16. "World Bank Economist Urges Flexibility," *Wall Street Journal*, February 29, 2008.

17. Shi Yanchan, "Zhong Xu youyishen, lili zai xintou" (The Friendship between China and Syria Is So Deep-Rooted That Everything Is Fresh in People's Minds), *Alabo Shijie* (2005:2), pp. 2–4.

18. "Damashq wa Bikin aqrab ila ba'dihoma ba'dan min ayy waqt mada qafza nau'iya fi 'alaqat al siyasiya wa al iqtisadiya" (Damascus and Peking Are Closer to Each Other Than at Any Point in Time. a Qualitative Leap in Political and Economic Relations), Syrian Embassy in China Website, *www.syria.org.cn*

19. Central Bank of Syria website, *www.banquecentrale.gov.sy*

20. "Zhong Xu jingmao hezuo jianjie" (A Brief Introduction to China–Syria Economic Cooperation), *Zhu Xu Jingshangchu* February 26, 2006.

21. Ibid.

22. "The Huawei Way: The Telecom Giant Is Either a Security Menace or a Real Comer – or It Could Be a House of Cards. or All of the above," *Newsweek International*, January 16, 2006.

23. Isam Al Za'im, "at tawajjuhat as stratijiya fi tanmiya al iqtisad as suri iza'a mashari' al 'ulama wa al tanmiya" (Strategies in Developing Syria's Economy Alongside Globalization's Projects and Regional Development), *Jam'iya Al U'lum Al Iqtisadiya As Suriya*, March 23, 2004.

24. *China Statistical Yearbook*, National Bureau of Statistics of China, 2006.

25. "Hu Jintao zai Shate Alabo Wangguo Xieshang Huiyi de yanjiang" (Speech delivered by Hu Jintao to the Saudi Arabia Consultative Assembly), *Xinhua*, April 23, 2006.

26. "Xuliya: Zhongguo qiche de da shichang" (Syria: a Big Market for Chinese Cars), *Xinhua She Jingji Xinxi*, June 15, 2006.

27. "Guiguo renyuan jiangshu cheli jingli: Cong Beirute dao Shanghai zou le wu tian" (Those Who Return Home Recall Their Retreat: It Took Five Days from Beirut to Shanghai), *Xinwen Chenbao*, July 20, 2006.

28. *Direction of Trade Statistics*, International Monetary Fund.

29. *Fact Sheet: Egypt–China: Economic and Trade Relations*, Egyptian Ministry of Trade and Industry, 2007. The figure is for the period from 1970 to March, 2006. Chinese companies reportedly hold stakes in 203 inland investment companies.

30. For instance, Egyptian academics invited to speak by universities in Europe have periodically had trouble obtaining visas. Author's interviews. Also, see *Nonimmigrant Visas Issued by Nationality (Including Border Crossing Cards): Fiscal Years 1998–2007*, Report of the Visa Office, U.S. Department of State, 2007. And, *Entry Clearance Statistics, UK visas*, 2000 & 2006.

31. "Global Unease with Major World Powers," *The Pew Global Attitudes Project*, (June 27, 2007), p. 39. A majority of respondents in Kuwait (67 percent), Jordan (57 percent), Egypt (50 percent), Palestine (42 percent), and Lebanon (61 percent) thought China's growing economy was a good thing for their country.

32. Shi Guangsheng, "Shishi 'Zou Chu Qu' zhanlue tigao duiwai 'Kaifang' shuiping" (Implement the Strategy of Go Global. Enhance the Level of "Opening Up"), *Qiu Shi*, November 1, 2002.

33. *Chinese Embassies*, Ministry of Foreign Affairs of the People's Republic of China, March, 2008.

5 Young women and the future of the Arab world

1. Shi Yanchan, "Zhong Xu youyishen, lili zai xintou" (The Friendship between China and Syria Is So Deep-Rooted That Everything Is Fresh in People's Minds), *Alabo Shijie* (2005:2), pp. 2–4.

2. *Zhongguo Shenzhen fazhan baogao* (China Shenzhen Development Report), Shehui Kexue Wenxian Chuban She (Beijing, 2004).

3. Shortages of skilled workers first emerged in the second half of 2002. The first shortages of nonskilled workers appeared in 2004. For more details see, "Wuguo laodongli liudong de xinqushi" (New Trend in Our Country's Labor Flow), *Guangzhoushi Shehui Kexueyuan*, March 17, 2006. Also see, "Shei zai wei rengong huang er huang?" (Who Is Panicking about Labor Shortages), *Nanfang Wang*, March 3, 2005.

4. "Zhongguo Wenzhou nulaoban chuangye zai Dibai" (Female Entrepreneurs from China's Wenzhou Are Launching Their Careers in Dubai), *Xinhuashe Zhongwen Xinwen*, March 8, 2007.

5. Ragui Assaad and Farzaneh Roudi Fahimi, *Youth in the Middle East and North Africa: Demographic Opportunity or Challenge?*, Population Reference Bureau (April, 2007), p. 3.

6. Shenzhen's economy has grown from $26 billion to $89 billion between 2000 and 2007, while Syria's economy has grown from $20 billion to $37 billion in the same period. Data from International Monetary Fund and National Statistics Bureau of China.

7. *The Status and Progress of Women in the Middle East and North Africa*, The World Bank (Washington, 2007), p. 19.

8. *Farzaneh Roudi Fahimi and Mary Mederios Kent, Fertility Declining in the Middle East and North Africa*, Population Reference Bureau (April, 2008).

9. Joyce Jennings Walstedt, "Reform of Women's Roles and Family Structures in the Recent History of China," *Journal of Marriage and Family*, 40:2 (May, 1978), p. 380.

10. Ibid., p. 382.

11. Ibid., p. 383.

12. Ibid., p. 386.

13. Ibid., p. 385.

14. *Arab Human Development Report 2005*, United Nations (Washington, 2005), p. 86.

15. Ibid., p. 87.

16. Ibid., p. 110.

17. *The Status and Progress of Women in the Middle East and North Africa*, The World Bank (Washington, 2007), p. 20.

18. *Arab Human Development Report 2005*, United Nations (Washington, 2005), p. 110.

19. *Women Entrepreneurs in the Middle East and North Africa: Characteristics, Contributions, and Challenges: Executive Summary*,

The Center of Arab Women for Training and Research and the International Finance Corporation (June, 2007).

20. Michael Ross, *Oil, Islam, and Women*, UCLA Department of Political Science (August, 2007).

21. Ibid., p. 22.

22. Ragui Assaad and Farzaneh Roudi Fahimi, *Youth in the Middle East and North Africa: Demographic Opportunity or Challenge?*, Population Reference Bureau, (April, 2007).

23. Ibid. Note that Kuwait, for instance, has a lower rate, but only because the large female expatriate population is included in the figure.

24. Ibid.

25. *World Population Prospects: The 2006 Revision*, Population Division, United Nations (2006). Author's calculations based on 2000 and 2005 data.

26. Nader Kabbani and Noura Kamel, *Youth Exclusion in Syria: Social, Economic, and Institutional Dimensions*, Wolfensohn Center for Development and Dubai School of Government (September, 2007), p. 31.

27. Diane Singerman, *The Economic Imperatives of Marriage: Emerging Practices and Identities among Youth in the Middle East*, Wolfensohn Center for Development and Dubai School of Government (September, 2007), p. 33.

28. Ibid., p. 13.

29. "Dreams Stifled, Egypt's Young Turn to Islamic Fervor," *New York Times*, February 18, 2008.

30. Author's calculations using data from *Egyptian Labor Market Panel Survey*, Central Agency for Public Mobilization and Statistics.

31. *National Occupational Employment Wage Estimates*, Bureau of Labor Statistics, United States Department of Labor, (May, 2006). Assumes median annual wage of $39,190. Also, *2007 Annual Survey of Hours and Earnings*, United Kingdom National Statistics (November, 2007). Assumes median gross annual earnings for full-time men at £26,300.

32. *Statistics on Displaced Iraqis around the World*, The UN High Commissioner for Refugees (September, 2007). There were an estimated 1.2–1.4 million Iraqi refugees living in Syria.

33. "Dreams Stifled, Egypt's Young Turn to Islamic Fervor," *New York Times*, February 18, 2008.

34. "Hamas Sponsors Mass Wedding in Palestinian Refugee Camp in Syria," *Associated Press Newswires*, August 4, 2007.
35. James Wolfensohn, *A New Commitment for Securing a Prosperous Middle East*, Middle East Youth Initiative, Wolfensohn Center for Development at Brookings, December 12, 2007.
36. *King Abdullah Economic City Launched by Custodian of Two Holy Mosques,* Emaar and Saudi Arabian General Investment Authority (December 20, 2005).
37. Unemployment rate is for male youths aged between 15 and 29. See, *Labor Force by Age Group and Sex*, Saudi Arabia Central Department of Statistics, 2006.
38. *Article IV Consultation with Saudi Arabia*, International Monetary Fund, 2003. This puts government domestic debt at 97 percent of GDP by end-2002. Adjusting for net foreign assets would reduce the share to 75 percent. *Article IV Cconsultation with Turkey,* International Monetary Fund, 2005, puts net public debt at 76 percent of GDP by end-2001.
39. "Mideast Airlines Face Crowded Skies, Staff Shortfalls," *Dow Jones*, January 30, 2008.
40. "Press Release on Labor Force Survey Results," Palestinian Central Bureau of Statistics (October–December, 2007).
41. "Monthly Bulletin," Central Agency for Public Mobilization and Statistics. Chinese arrivals in 2007 accounted for 0.7 percent of total arrivals.
42. "Xuliya zhengshi chengwai Zhongguo gongmin chuguo luyou mude diguo" (Syria Formally Becomes a Chinese Tourist Destination), *Zhonguo Renmin Gongheguo Zhu Alabo Xuliya Gongheguo Dashiguan Jingji Shangwu Zanchu,* August 21, 2007.
43. *Regional Wheat Imports, Production, Consumption, and Stocks*, Foreign Agricultural Service, U.S. Department of Agriculture (March, 2008).
44. *General Customs Administration of China.* China's exports to Europe rose from $54 billion to $294 billion between 2000 and 2009. Its exports to the United States were worth $262 billion in 2009. These figures adjust for China's re-exports through Hong Kong.
45. David E. Bloom, David Canning, and Jaypee Sevilla, "Banking the 'Demographic Dividend': How population dynamics can affect economic growth," *Rand Corporation*, 2002.

6 The new public relations war: "Al Jazeera" in China

1. Author's interview with Ezzat Shahrour, Al Jazeera's Beijing correspondent.
2. "Global Unease with Major World Powers," *The Pew Global Attitudes Project* (June, 2007).
3. *Economics of Basic Cable Networks 2006*, Kagan Research, LLC, June, 2005.
4. Author's interview with Ezzat Shahrour, Al Jazeera's Beijing correspondent.
5. "Yazhou Dongxi liang ge daguo de xieshou" (The Cooperation of Two Big Nations from East and West Asia), *Xinhua*, March 19, 2006.
6. "Xia jueding tigao xinhuashe jingji xinxi chanpin de guoji jingzhenli" (Determined to Raise the International Competitiveness of Xinhua's Economic Information Products), *Xinhuanet.com*, August 1, 2006.
7. "China's Media Curbs Bolster State Agency – Beijing Hopes to Strengthen Xinhua as Global News Competitor and Political Tool," *The Wall Street Journal*, September 13, 2006.
8. "Xinhuashe Zhongdong zongfenshe xinbangonglou qiyong" (Opening of the New Office Building of the Middle East Regional Office of the Xinhua News Agency), *Xinhua Zhongwen Xinwen*, November 27, 2005.
9. Gautier Battitstella, "The World's Biggest Propaganda Agency," *Reporters Without Borders* (October, 2005).
10. *U.S. International Broadcasting: Management of Middle East Broadcasting Services Could Be Improved*, U.S. Government Accountability Office (August, 2006), p. 9.
11. Author's interview with Hugh Miles.
12. "BBC Arabic-Language Television Channel to Be Launched 11 March," *BBC Monitoring Middle East*, February 15, 2008.
13. Hugh Miles, *Al Jazeera: How Arab TV News Challenged the World* (London, 2005), p. 93.
14. Peter Fueilherade, "Analysis: France 24 Global News Channel Adds Arabic Broadcast," *BBC Monitoring Media*, April 2, 2007.
15. Edward Djerejian, "Changing Minds and Winning Peace: A New Strategic Direction for U.S. Public Diplomacy in the Arab and

Muslim World," *Report of the Advisory Group on Public Diplomacy for the Arab and Muslim World* (Washington, 2003).

16. Adel Darwish, "The BBC Arabic Channel: Welcome Back," *Asharq Alawsat*, November 2, 2005.

17. "Global Unease with Major World Powers," *The Pew Global Attitudes Project* (June, 2007).

18. " Zhu Aiji Shiguan Linshi Daiban Li Chen Chuxi Xinhuashe Zhongdong Zongfenshe Yu Aiji (Shi Yue) Zazhi Qianyue Yishi" (Li Chen, the Charge D'affaires of Embassy of PRC in Egypt, Attended the Signing Ceremony of Xinhua News Agency's Middle East Regional Office and *October* Magazine of Egypt), *Zhonghua Renmingonghe Guowai Jiaobu*, August 16, 2006.

19. "Zhuazhu huangjin shangji...dahao chendezhan...Xuliya ji Zhongdong diqu dui Zhongguo qiche fanxiang qianglie" (Grasp the Golden Business Opportunities...Establish a Stragtic Position...Chinese Cars Are Enjoying a Strong Reaction in the Syria and Middle East Region), *Guo Ji Shang Bao*, May 29, 2006.

20. "Zhejiang shangren ba shengyi zuodao le yi zhan xian pang" (Zhejiang Businessmen Are Taking Their Business to the Battlefront of the Lebanon–Israel War), *Zhongguo Maoyibao*, August 22, 2006.

21. Ma Xiaolin, "Zhongguo meiti zhong de Shate Alabo xingxiang" (Impressions of Saudi Arabia in the Chinese Media), Paper originally presented at the Guoji Taolun Nianhui, April 31, 2004.

22. "Alexa Top 500 Sites," *www.alexa.com*

23. Jess Ford, *U.S. Public Diplomacy: Strategic Planning Efforts Have Improved, but Agencies Face Significant Implementation Challenges*, U.S. Government Accountability Office, April 26, 2007.

24. "Global Unease with Major Powers," *Pew Global Attitudes Survey* (June, 2007), p. 13.

7 Arabic and the language of globalization

1. "Alaboyu fanyi cheng Huizu qingnian de remen zhiye" (Arabic Translation Has Become a Desirable Profession among the Hui Youth), *Xinhua*, October 17, 2005.

2. *China: International Religious Freedom Report*, Bureau of Democracy, Human Rights, and Labor, U.S. State Department (2004).

3. Ibid.

4. "Alaboyu fanyi cheng Huizu qingnian de remen zhiye" (Arabic Translation Has Become a Desirable Profession among the Hui Youth), *Xinhua*, October 17, 2005.

5. "The Sino-Saudi Connection: The Two Countries Have More to Offer Each Other Than Oil and What It Buys," *Forbes Asia*, April 17, 2006.

6. Zhang Hong, "Zhongguo de Alaboyu jiaoxue" (China's Arabic Language Teaching), *Zhonghua Renmin Gongheguo Zhu Shate Alabo Wangguo Dashiguan* (September, 2001).

7. Author's interview with former Chinese journalist for the Guangming daily who was a student in Damascus during the 1960s.

8. Author's interview.

9. *U.S. Official Fernandez Admits "Arrogance" in Iraq*, BBC Monitoring Middle East, October 24, 2006.

10. Author's interview with Edward Djerejian, Chairman of the Advisory Group on Public Diplomacy for the Arab and Muslim World.

11. *Staffing and Foreign Language Shortfalls Persist Despite Initiatives to Address the Gap, Report to the Chairman, Committee on Foreign Relations, U.S. Government*, U.S. Government Accountability Office, (August, 2006), p. 25.

12. Ibid.

13. Furman, Nelly, Goldberg, David, and Lusin, Natalia, *Enrollments in Languages Other Than English in United States Institutions of Higher Education*, Modern Language Association (Fall, 2006).

14. *National Security Language Initiative*, Bureau of Educational and Cultural Affairs, U.S. Department of State.

15. "Our Diplomats' Arabic Handicap," *The Washington Post*, October 16, 2005.

16. *Arabic Speakers Embassy Baghdad*, Taken Question, Office of the Spokesman, U.S. Department of State, June 19, 2007.

17. *State Department Efforts to Engage Muslim Audiences Lack Certain Communication Elements and Face Significant Challenges*, United States Government Accountability Office (May, 2006), p. 36.

18. "Global Unease with Major World Powers," *Pew Global Attitudes Survey* (June, 2007), p. 13. A minority of respondents in Egypt (21 percent), Jordan (20 percent), Morocco (15 percent), and Palestine (13 percent) had favorable views of the U.S.

19. Related in Mohamed Maamouri, *Language Education and Human Development*, International Literacy Institute (1998), p. 35.
20. Li Jian Biao, *Zhi zhu luo yue* (Xian, 2000).
21. Tao-Tai Hsia, "The Language Revolution in Communist China," *Far Eastern Survey*, 25:10 (October 1956), pp. 145–154.
22. Ibid.
23. "Banshu yishang de Zhongguoren nengyong putonghua jiaoliu" (More Than One-Half of Chinese Are Able to Use Putonghua to Exchange), *Xinhua She Zhong Wen Xin Wen*, December 26, 2004.
24. Assuming 53 percent of the population speak Putonghua.
25. Beijing Foreign Studies University website. The university started in 1941 as the Yanan school of Foreign Languages.
26. "China Moves to Meet Surging Demand for Chinese Language Teachers," *Xinhua's China Economic Information Service,* March 20, 2007.
27. See earlier discussion in this chapter.
28. *World Economic Outlook*, International Monetary Fund (October, 2007), p. 7.

8 Implications for the West: A new center of gravity

1. "Jingmao wanglai cucheng qijing: Zhongguo chuxian Zhongdong jie," (Trade Brings about a Wonderful View: China Emerges as a Middle East Street), *Yazhou Xinwentai*, March 14, 2008.
2. *China Statistical Yearbook*, National Bureau of Statistics of China, 2009.
3. *Direction of Trade Statistics*, International Monetary Fund, 2010.
4. Niall Ferguson, *Colossus* (London, 2005), p. 2006.
5. *The Royal Opening of RBS Gogarburn: Media Factsheet*, Royal Bank of Scotland, September 14, 2005.
6. "Members and Observers," *www.wto.org*
7. *Staffing and Foreign Language Shortfalls Persist Despite Initiatives to Address the Gap, Report to the Chairman, Committee on Foreign Relations*, U.S. Government, U.S. Government Accountability Office (August, 2006), p. 15.
8. *Compensation and Benefits*, Office of Recruitment, Examination, and Employment, U.S. Department of State (March, 2008).

9. Donald Rumsfeld, "The Smart Way to Beat Tyrants Like Chevez," *Washington Post*, December 2, 2007.

10. Robert M. Gates, "Landon Lecture," A speech at Kansas University, November 26, 2007.

11. Author's interview with Edward Djerejian who chaired The Advisory Group on Public Diplomacy for the Arab and Muslim World.

12. "Hughes Tries Fine-Tuning to Improve Diplomatic Picture," *The Washington Post*, April 19, 2006.

13. Shenzhen's economy has grown from $26 billion to $89 billion between 2000 and 2007, while Syria's economy has grown from $20 billion to $37 billion in the same period.

14. Edward Djerejian, *Changing Minds Winning Peace: A New Strategic Direction for Public Diplomacy in the Arab and Muslim World,* The Advisory Group on Public Diplomacy for the Arab and Muslim World, (October 1, 2003).

15. Shafeeq Ghabra and Margreet Arnold, *Studying the American Way: An Assessment of American-Style Education in Arab Countries*, The Washington Institute for Near East Policy (June, 2007).

16. Edward Djerejian, *Changing Minds Winning Peace: A New Strategic Direction for Public Diplomacy in the Arab and Muslim World*, The Advisory Group on Public Diplomacy for the Arab and Muslim World, Washington, October 1, 2003, p. 33.

17. Johnson, Simon, "The Rise of Sovereign Wealth Funds," *Finance and Development*, International Monetary Fund (September, 2007), p. 56.

18. Tim Weber, "Who's Afraid of Sovereign Wealth Funds?," BBC news website, January 24, 2008.

19. Official Kuwait Investment Authority website. Also, "Big Spenders – How Sovereign Wealth Funds Are Stirring up Protectionism," *Financial Times*, July 30, 2007.

20. Angus Maddison, *The World Economy: Historical Statistics*, OECD (Paris, 2003).

21. "Europe – Far East (AE8) – Eastbound," *Maersk Line website* (March, 2008).

22. Angus Maddison, *The World Economy: Historical Statistics*, OECD (Paris, 2003).

23. For more details see, Willem Floor, *The Persian Gulf: A Political History of Five Port Cities 1500–1730* (Washington, 2006).

24. "Emirates Aims to Redraw World Aviation Map," *International Herald Tribune*, July 5, 2007.

25. "China Construction Bank Announces Plans for Overseas Branches," *Xinhua's China Economic Information Service*, December 24, 2007.

26. "Ernst & Young Islamic Fund & Investment Report," *Ernst & Young* (2010).

27. *Direction of Trade Statistics*, International Monetary Fund, 2008.

28. "London: Financial Capital of the Universe," *International Herald Tribune*, October 26, 2006.

29. "Islamic Finance," *IFSL Research*, January, 2010. London hosted 22 Islamic banks. New York hosted 9 Islamic banks.

30. *Triennial Central Bank Survey of Foreign Exchange and Derivatives Market Activity in April 2007*, Bank for International Settlements, September, 2007.

31. *Direction of Trade Statistics*, International Monetary Fund, 2008. Author's calculations. The share of the Arab world's oil and gas exports to China is based on national sources.

32. *World Energy Outlook 2007*, International Energy Agency (Paris, 2007), pp. 80 and 82. Figure for Arab world includes Iran.

33. *A New Phase in Iea Work with China and India*, International Energy Agency, December 6, 2007.

34. *U.S. and China Sign Agreement to Increase Industry Energy Efficiency*, Office of Public Affairs, United States Department of Energy, September 14, 2007.

35. John Keefer Douglas, Matthew B. Nelson, and Kevin Schwartz, "Fueling the Dragon's Flame: How China's Energy Demands Affect Its Relations in the Middle East," presented to the U.S.–China Economic and Security Review Commission, September 14, 2006.

36. Estimate is based on the *2000 China 5th Population Census*, National Bureau of Statistics. The census does not ask respondents to specify their religion. However, the Chinese government typically divides its "Muslim" citizens into ten ethnic categories distinguished by common territory, language, and economy. The ten ethnic categories have a total population of 20.3 million.

37. Ibid.

38. "Zhongguo Chaoguo 1.2 Wan Ming Musilin Fu Maijia Chaojin" (China surpases 12,000 Muslims Making Hajj to Mecca).

39. "Hu Jintao Zai Shate Alabo Wangguo Xieshang Huiyi De Yanjiang" (Speech delivered by Hu Jintao to the Saudi Arabia Consultative Council), *Xinhua*, April 23, 2006.
40. "Gulf nations tighten investment ties with China," *Financial Times*, April 8, 2008.

INDEX

Abdul Midani, 19, 20, 80
Abu Dhabi, 55, 71
  Al Nahyan, rulers of, 55
Africa, 40
  American military command in, 46
  Chinese aid to, 40, 45
  visit by Chinese President Hu Jintao to, 40
Al Faisal, Turki, 37
Al Jazeera, 116, 117, 118, 119, 120, 121, 122, 123, 124, 139, 140, 141, 144, 146, 147, 159, 166
  documentary 'Eye on China', 116, 117, 139, 140
  interview of Zhai Jun, 118
Al Naimi, Ali, 33
Alibaba, B2B website, 25, 26, 94
Arab, 56
Arab and the Arab world
  Chinese female traders in, 100, 101
  economic growth in, 11
  failure to lobby the Chinese media, 126
  female entrepreneurs in, 107
  food prices in, 113
  historic decline of, 79
  investment in China, 68, 69
  marriage costs in, 109, 110, 111
  saves its oil windfall, 52
  social stability in, 115
  threat from Chinese imports in, 113
  tourism in, 113
  visas for, 10, 11
  wasta in, 109, 111, 161
  youth unemployment rates in, 102, 109
Arab Human Development Report, 104, 106
Arab wealth funds, 54, 56, 66, 69, 70, 73, 163, 164, 165, 166, 167
  Abu Dhabi Investment Authority, 55, 60, 65, 69, 71, 72
  investment in the Arab world, 67
  investment in the developing world, 65, 66
  Kuwait Investment Authority, 56, 60, 165
  lobbyists for the, 60
  Qatar Investment Authority, 56, 64
Arabic language
  Fusha, 146, 147, 148, 149, 152
Asia
  demographics in, 114
Assad, Bashar, 83, 84

Bahlaiwa, Omar, 36, 37
Bahrain, 46, 112
Berkshire Hathaway, 65
Bernanke, Ben, 71